ROCKWELL KENT

ROCKWELL KENT

AN ANTHOLOGY OF HIS WORKS
EDITED, WITH AN INTRODUCTION,
BY FRIDOLF JOHNSON

ALFRED A. KNOPF · 1982 · NEW YORK

TO HEIDI

THIS IS A BORZOI BOOK PUBLISHED BY ALFRED A. KNOPF, INC.

Copyright © 1981 by Fridolf Johnson. Previously unpublished Rockwell Kent material copyright © 1981 by Sally Kent Gorton. Foreword copyright © 1981 by Jamie Wyeth. All rights reserved under International and Pan-American Copyright Conventions. Published in the United States by Alfred A. Knopf, Inc., New York, and simultaneously in Canada by Random House of Canada Limited, Toronto. Distributed by Random House, Inc., New York.

Grateful acknowledgment is made to the following for permission to reprint from previously published text by Rockwell Kent:
Astor-Honor, Inc.: Excerpts from Greenland Journal *by Rockwell Kent.*
Copyright © 1962 by Rockwell Kent. Reprinted by permission of the publishers, Astor-Honor, Inc.
Hawthorne Properties (Elsevier-Dutton Publishing Co., Inc.): Excerpts from This Is My Own *by Rockwell Kent. Published by Duell, Sloan & Pierce. Copyright 1941, 1969 by Rockwell Kent. Reprinted by permission of Hawthorne Properties (Elsevier-Dutton Publishing Co., Inc.).*
Wesleyan University Press: Excerpts from N by E *by Rockwell Kent. Copyright 1930 and renewed 1958 by Rockwell Kent. Reprinted by arrangement with The Rockwell Kent Legacies and by permission of Wesleyan University Press, 1978.*
Unless noted above, all text by Rockwell Kent is the property of The Rockwell Kent Legacies, and is reprinted with their permission.

Grateful acknowledgment is made to the following for permission to reprint previously published artwork by Rockwell Kent:
American Artists Group, Inc.; American Car & Foundry Co., Inc.; Astor-Honor, Inc.; Chicago Tribune; Conde Nast (Vanity Fair); Crown Publishers; A. B. Dick Co., Inc.; Doubleday & Co., Inc. (The Literary Guild); Esquire; Hawthorne Properties/Elsevier-Dutton Publishing Co., Inc. (Duell, Sloan & Pierce); Horace Hart (The Printing House of Leo Hart); The Limited Editions Club; Liveright Publishing (Albert & Charles Boni); Marshall Field; M.B.I. Corporation (The Heritage Club); The National Council of Soviet-American Friendship; Random House, Inc.; The Schering Corporation; United States Pipe & Foundry Co.; Wesleyan University Press; Whitney Communications (Tribune).

LIBRARY OF CONGRESS CATALOGING IN
PUBLICATION DATA

Kent, Rockwell [date].
Rockwell Kent.

Bibliography: p.
Includes index.
1. Kent, Rockwell [date]. I. Johnson, Fridolf.
N6537.K44A4 1982 760'.092'4 81-47477
ISBN 0-394-41771-2 AACR2

Manufactured in the United States of America
First Edition

CONTENTS

LIST OF PAINTINGS & DRAWINGS

Many of Rockwell Kent's records were lost in a fire in 1969. Every effort has been made to trace and properly attribute the current ownership of the art used in this book. The editor, publisher, and The Rockwell Kent Legacies express their regret for any inadvertent error, and will be happy to make the necessary correction in future printings.

PAINTINGS REPRODUCED IN COLOR

PAINTINGS REPRODUCED IN BLACK & WHITE

DRAWINGS

ACKNOWLEDGMENTS

Rockwell Kent's autobiographic writings are often ambiguous and misleading as to circumstances and chronology. Also, stories about him have been distorted—sometimes maliciously—and copied repeatedly by so many writers that they have become much more legendary than factual. By carefully sifting through masses of papers, I have succeeded, I believe, in establishing correct dates and in setting the record straight in some matters which have frequently been subject to invidious interpretations. Where Kent has hidden identities under pseudonyms, I have provided actual names when anonymity seemed no longer called for. Many interesting particulars revealed in my researches have been left to future biographers who may no longer be bound by discretion.

From the outset, I have enjoyed the full support of Rockwell Kent's widow, Sally Kent Gorton, and her late husband, John F. H. Gorton, director of the Rockwell Kent Legacies. During my frequent visits to Asgaard, in Au Sable Forks, New York, they gave me free access to the wealth of material in their possession, including sections deleted from the published version of *It's Me O Lord* and the rough draft of the manuscript for the continuation of Kent's autobiography, left unfinished at his death. Through taped interviews, by telephone, and by correspondence over several years, both Sally and John supplied insights and information not likely to be obtained anywhere else. Furthermore, it is largely through them that the pictorial contents of this book were made available. Happily, Scott Ferris, recently appointed successor to John Gorton as director of the Legacies, assumed his post in time to be of inestimable service in many ways. Another important source of documentary material has been the Archives of American Art, Washington, D.C., where the overwhelming bulk of Rockwell Kent memorabilia has been classified and stored.

For much help and valuable advice I am especially beholden to Dan Burne Jones, Kent's official bibliographer and the leading expert on the artist's prints, and to George Spector, editor and publisher of *The Kent Collector*, a quarterly replete with Kentiana. My thanks also to Hayward Cirker, of Dover Publications, for the extended loan of many hard-to-find Kent books, and for permission to reprint certain passages from my introduction to *The Illustrations of Rockwell Kent* (1976).

Many others have been helpful in various ways: of these I would like to mention the print craftsman Letterio Calapai, of the Workshop Gallery, Glencoe, Illinois; Clarence P. Hornung; Kathleen Kent; the late Georgina Klitgaard; Kenneth A. Lohf, librarian of rare books, Columbia University Library; Robert Nikirk, librarian of the Grolier Club of New York; Dale Demy, production editor, and Naomi Osnos, designer, at Alfred A. Knopf; Richard Larcada, of Larcada Gallery–One Art Service; David Preiss; Andrée Ruellan; Richard V. West, director of the Crocker Art Museum, Sacramento, California, and an authority on Kent's paintings; and Karel Yasko, counselor for Fine Arts and Historic Preservation, General Services Administration, Washington, D.C. Some of Kent's letters were included in the anthology through the kind interest of Kathleen Kent Finney, Dan Burne Jones, Mrs. Albert E. Kahn, Victor and Ellen Perlo, and Paul Robeson, Jr. To the late Louis Untermeyer I owe the privilege of including a limerick he wrote on a greeting to Kent.

The preliminary task of considering Kent paintings for reproduction was considerably lightened by prompt responses from many museums. Acknowledgments for these are noted on pages 7 - 8 or the copyright page. For valuable help, particularly with respect to paintings in Soviet museums, my thanks to Herbert McCoy, Dr. Richard Stowe, Ed Brohel, and Bruce Stark, all of the State University of New York College at Plattsburgh, another important repository of Kentiana.

I am especially indebted to three private Kent collectors: Peter Brady (Oak Ridge Collection), Peter Bergh, and Joseph M. Erdelac, each of whom generously provided photographs of works in their possession. Also to Richard Lynch, of Hammer Galleries, for the use of many color transparencies.

To Angus Cameron, vice president of Alfred A. Knopf, warm thanks for his invaluable suggestions for this project, of which the first and most gratifying to me was that I should be the one to undertake it. Warm thanks also to Barbara Bristol for her fine-tuned judgment as my editor, and for her unfailing tact in dealing with her charge. To the efficiency and resourcefulness of Alice Gordon should be attributed the success of intricate arrangements connected with the reproduction of so many Kent paintings at so many places, including permissions and the tracking down of elusive examples and their owners. Inevitably, numerous inaccuracies and other faults resulted from my typing and retyping the manuscript; mercifully for everyone, and in the nick of time, my crimes against truth and syntax were rooted out by the vigilantes at Knopf. Those that remain are mine alone.

It was Robert Scudellari, art director and designer of this volume, whose skill at graphic organization transformed a huge, chaotic pile of assorted material into a superb format. And for me, especially, having this handsome book open with such a perceptive foreword by Jamie Wyeth was like frosting on the cake. My sincerest thanks to both.

And finally, deepest gratitude goes to my wife, Heidi Lenssen, who excels in every attribute truly worthwhile.

Woodstock, New York   *Fridolf Johnson*

MONHEGAN, MAINE: A SMALL ISLAND

FOREWORD

I am, perhaps, an odd choice to write a foreword to this large book on Rockwell Kent. First, because I am a painter, and not a writer. Second, the Rockwell Kent that has touched and deeply influenced me is but a small part of that man and his rich life. Nonetheless, it is that "small part" I shall attempt to share.

I am writing this on Monhegan, a small, windswept, North Atlantic island. It is on this island that Rockwell Kent lived and worked for several years. Just as an island can be viewed as a microcosm of the mainland, those few years are, in a sense, a microcosm of his entire life.

He first arrived on Monhegan in the spring of 1905, a twenty-three-year-old, fairly bursting with energy. Here was an island, beautifully picturesque, quaint, and, to all outward appearances, sweet. Kent looked deeper. His early paintings were almost elemental in their power. None of the pretty blue sky and sailboat-dotted sea for him. Kent painted the stark headlands and rugged fishermen. He remained after the summer people departed, to paint the island during the ravages of winter.

Monhegan was more to Kent than a place to paint. It was freedom, financially and psychologically. This was the first time he supported himself, earning a meager sustenance by well drilling, lighthouse keeping, carpentering, and, finally, by fishing alongside the islanders.

As one studies his life on the island, one finds two men. First, the ambitious young man with barely enough hours in the day to paint. Such was his excitement over his work that, for a period, he suffered from insomnia. Gradually, another man emerges. A man not content to just observe and paint, but one that felt the need to participate, to better understand his "fellow worker." His sense of social injustice grew, and it is here that he first struggled with his life-long philosophy: "Fundamental to all consideration of art is its purpose. To be entitled to the honor that society bestows upon it, it must unquestionably have a social value; that is, as a potential means of communication it must be addressed, and in comprehensible terms, to the understanding of mankind."

The Monhegan years were a major turning point for Kent. Eventually his world outgrew what he would later describe as "that world unto itself, Monhegan," and he left in the fall of 1910. He would return for brief visits in the fifties, but his time here was finished.

He went on, of course, to become an accomplished writer, explorer, sailor, lithographer, engraver, architect, farmer, and political activist; and he traveled to and lived in Greenland, Labrador, Alaska, Ireland, and Tierra del Fuego. All of which brought him fame and controversy.

As I sit writing, in this house that he built, I look around the walls, at the paintings he painted, and I think: What Kent accomplished in those five island years would satisfy most as a lifetime's accomplishment. But Rockwell Kent, as you will see in this book of his work, was forever a restless searcher, in his life and in his art.

Kent House, Monhegan Island   *Jamie Wyeth*

INTRODUCTION

He was not exactly tall — three inches short of six feet, to be precise — and one saw that his chin was not particularly prominent. His mouth was generous. (His mother once said that in profile he had the look of "a duck about to quack.") But the firm lines of his mouth and the burning brown eyes under bushy brows gave instant notice that his gentle and humorous manner was a cover for an aggressive mind and will. He could be impressively angry and assertive, and often was. His premature baldness and thin mustache, gray in his later years, added to his look of distinction. Nearly everything he did was newsworthy; his name was familiar, for a variety of reasons, to newspaper readers everywhere. He was at ease in the world, in public appearances, in highly publicized courts of law or inquisition, on radio and television, as well as in the company of the working classes he championed so often, and in sharing the hardships of primitive peoples. He was a remarkable, many-sided man; hard to forget.

Rockwell Kent was one of those who truly lived more lives than one. Into his long life he crammed more careers than any ordinary man would seriously contemplate. Painter, muralist, illustrator, printmaker, book designer, graphic artist, architect and builder, writer and editor, speaker and lecturer, navigator and restless traveler, political and social activist — he was all these and much more.

This is not to say that he was merely a jack-of-all-trades. As a painter, he won critical acclaim and his canvases were acquired by important museums and discriminating collectors. He was the first artist to incorporate himself, paying his shareholders handsome dividends. From long sojourns in Alaska, Tierra del Fuego, and Greenland, among other places, he brought back powerful paintings and vivid accounts of his experiences. The romantic appeal of the paintings and the circumstances of their production in faraway places brought large crowds to see them. Perhaps no other American artist before him had so graphically expressed the sense of remoteness and awesome splendor of the arctic.

As a wood engraver and lithographer, he was enormously successful, achieving international recognition as a master of the print. Somehow he found time to produce well over 150 engravings and lithographs, many as illustrations for fine books.

He was undoubtedly the most important American book illustrator of his time. Limited editions of the classics he illustrated during the twenties and thirties were enthusiastically snapped up at high prices by collectors and libraries. Trade editions of these, as well as his own heavily illustrated books on his adventures, reached additional thousands through distribution by influential book clubs.

Kent was equally distinguished as a designer of book jackets, bookplates, and campaigns for national advertisers, and for his unerring taste in fine typography. His distinctive style was extravagantly admired, assiduously imitated by amateurs and other professionals. All his drawings had the unmistakable stamp of his personality; thus his work was instantly recognizable, even to those not particularly concerned with such matters. Continual exposure in so many places and media made his work familiar to a much wider public than is ordinarily achieved by an artist. He became a cult figure; to this day there is a large body of collectors who hunt for and preserve every scrap of Rockwell Kent memorabilia. *The Kent Collector,* a quarterly, is the current focus for such activities.

Kent was driven by an almost uncontrollable urge to accomplish things, to succeed in everything, to seek out and overcome obstacles. He was continually at war with himself: "I suspect that I get up early in the morning because I want to lie in bed, that I exercise because I want to sleep, that I work because I am essentially lazy, that I want to accomplish something because I have profoundly a contempt for accomplishment." He had boundless energy, a strong back. When he was a young painter, he supported himself as a well-digger, a lobsterman, a carpenter and builder. He could hew timber for beams and build a house from the ground up. He could improvise a workshop for himself in the most unlikely places; a great number of his paintings and illustrations were made far from the conveniences of his studio.

OPPOSITE: FLAME, 1928, WOOD ENGRAVING ON MAPLE, 8 x 5-1/2"

ROCKWELL KENT

Kent's personal life furnished intriguing counterpoints to his multiple professional and public careers. His response to life was passionate and unequivocal. Kent admitted that throughout his life he had been governed chiefly by his emotions, and they were to cause him considerable trouble in his public as well as his personal relations. The erotic side of his nature surfaced early, coming to him, as he wrote in his autobiography, as premonitions "of future ecstasy and shame." These tendencies were long held in check by moral influences at home and unrealistic perceptions of love and marriage. He was in his middle twenties when he had his first sexual experience, and he was disappointed and confused by it. But he soon "made up for lost time," as he remarked much later, and his love life embraced three marriages and a heroic succession of affairs.

In time, Kent made little effort to conceal his connubial deviations from those who loved him, blandly describing a few of the more interesting ones in his books. Actually, there were a great many more — interludes of the moment or affairs of some duration. For him, the attraction of a desirable woman was seldom to be resisted. Predictably, complications often ensued, and it has been asserted — and he himself admitted — that his trips to the edges of the world were partly strategic withdrawals from emotional entanglements.

Prosperity and a greatly expanded social circle put an end to the Spartanism of his early years, when he was a strict vegetarian and baked his own bread. He loved fine food and good company, could outdrink his companions without succumbing, was a generous and resourceful host, played the flute well, wrote delightful verses for special occasions, was an ingenious practical joker. The attraction of his personality and accomplishments was magnetic, and the roster of his friends, infinite in its diversity, ranged far and wide, though subject to sudden omissions; he preferred those who accepted him as he was, never hesitating, for a time at least — or permanently — to cut off those he felt were not punctilious in their relations with him.

Kent was not one to turn the other cheek; his first reaction to the slightest infringement on his rights was to phone his attorney. Palpable imitations or unauthorized use of his work brought instant reprisal. His eminently numerous and sometimes spectacular legal battles included suits against a railroad (for discontinuing service) and a steamship line (for misplacing his son); he won them both. He engaged in a personal vendetta against roadside signs, chopping them down at night; he had himself appointed game warden to protect songbirds from promiscuous killings. From his youth he was a nonconformist, a champion of unpopular causes, giving much of his time and substance fighting for social justice, bringing down upon his head public and official abuse that now appears to have been in large part unjustified. His suit against John Foster Dulles and the State Department over his Constitutional right to travel was a *cause célèbre*. In 1958, the United States Supreme Court rendered a landmark decision in his favor.

In his hometown of Tarrytown, New York, Kent attended his first Socialist meeting in 1904, and became a member, paying his initial monthly dues of twenty-five cents. He had just passed his twenty-second birthday. From this small beginning proceeded an almost continual involvement in political and social reform movements throughout his life. For principles he believed in, Kent was always willing to stand up and be counted, joining and supporting scores of organizations; and because so many of them were suspected of being subversive, he was for many years burdened with a notoriety which effectively eclipsed his popularity as an artist. Later in life he developed a strong empathy with the Russian people, but he consistently denied his ever being a member of the Communist Party, declaring that he couldn't imagine himself being one because he felt that the Russian brand of Communism was quite contrary to his democratic notions. Nevertheless, he regularly suffered the hostility known to so many artists and writers of his time.

Since his youth, Kent had been an omnivorous reader and was well informed on many subjects. As one who frequently figured in the public press, he regularly subscribed to clipping services, carefully preserving his notices in huge scrapbooks. And he carried on a voluminous correspondence, which he systematically filed along with windrows of other records and ephemera. His secretaries were not allowed to throw anything away without his permission. Secure in the estimate of his lasting importance, and wishing to preserve all this material for posterity, at his death in 1971 he left behind an incredibly large amount of correspondence and memorabilia. It is a fascinating and instructive assortment.

FROM THE FIRST, Rockwell Kent revealed strong indications of an ancestry notable for independence and enterprise. No doubt in his genes he also carried accumulated vestiges of manual skills and pragmatic attitudes which he nurtured and put to good use. Independence of mind surfaced early in the person of William Rockwell, a deacon of the Congregational Church, who came from England in 1630 and settled at Dorchester, in the Massachusetts Bay colony. The deacon took exception to Governor Winthrop's negative ideas on democracy and soon moved, along with about half the population of Dorchester, to Windsor, Connecticut.

Little is known about Thomas Kent except that he came from England to Massachusetts before 1643. Significantly for our theme, one of his descendants, Zenas Kent, was a carpenter and joiner by trade, as was his son Zenas Kent II, who took a carpenter's daughter to wife. Zenas Kent II had a good head for business and grew wealthy and highly respected as a citizen of Mantua, Ohio. He and the abolitionist John Brown, who was to lead the raid at Harper's Ferry, were for a time partners in a tannery at nearby Franklin Mills.

The name of Zenas Kent lives on in the community; Franklin Mills was renamed Kent in his honor, and it was his son George Lewis Kent who drew the Rockwell line into his family's orbit by marrying Matilda Rockwell. In 1853, the young couple epitomized the union of the two lines by naming their baby George Rockwell Kent. The elder Kent prospered as a wholesale merchant in the city of New York and as owner of the Buckingham Hotel, which once stood on a site later occupied by Saks & Co. His son received an extensive education in mining engineering and law, and eventually became a junior partner in the New York firm of Lowry, Stone & Auerbach, with interesting peripheral consequences bearing upon a certain Sara Ann Holgate and the yet unborn second Rockwell Kent.

Sara Ann's father, Alexander Lindsey Holgate, had come from Manchester, England, and married a well-endowed widow, Clara Ann Guilmartin, daughter of John Gottsberger, from Vienna. Sara had an older brother, Frank, and a younger sister, Jo. When Sara was eleven, she was sent to live with her uncle James Banker and his wife, Aunt Josie. Her uncle's name was quite appropriate; his preoccupation was money and power, of which he had more than enough, and he was an intimate associate of Commodore Vanderbilt.

Superficially, Sara's good fortune had all the elements of a fairy tale: a huge mansion full of servants to spoil her, a palatial summer estate on the Hudson, a yacht, fashionable schools, and a will made by Uncle James leaving half of his wealth to her as an adopted daughter. But Uncle James was a tyrant, Aunt Josie cold and unapproachable, and the unhappy girl was too shy and intimidated to protest the stifling of her natural instincts. Then, in due course and again as in a fairy tale, came a handsome prince to rescue the beautiful girl from her thralldom.

Young Kent's firm had a client, Thomas Edison, seeking financial backing for an invention he called an incandescent lamp, and Uncle James agreed to meet him at the Tarrytown estate of Grosvenor Lowry. This was in the late summer of 1880; the day being ideal for a carriage ride, Uncle James invited his niece to come along—an uncharacteristically thoughtful gesture he was soon to regret. For it was at this meeting that Sara met the attractive junior partner.

A serious romance blossomed—secretly. When Uncle James got wind of it, he issued a ferocious ultimatum to Sara Ann: if she married the young attorney, he would not give them one cent, nor would he want to ever see his niece again. But Sara's will proved to be equal to that of her uncle, and on July 17 of the following year the pair ran off to New York City and were married.

RIGHT: BOOKPLATE DESIGN

R O C K W E L L   K E N T

OTTO J. FRANK, S. W. COR. 125 ST., & 3 AVE.

Father (in his prime)
to Kathleen (in hers)
Christmas
1933.

Apparently without much regret, Sara Ann shed her temporary name of Banker and relinquished her share of her uncle's fortune and the doubtful benefits of his solicitude. The newlyweds found a friendly haven in the gatehouse of Grosvenor Lowry's estate, and their first child (our Rockwell) was born there June 21, 1882. That he chose to come into the world so early as four o'clock in the morning was perhaps a presentiment of his lifelong habit of "getting things done." His brother Douglas was born two years later.

In the spring of 1883, the Kents moved into a quaint neo-Tudor house in Tarrytown, on the heights above the Hudson, where Rockwell spent the next ten years of his life. James Banker died in 1885, leaving his entire estate to his widow, but certain benefits filtered through to Sara Ann and her children in later years. Then, in September of 1887, Rockwell's father died, leaving almost nothing to the family that was soon to be joined by a baby girl, Dorothy. The Kent ménage almost foundered thereafter; but for the next fifteen years Sara, mostly by her own efforts, managed to maintain the household in an atmosphere of gentility. Her almost feudal concept of the family's superiority meant private schools for the children and a tacit quarantine against those on "the other side of the tracks." As Rockwell expressed it, "The tracks, to us, ran past our gate," and he had very few playmates.

Rockwell was thirteen when Sara's sister Jo took him to Europe for four months. Auntie Jo (not to be confused with the formidable Aunt Josie Banker) was not only strikingly beautiful but had practical abilities rare in a woman of her place and period, and also a modest reputation as a watercolorist. Their ship, the great Cunard *Umbria,* with its labyrinth of corridors and stairways, was endlessly fascinating to the boy. He was deeply stirred — prophetically — by the dense fog of the Newfoundland Banks, the limitless sea, the rolling and pitching of the ship on the high waves during a storm; thrilled by the unfamiliar sights and sounds of London, Liverpool, and The Hague. Their principal destination was Dresden, where Auntie Jo was to take lessons in painting Watteau vignettes on china.

It was at Dresden that Rockwell came face to face with another part of his nature: "The stairway to the floor on which we lived was in an open well and was entered from the street through an archway to a court. One day I burst in unexpectedly upon three little street girls who were seated on the lower steps, and one of whom had at that instant pulled her dress far up above her waist. The impact of her lovely nakedness upon me sent me rushing past them in a state of wild confusion and furious desire. Upstairs and all alone, I realized for the first time one thing, at least, that life was all about. If for no other memory, Dresden will be forever dear to me."

Rockwell returned to school in the fall with all the marks of an incipient man of the world. The boy's intractable spirit had apparently been too much to handle at home, and when he was about ten he was sent to a strict boarding school in North Tarrytown. Presumably he learned there, if nothing else, a few lessons in discipline. He had learned some other lessons, more useful in his opinion, after he had been enrolled, in 1893, at the Episcopal Academy of Connecticut, in the little town of Cheshire, near New Haven.

Here, also, discipline was strict, and as in most such schools of that period, between masters and pupils there was no friendliness or trust, but over all a chilling pall of overt surveillance. Rockwell later described his years at boarding school as "tantamount to seasonal orphanage." Authority, in his mind, became something to mistrust or repudiate. His prejudice against Latin exasperated the teachers and no amount of punishment or reasoning had any effect. But he enjoyed English, delighting in the intricacies of sentence structure, a predilection apparent to readers of his prose. As he later expressed it: "I think I liked it particularly because, as it was then taught, we diagrammed our sentences, made pictures of them, showing them to be somewhat like living trees having the power to grow and, branching out, bear leaves and blossoms. And the more intricate a sentence was, the more I delighted in the interrelationship of its parts, articulating them, and making sure the sap could reach and nourish every least last branch."

OPPOSITE, CLOCKWISE FROM TOP: YOUNG ROCKWELL; ROCKWELL'S UNCLE, JAMES BANKER;
AUNTIE JO; ROCKWELL (LEFT) AND BROTHER DOUGLAS WITH THEIR MOTHER, SARA KENT,
TARRYTOWN, N.Y., JUNE 1885; ROCKWELL'S FATHER, GEORGE ROCKWELL KENT, WITH HIS
SILVER FLUTE; AUNT JOSIE BANKER. CENTER: ROCKWELL AS A CHILD
(PHOTO INSCRIBED IN 1933 TO HIS DAUGHTER KATHLEEN)

ROCKWELL KENT

At the academy, prayers and worship were obligatory, and as Rockwell soon discovered, "There religion was organized, ordained to be a daily diet." At night, lying in the dark, he would ask himself unanswerable questions about what it all meant — the earth and all it held, the unreachable spaces above it, with its stars, and the invisible Spirit his elders confidently asserted was their sole Creator and Master. Faithfully he said his bedtime prayer; sometimes he was unaccountably stirred by the solemn ritual and music of the Sunday services. "But what has such religion got to do with sitting in hard seats or pews, sitting till your bottom ached, and listening to manufactured prayers and all that sort of thing out of a book by professional pray-ers, by clergymen who, just like us choir boys, wore their real clothes under their gowns (their trousers showed) and their real, everyday voices under the holy ones they used in church?" In time, Rockwell rejected what he conceived to be only mumbo jumbo, forming in its place a more personal but deeply reverential response to the cosmos.

In 1895, Rockwell was enrolled in the Horace Mann School in New York, to which he commuted from Tarrytown every school day. It was a private school, modern in every respect. To Rockwell and some of the other boys, previously conditioned to the artificial segregation in boarding schools, the presence of girls in class was obnoxious. In later years, of course, Rockwell would be infinitely more tolerant. At Horace Mann he developed skills and aptitudes that were to play a major role in his future life and career.

Meanwhile the vexing problem of family finances continued. Rockwell's mother and Auntie Jo were driven to such expedients as needlework, cooking, baking, and candymaking for sale at the Tarrytown Woman's Exchange. Auntie Jo set up a charcoal kiln, putting to good use what she had learned in Dresden, and on weekends and holidays Rockwell helped out by painting simple designs on chinaware. By the time he was fifteen, he was already practicing as a professional, making, among other small items, sets of dinner cards on commission.

It was plain to see that Rockwell had exceptional talents and drive. His natural bent came into sharper focus when he attended the summer art school at Shinnecock Hills, near Southampton, Long Island. His mother and Auntie Jo had a cottage nearby. It was the first out-of-doors summer art school in America. William Merritt Chase (1849 – 1916) had founded it in 1891. Even before 1878, when Chase returned from six years of study at the Munich Royal Academy, he had won popular and critical acclaim, and the summer school attracted pupils from across the country. Though he was sometimes labeled an Impressionist and, like the Impressionists, believed in painting directly outdoors, he considered himself a realist. Avoiding the "little dabs of color" characteristic of some Impressionists, he worked with a loaded brush in generous sweeps that conveyed impressions quickly and succinctly; he could finish a still life of fresh fish in time to have his subject still fit to be prepared for dinner. Chase was a master of atmosphere, particularly adept at rendering highlights and surface qualities.

Dapper, immaculately turned out, and with a flair for showmanship, Chase was the perfect image of the successful artist of that time. His huge studio at 15 West Tenth Street, in New York,

ABOVE: THE CHESHIRE ACADEMY, 1947, LITHOGRAPH ON STONE, 10-7/8 x 14-7/8"

ROCKWELL KENT

was tastefully crowded with bizarre art objects, armor, weapons, exotic musical instruments, and richly carved furniture. The walls were hung with tapestries, lined with innumerable pictures in large gilt frames. On the floor stood palms in huge brass pots.

But American artists were generally not as prosperous as they had been a decade or so before. They had suddenly found themselves forsaken in favor of the salon art of the French Academicians, to which some nine or ten million visitors had been exposed at the 1876 Philadelphia Centennial Exposition. The lure of "anything French" was too strong, and few art patrons bought the work of their American contemporaries. Chase, though fairly successful, largely supported himself in a brilliant career as a teacher in various places, including the Pennsylvania Academy of the Fine Arts. By the time he died, he had taught literally thousands, leaving in his wake an impressive roster of important twentieth-century American artists.

At Shinnecock, inspired by Chase, Rockwell devoted himself to painting with enthusiasm. Loving the outdoors and imbued with the conviction that nature was the fountainhead of all art, he set up his easel in some field or grove or barnyard every morning and afternoon. At classroom critiques, Chase often praised his work, and the second summer awarded him a picture painted before the class by the master himself. Furthermore, Chase was so impressed with Rockwell's abilities that he offered him a full scholarship to the New York School of Art.

Rockwell's mother and aunt were dismayed; the family was too poor to afford an impecunious artist. Besides, how would he resist the immoral influences of a bohemian life? Could he willfully put a blot on the family escutcheon? Why couldn't he choose a career that was more respectable, one that would bring in an assured livelihood — architecture, for instance? Reluctantly he gave in to family pressure and registered in the School of Architecture at Columbia University in the fall of 1900. In the entrance examination he made the highest score and won a four-year scholarship.

At Columbia, Rockwell's natural aptitude and strong competitive instincts brought him marks as good as or better than those of his classmates. Without being a drudge or learning by rote, he ingeniously recorded the essentials of what he had learned on charts of his own devising. These consisted of pictures, diagrams, and various distinctive styles of lettering and colors which he could invoke visually in his mind at examination time.

Students were required to make a dozen architectural sketches during summer vacation to submit at the opening of the fall term. The majority of the sketches turned in were obviously dashed off at the last minute, passing muster simply because they had actually been made. But Rockwell made the summer's work a vocation, producing twelve very large paintings in oil. As they proved too cumbersome and expensive to ship from home, he submitted only one, with a letter from his master certifying that he had done all twelve. When an officious professor nevertheless still demanded to see them all, Rockwell blew up and threatened to cut the one canvas into twelve pieces and submit them on separate mounts. This, one of the more colorful of Rockwell's infractions of the school's standards of behavior, nearly caused his dismissal; the difficult boy had become a difficult young man.

At Columbia, architectural rendering was the only subject he could respond to with feeling, no doubt because it was more like painting, and he desperately wanted to be a painter. To him, architecture was a dead end, and in the middle of his fourth year he had had enough; he retrieved the scholarship Chase had offered him in 1900. As though the stars had ratified his act, his mother inherited enough money from Aunt Josie's estate to maintain her in financial security for the rest of her life, and he now had no reason to feel guilty about his revolt.

While Rockwell was studying at Columbia, he also attended Robert Henri's evening life-classes at the New York School of Art. Originally known as the Chase School, it had been founded in 1896 by Chase himself, but under his management the school ran into the red; the school was renamed and came under the direction of an associate, Douglas John Connah, who had persuaded Henri to teach there also.

Connah, a fine man and a painter of portraits and large nudes, was noted for his rendering of beautiful, pearl-like skin tones, a faculty perhaps reflective of his consuming interest in women. Tall, handsome, and elegant, he was irresistible to feminine hearts, and apparently exerted very little resistance in his own behalf. It was rumored that while studying in Europe, he had had a serious romance with a relative of Kaiser Wilhelm.

Besides the inevitable financial difficulties, Connah had problems with Chase and Henri, who differed widely on teaching methods, Chase asserting that Henri's viewpoint was vulgar. The majority of the students sided with Henri, and flocked to his classes in such overwhelming numbers that in 1907 Chase resigned and returned to his former post at the Art Students League. Henri, weary of waiting for back payment of his salary, resigned in January of 1909 and immediately set up classes of his own in the old Lincoln Arcade Building at Sixty-sixth and Broadway.

Auntie Jo had once studied with Abbott Thayer, the naturalist-painter, and through her influence he agreed to accept Rockwell as an apprentice. Thayer (1849–1921) had gone to Paris in 1875 to study under Gérôme; after his return home he had a brief success as a figure painter, working in a semi-classical idiom — chaste, ideal, impersonal — that also brought him some mural commissions. But in 1901, discouraged and suffering from recurring fits of depression, he retreated to a house near Dublin, New Hampshire, at the foot of Mount Monadnock. When Rockwell joined him in the summer of 1903, Thayer found little for him to do, and most of the time he was free to paint for himself.

The Thayer home was an absurd though amiable establishment, isolated from all but a carefully chosen few. The drafty, nondescript house, buried in the dark woods, was sparsely furnished; sleeping arrangements were in separate lean-tos nearby. The austere and lofty-minded Thayer was the master; his disciples were his wife Emma, his son Gerald, his daughters Gladys and Mary, and everyone else admitted to the sacred circle. Mealtime conversation was intellectually rarefied and resolutely moral; Thayer, growing more and more eccentric, was completely removed from any political or social realities, and Rockwell kept his liberal ideas to himself, but later wrote that his association with the Thayers was one of the richest cultural experiences of his life. Another benefit was that he sold a painting for the first time — two, in fact. They had been painted at Dublin in 1903 and exhibited at the winter show of the National Academy. *Dublin Pond* (page 256) was bought by Smith College, and *Monadnock* by Charles Ewing, eldest son of a Tarrytown family. Rockwell felt that his student days were over.

With some of the proceeds of her inheritance, Rockwell's mother decided to build a house, and bought land in Tarrytown. Naturally, she turned to Rockwell for suggestions as to its design, and just as naturally, he mentioned this to his friend Charles Ewing, who was head draftsman for a large New York architectural firm. Charles saw it as a golden opportunity to set up a firm of his own, and with George Chappell, another Beaux Arts student, opened an office in New York and promptly hired Rockwell as draftsman to work on the new firm's first and at that time only commission — the Kent residence. Typically suburban, slightly pretentious, and costing much more than expected, it had an impressively large studio for Rockwell, but, as he later remarked, "reflecting the happy transient domestic relations of that period, the servant rooms resembled prison cells in size."

ABOVE: SARA KENT'S HOUSE IN TARRYTOWN, N.Y. KENT'S
FIRST JOB AT EWING & CHAPPELL WAS TO WORK
ON THE DRAWINGS FOR HIS MOTHER'S NEW HOUSE

ROCKWELL KENT

The firm of Ewing & Chappell had good connections and prospered. For many years, as a capable draftsman and warm friend, Rockwell was always welcome to use the office as his headquarters and to work there whenever he needed to earn some money.

Late in 1904, Rockwell enrolled in the daytime classes at the New York School of Art; mornings he painted from life under Henri and afternoons he studied under Kenneth Hayes Miller. Robert Henri (1865 – 1929) had first studied at the Pennsylvania Academy of the Fine Arts under Thomas Anshutz, then for three years in Paris. After a period of travel and painting in Europe and of teaching at the School of Design for Women in Philadelphia, Henri settled permanently in New York in 1900. John Sloan, George Luks, William Glackens, and Everett Shinn had also studied with Anshutz in the early nineties. Through Anshutz, all were inspired to turn toward contemporary subjects, shocking the world of art with their paintings of the seamier side of life — laborers, street characters, barrooms, tenements, alleyways. Collectively they were later dubbed the "ashcan" school of art, and Henri was its leader. Henri's paintings, though often superficial, were done with remarkable facility and brilliant brushwork; his importance lies more securely in his gifts as a teacher and writer on art. His book, *The Art Spirit,* first published in 1923, has become a classic and has been an inspiration to generations of artists.

Kenneth Hayes Miller (1876 – 1952) had a reputation as a teacher almost on a par with that of Henri. He had studied under Chase and Kenyon Cox, but had also turned to the New York scene for subjects. His concern was more with form and composition than with light, shading, and bravura brushwork. One may see the influence of Miller overshadowing that of Henri in Kent's later style of simple, crisply defined shapes and formalized patterns of dark and light colors and tones. But it was Henri who, by chance, was to have a profound effect upon Rockwell's immediate future.

In 1903, Henri had spent the summer happily painting at Boothbay Harbor, a picturesque fishing village on the coast of Maine, but when he discovered the more dramatic configurations of Monhegan Island, ten miles from the mainland, he was ecstatic. Rockwell, infected by Henri's enthusiasm, was eager to go there; he first saw Monhegan in June of 1905 and promptly fell in love with it.

ROBERT HENRI'S LIFE CLASS, NEW YORK, 1907; KENT, AT EXTREME LEFT

ROCKWELL KENT

In those more spacious days, the village of Monhegan consisted of perhaps less than thirty houses, as simple and unpretentious as their occupants, most of whom depended upon fishing and, in particular, lobstering, for subsistence. The year-round villagers were not unfriendly but preferred to mind their own business, leaving painters and tourists to shift for themselves. As Rockwell came to know the fishermen, he learned to admire them for their skill in handling boats and their intimate knowledge of the rough seas that dashed against the rocky shores. And he envied them, too; compared to them, he was a useless painter of pictures. It was here that he truly began to appreciate the dignity of labor, to discover a latent affinity to the working classes he had been exposed to so frequently while studying with Henri. He wrote that he, too, would be a laborer, see and feel what *they* saw and felt. How much of this was born of conviction or was merely circumstantial is not clear, but the hard fact was that he would soon run out of money, and he wanted to stay longer.

At the end of the summer season he found a cheap room and took a job as assistant teamster, longshoreman, and well-driller to a man named Hiram Cazallis. An eight-hour day at various jobs netted him eight dollars — enough to pay room and board and to buy essentials. An occasional job to clean a privy for ten dollars was a windfall. Digging wells into solid rock was the hardest labor of all; even so, as his muscles hardened he retained enough strength and energy to paint every free moment.

When, in December of 1905, Rockwell left Monhegan, he was proud of his horny hands and tough muscles, his mind stimulated by his newfound empathy with the working classes. His experience at hard labor had begun to confirm attitudes he was gradually absorbing from serious books. Reading Herbert Spencer, he was grateful to be told that infinity and eternity were essentially unthinkable and unknowable, and not to be thought about. He said that this set his "Victorian mind completely and lastingly to rest." He also read Haeckel and Darwin, imbibing from them a mechanistic conception of the world that precluded what he considered an evolutionary aberration (as he put it): " . . . the origin and existence of privilege and its transmission to unworthy heirs; the concentration of great wealth in hands which did not labor to create it; the existence of poverty in a land of plenty." For Rockwell, the issues were simple; the workers must be given an even break, and he had joined the Socialist Party in 1904 as the best instrument for achieving labor reform through orderly, legal tactics.

The transitory joy of being home again soon gave way to an uncomfortable sense of alienation from the family, who felt that he had sinned by turning his back on a respectable career as an architect and by displaying an unaristocratic solicitude for the anonymous masses who existed on a much lower plane and should therefore be ignored; and his silly vegetarianism could only end in physical and moral collapse.

By April of 1906, he was back on Monhegan again, and that summer he built himself a house on Horn's Hill. It was small, but good enough for a self-sufficient bachelor with no money to speak of, and he found odd jobs to keep him going. Despite hard labor and his vegetarian diet, he remained exceedingly healthy.

He stayed on Monhegan all through that winter, and by March of 1907 he had managed to produce enough paintings for an exhibition. On the first of April, a show of fourteen fairly large canvases, modestly priced at from $200 to $600, opened in the gallery of William Clausen at 381 Fifth Avenue. Reviews were encouraging, but nothing was sold. However, a number of the paintings eventually gravitated to important collections; notably, *Winter, Monhegan Island* (page 254), to the Metropolitan Museum of Art, and *Toilers of the Sea* (page 243), to the New Britain Museum of American Art.

In early summer of 1907, he returned to Monhegan flushed with his New York "success" but with empty pockets. Relief came unexpectedly in the form of a partnership in the building of two houses. By this time, he had come to be accepted on the island almost as though he belonged there, but he seldom resisted an urge to air his views on religion or any other controversial subjects, and in time he became somewhat notorious; clearly he had no ambition to become a consummate public-relations man.

ROCKWELL KENT

With children he was a great success, though some were forbidden to go near him. The less conservative younger set liked him well enough, and he frequently joined their evening gatherings, where they sang and played games, and where he often saw a girl we shall call "Janet." A faded snapshot shows her modestly dressed in a white middy blouse and a full dark skirt to the ground; over her round, sweetly smiling face is an abundance of dark hair crowned with a bun. Rockwell was intrigued by this plain, unalluring girl's uncanny ability to read his mind at games, touched to the heart by her artless singing, and he taught her some of his favorite German songs. In the early part of his autobiography, he several times mentions his "better self," that priggish alter ego of his that invariably surfaced whenever the juices of his youth showed signs of erupting. Thus, in his middle twenties, he was still the embryonic lover. Now physical attraction and clandestine meetings on secluded paths proved to be too much for both of them.

Though Rockwell loved Janet, he was not yet ready for a lasting relationship, and his departure from Monhegan in December of 1907 may have been partly a strategic retreat. After the holidays he shared the old farmhouse of George de Forest Brush, near Dublin, with Gerald Thayer. They were joined later by young George Palmer Putnam. Though the Brush house, meant only for summer use, was frigid, they enjoyed the isolation, and Rockwell painted constantly. Of the paintings he made that winter the best known is *Road Roller* (page 255), first shown under the title *Road Breaking* at the Independent Artists Exhibition of 1910 and now in the Phillips Collection in Washington, D.C.

Rockwell's aim to paint as much as possible that winter was deflected somewhat, in February of 1908, by the unexpected entry into his snowbound Eden of a beautiful young girl. Her name was Kathleen Whiting; she was Abbott Thayer's niece, and she had come to the Thayers in Dublin for a short visit. There was instant rapport between them; both promised to write, and Kathleen invited him and her cousin Gerald to visit her family in the Berkshires in March.

At dawn of what promised to be a clear March day, the young men set out from Dublin on horseback. The catch was that they had but one horse to ride on, and they used the "ride and tie" method, a time-honored expedient in which one would ride ahead for about ten miles while the other walked, then leave the horse at an appointed hostelry for his partner and proceed on foot for another ten miles or so. Alternately riding and walking in the heavy snows for several days was an ordeal, and when they finally arrived in Berkshire, Rockwell could barely walk; he spent the first full week in bed. As in the old tales of wounded knights and pure maidens, he had the delicious compensation of having the lovely Kathleen to nurse and comfort him.

It was a situation for which he was poorly prepared. Later he wrote, "If, in my boyish experience, I could only have known — if, with her young girl's trustfulness, Kathleen could only have known — how little the judgments and the promises of the innocent are to be relied upon; if she, or I . . . could have had a premonition of the excesses to which my first real taste of the good wine of life would lead me, what endless sorrows might have been averted!"

They were thrilling weeks of courtship, of "fervent, passionate anticipation." Because Kathleen was so young — only seventeen — her parents insisted that the wedding be deferred until New Year's Eve, nine months away. Early in the summer, Rockwell went to Monhegan to prepare the house for his bride.

It could not have been easy to tell Janet of his engagement; she was crushed, but he naïvely hoped that she and Kathleen would accept the situation and become friends. As he was to demonstrate repeatedly in subsequent triangles, his inflated expectations of feminine forbearance never diminished. His relationship with Janet was hardly interrupted, as later events proved.

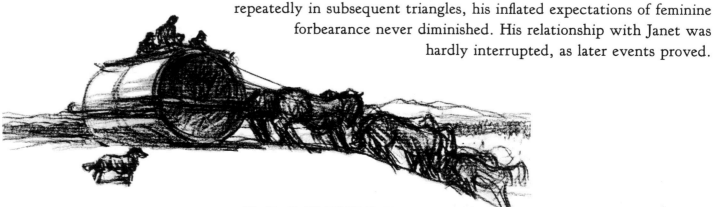

R O C K W E L L   K E N T

Rockwell added a room to his house and built a porch, restored old furniture, and started a big garden for vegetables. He took any kind of odd job to bring in extra money, hoping to have at least $250 saved up by the time they were married. His impatience for the consummation of his desires was intensified by uneasiness over Kathleen's parents, who, he knew, were not very happy about the match. At the risk of alienating them still more, he insisted on a civil ceremony, on the grounds that he was a non-believer. On December 31, 1908, and in the Whiting home, the wedding service was read by an indulgent Unitarian pastor from a script written by the groom himself.

Kathleen's anxious parents decreed that the couple spend at least the remainder of the winter nearby, and a cottage was found for them in Berkshire. The bride's expectation of an idyllic domestic life, with endless hours of leisure and romantic communion, was soon dissolved by her husband's insistence on a strenuous household routine; for him, love requited was incidental to "getting things done." Furthermore, he left her alone often while he was out painting, and finally every day, when he took a job with an architect in Pittsfield.

Together they went to Socialist meetings in Pittsfield. The speaker one night was J. Graham Phelps Stokes, a prosperous man with radical leanings which he shared with his wife, Rose, who also attended. The four became good friends, and as Kathleen was already pregnant, the Kents were invited to await the arrival of their child in a separate house on the Stokes estate on Caritas Island, near Stamford, Connecticut.

By the end of September, 1909, the Kents were settled there, and Rockwell resumed his job at Ewing & Chappell; he also enrolled again in Henri's evening life-class, which meant that Kathleen would be alone six days a week, from breakfasttime until her husband got home from New York late at night. Generously he devoted most of his one day of rest to her, but he was preoccupied much of the time with another matter: plans for the Exhibition of Independent Artists, scheduled to open in New York on April 1, 1910.

Kent, like many other artists, resented the consistent rejection by the National Academy of any art that was not safely traditional. An earlier manifestation of revolt against Academic prejudice had been the widely publicized group show of eight angry artists — John Sloan, George Luks, William Glackens, Everett Shinn, Robert Henri, Maurice Prendergast, Ernest Lawson, and Arthur B. Davies — held at Macbeth's Gallery, on Fifth Avenue. Known as an exhibition of "the Eight," it ran through the first two weeks of February, 1908, racking up an impressive record of about seven thousand visitors and the sale of seven pictures for a total of $4,000.

Inspired by the show's success, early in January of 1910 Henri had suggested to John Sloan that they start a society with its first purpose to present a no-jury exhibition completely free of Academic shibboleths. The idea immediately took fire; Kent and Walt Kuhn joined in and they found a suitable exhibition site on three floors of a building on West-Thirty-fifth Street.

Minimal entrance fees and the absence of a jury attracted a motley assemblage of nearly five hundred works of art. More than two thousand people jammed the opening, and comment varied from favorable to scornful. Yet the show made a lasting impression on the world of art and planted the seeds for the future Armory Show of 1913 and, ultimately, in 1916, for the establishment of the Society of Independent Artists. The catalogue lists four paintings by Rockwell Kent; they won considerable praise, and *Art News* described the artist as "in a way, a younger Winslow Homer in his somewhat hard and crude color but dramatic intensity."

Rockwell's minor success as a painter did little to assuage Kathleen's pain over his involvement with Janet. How she found out about it and when is not clear, but that it was quite early is revealed in a letter she wrote to her husband in February, 1911: "It is as though you had plunged a knife into my heart four months after our marriage." He had confessed all, in what he wrote was the "quaint and disastrous illusion that it is best to tell the truth . . . self-righteousness, that cloak of perfidy!" Pros and cons of confession aside, the natural result of the revelation was unhappiness for both, even

OPPOSITE: ROAD ROLLER, 1907 – 09, CHARCOAL STUDY, 7-7/8 x 9-7/8″,
THE PHILADELPHIA MUSEUM OF ART

ROCKWELL KENT

A SUMMER SCHOOL OF ART
ON MONHEGAN ISLAND
COAST OF MAINE
School prospectus, summer of 1909.

after the birth of their son, Rockwell III, on October 25, 1909. In May, Kathleen, bewildered and still unhappy, took the baby and retreated to the comfort of her family in Berkshire. Rockwell, knowing that Janet was away from Monhegan, went there and — with Julius Golz, a classmate of his at the Henri school, as partner — threw himself into the establishment of a summer school of art. The school attracted some fifteen or twenty pupils that year.

Their marriage hung in the balance for several months before Kathleen agreed to join Rockwell on Monhegan, but with the conditions that he give up Janet and leave forever the scene of his first fall from grace. Early in October of 1910, they returned to New York, but the reunion was an uneasy one and Rockwell, though contrite, was inwardly defensive. He had tried his wings too soon and had landed in a patch of nettles, but he had his career to think of. Characteristically, he found a geographic solution to his dilemma by going away for a while. The higher latitudes had always appealed to his adventurous spirit; perhaps he and Kathleen could find a new life in Newfoundland! Barely two weeks after they had come to New York, Kathleen and the baby had moved in with friends on Pacific Street, in Brooklyn, and Rockwell had packed his bags.

He arrived in Boston on October 14, expecting to get cheap passage on a herring-fishing boat bound for Newfoundland, but the sailing had been postponed for two weeks; he could not afford to wait that long and he decided he would have to go by rail to North Sydney, Nova Scotia, and take a regular boat from there. Knowing that Janet and her sister were then living in Boston, he went to see them on Saturday afternoon and later took Janet to dinner. It was all innocent enough; they would not see each other again. His "better self" had triumphed, but Sunday morning brought another trial when he found that there was no train to North Sydney that day. Disgusted, he turned away from the gate — and ran into Janet outside the station. They spent the night together in a small hotel across the street and bid each other a poignant farewell the next morning.

Newfoundland was a glorious adventure, with its magnificent, mountainous shoreline and its rough seas.[1] What is more, he had discovered an abandoned fishing establishment — a perfect site for a school of art! Excitedly he wrote to his friend Bayard Boyesen, who had plenty of money to help finance it and with whom he had often discussed just such a project. Full of bright dreams, he started for home after being away for a month.

---

[1] On October 19, Kent sent a postcard to Kathleen: "Dear K. Here I am at N. Sydney. Leave here tomorrow. Am in a very cheap and dirty hotel. Went down a 700-ft. coal mine this morning. Wonderful. Took sleeper last night & slept splendidly. Rockwell." He painted two small pictures. His hotel bill, including five meals, was $1.50, which he paid off by painting a satin sofa pillow for the proprietor's daughter.

ABOVE: COVER DESIGN FOR ART SCHOOL PROSPECTUS, MONHEGAN, 1909

The Kents then moved into a walk-up studio in an old brownstone at 165 West Twenty-third Street. John Sloan, who lived with his wife, Dolly, just above them on the top floor, was not too pleased to have Rockwell for a neighbor, having seen enough of Kathleen's unhappiness. However, they got along well enough, and Sloan taught Rockwell the rudiments of etching.

Early in December of 1910, Rockwell went alone to Monhegan to finish some paintings and prepare his house for sale. While there, he received a disturbing letter from Janet — she was three months pregnant — and he hurried to Boston to meet her in the railroad station. Janet wanted to keep the baby for herself, and the family for whom she worked as a nursemaid offered to let her stay with them as long as necessary. When Kent came home and broke the news to Kathleen, they decided there was only one thing to do: liquidate all available resources, and together with their savings, send every penny of it to Janet. Rockwell's practical response to this financial calamity was to show up for work at Ewing & Chappell at nine o'clock the very next morning.

By frugal living and on a vegetarian diet, the Kents managed on $25 a week. Resilient and confident as usual, Kent, having been offered free use of the loft in the building of the Society of Beaux Arts Architects, decided to be the entrepreneur of another art show similar to the 1908 exhibition of "the Eight." Because he adamantly refused to include any artist who was willing also to exhibit at the Academy, Henri, Sloan, Glackens, Bellows, Davies, and some other fine artists withdrew under protest. Of the final muster the most notable were: Guy Pène du Bois, George Luks, Marsden Hartley, John Marin, and Maurice Prendergast. The show, billed as "An Independent Exhibition of the Paintings and Drawings of Eleven Men," ran from March 26 to April 21, 1911. Not so controversial as the previous show, it drew less attention, but Kent felt that his time had been well spent, and after receipts and expenses had been figured, the eleven men were each out of pocket only $23.44. As there had not been enough entries to fill the huge loft, Kent had hung fifteen paintings and twenty-four drawings of his own, all never shown before; among them: *The Seiners* (page 242), later bought by Henry Frick; *Down to the Sea* (page 245), now in the Brooklyn Museum; and *Men and Mountains* (page 258), now in the Columbus Museum of Art in Ohio.

Publicity and favorably inclined art critics do not necessarily add to an artist's bank account. For some time, Kent had been hoping to find a patron, and in his papers is a heavily altered and re-altered rough draft of what seems to be a form letter written in 1910, in which he voices a complaint common to so many artists: "Today, in the prime of my life, it is absolutely impossible to give any but a few occasional days to my painting. These years which should be the most productive in a man's life are thus wasted and going by. You know the value of art. . . . What I want is this — enough money to enable me to paint continually. I can support my family, I think, on eight hundred dollars a year."

The Kent's second child, Kathleen, was born a month prematurely on April 19, 1911. Both the weakened mother and the frail baby sorely needed rest and fresh air in the country. Rockwell also knew that his wife's decline in spirit stemmed in great part from her being aware of the imminent birth of Janet's baby, inescapable evidence of her husband's infidelity. In desperation, and at the prompting of Arthur B. Davies, he appealed for help from the New York dealer William Macbeth, who had already shown an interest in his work. Macbeth offered to give him five hundred dollars, and Kent gratefully gave him the choice of as many paintings as he would consider equivalent to the money. Macbeth took thirteen of his best. Kent's versions of the transaction vary considerably — in one calculation he puts the value of the gold frames alone as greater than the sum he received. In any event, Macbeth got an unusual bargain, but Kent reasoned that the ready cash probably saved the lives of his wife and child. Janet's baby, born that June, was sickly at birth and died four years later.

On the advice of friends, Rockwell went to Richmond, New Hampshire, where he found an abandoned farm with an old ruin of a house that the owner was willing to let the Kents occupy rent-free in return for renovating it. Working stark naked in the sweltering heat of June, Kent made it again habitable, and a New York woman named Lily moved in with them to help Kathleen with the chores and the children. An attempt, again with Julius Golz, to start a summer art school at Richmond brought six pupils, but only three stayed, and Golz bowed out. Except for the improved health of Kathleen and the baby, the summer was a total loss. With the household goods packed and his family in the care of kindly neighbors, Rockwell returned to New York early in October and to his job at Ewing & Chappell; Barry Faulkner, a mural painter and nephew of Abbott Thayer, lent him his studio to live in until he could find a home for his family.

He found a ground-floor apartment, including basement, at 4 Perry Street, in Greenwich Village, where they lived quite comfortably. For a maid they had Lily, who had the basement in return for her services. They rented a grand piano for Kathleen and began to entertain, sometimes rather elaborately, but with an eye to economy. A constant visitor was the painter Marsden Hartley, a gentle, introspective man who envied their apparent happiness. And Carl Zigrosser, his distinguished career as an authority on prints still before him, came often. Carl, then about twenty years old, admired Rockwell immensely and was thrilled at his first penetration into the romantic life of the Village. Of the hundreds of friendships made through the years, Carl's proved to be one of the most enduring and fruitful.

Ewing & Chappell was very busy, and Rockwell made a lot of extra money for overtime, as well as on free-lance commissions for architectural renderings. Having no leisure to paint, he yearned for escape from his dull routine, and when in March of 1912 he was offered a year's work as a construction superintendent in the small town of Winona, Minnesota, he jumped at the chance to be free again.

The year in the small Minnesota town presumably had a steadying effect on their marriage, though in his autobiography Kent mentions Kathleen and baby, she returned to Perry Street with the children in March of 1913 while he remained behind to complete his job. Now he was free to do whatever he pleased, and he wrote that "despite the absence of Kathleen and the children, my last months there had been the best." In May, he had an exhibition of his paintings at the Winona Public Library, and before he left early in June there was a rousing Sunday picnic in his honor.

the children only obliquely. He remodeled a vacated schoolhouse for the family to live in and acquired a horse and carriage to ride to work and back. Through his employers he was accepted by the more prosperous members of the community, but he preferred the company of his fellow workers and took a prominent part in their disputes over wages. As Kathleen was to have another

The Kents' third child, Clara, was born June 30, 1913, and by that time Rockwell was back at Ewing & Chappell. His chosen career as a painter still suffered from what he felt to be the stupefying routine and unrewarding work of an architect's office. And simply because he had been working in faraway Minnesota at the time it was being planned, he had missed taking part in the spectacular Armory Show, which had run in New York from February 17 to March 15 of that year. The modest success of his exhibition at the Winona Public Library was poor compensation for the much greater one that would surely have been his had he remained in New York. However, he derived some satisfaction from the professional recognition he was winning with his architectural renderings. In watercolor, he could convey the exact color and texture of materials and at the same time, without compromising the structural verities, create compositions vibrantly suggestive of fine art. After all, it was more like painting, closer to his heart, and at the end of summer he resigned his job again and took space at 101 Park Avenue, advertising himself as an expert at "architectural rendering and general de-

signing in any medium." He also moved with his family to the mansion of his Uncle Percy and Aunt Frances, at Chappaqua, where they had free lodging in the servants' quarters in return for Kent's redesigning and remodeling an old house on the estate.

The move was not exactly Rockwell's idea of escape from his present condition, but at least he would not be tied down by daily routine, and he would go to his office only when he had a job to do. Still hankering to settle in Newfoundland, he went to Charles Daniel, a former bartender who had established himself as an art dealer in December of 1913. Kent, who had designed his gallery, told him about Newfoundland and suggested that if Daniel would finance him at the rate of two hundred dollars a month, he could have all the paintings and drawings Kent would make there. Daniel readily agreed, and Kent jubilantly wound up his affairs and made arrangements for the well-being of his family, who would join him in Newfoundland as soon as he could find a home for them.

Then Daniel suddenly changed his mind, explaining that the proceeds from his gallery would not warrant such a commitment. But Kent, though stunned, was determined to go regardless. A few days later, Daniel relented and offered to pledge fifty dollars a month, and Rockwell's mother offered to contribute an additional fifty a month.

Rockwell left from Brooklyn on a Red Cross liner early in March of 1914. A steward, sensing the discrepancy between his aristocratic bearing and his fifteen-dollar steerage ticket, kindly found him an unoccupied cabin on an upper deck and arranged for him to eat in the officers' mess. Arriving four days later at St. John's, Newfoundland, he was advised to settle at the little fishing village of Brigus, forty miles away, on Conception Bay. There he repaired a tiny house, added a studio, and then sent for his family.

In their cramped quarters, Kathleen had her hands full with the children; then she gave birth to another child, Barbara, on June 6, 1915, and spent several weeks recuperating in a St. John's hospital. Regularly prevented by bad weather from painting outdoors, Rockwell worked in his studio and brooded. His disconsolate mood is poignantly expressed in most of his paintings that have survived. The outbreak of war with Germany had also cast a pall upon his spirits.

On a happier note, though overshadowed by a sense of isolation, is *Portrait of a Child* (page 261). The infant Clara, naked, lies sleeping, behind her a vast panorama of land, sea, mountains, and clouds. It is now in the Pushkin Museum of Fine Arts in Moscow.

The insularity of the Brigus villagers was somewhat tempered by proximity to St. John's, the thriving North American seaport closest to Europe. At the same time, simply because Brigus was so near this center of wartime activity, it became a fertile seedbed for anti-German hysteria. To the villagers there was something sinister about a man who claimed he had come into their midst merely to paint pictures. He had been seen reading a German book; he had written a letter, partly in German, to a friend in Wisconsin; when he bought eight tons of coal, he was suspected of planning to supply a German U-boat with fuel; and he had been heard to say that he didn't think the British could reach Berlin in less than a year!

Kent's abrasive reactions to such foolish talk merely intensified suspicions that he was a spy. A joke that backfired was his posting on his studio door a sign with a German eagle on it and the words "Bomb Shop, Wireless Plant, Chart Room." He was accused of threatening a minor official, and rumors spread higher up. The authorities at first refused shipment of *Portrait of a Child* to Charles Daniel because "charts of forts and coast defenses were concealed among the lines that formed the composition." Police officials often dropped in on him unexpectedly, and finally, one day in mid-July of 1915, he was given twenty-four hours to leave the country. Appeals to the American consul failed, but he was granted a short postponement because all his children had whooping cough. In a formal letter to the immigration chief, Kent sarcastically requested permission for "six German spies" to leave.

ABOVE: NEWFOUNDLANDER

ROCKWELL KENT

There are two sequels to the story. In October of 1916, newspapers headlined the story of his eviction and of his attempt to sue the Canadian government for $5,000 damages. Secretary of State Lansing ruled that he had no grounds for action. And in 1967, fifty-two years after his eviction, Newfoundland's current Premier, Joseph Smallwood, having studied the case and wishing to make amends, invited Kent and his wife to St. John's as his guest. The Kents accepted and spent a week there the following July. Kent presented to Smallwood one of his paintings of the Monhegan coast.

THE RETURN OF Rockwell Kent and his family to New York was hardly triumphant. Without funds, his fourth child little more than two months old, Rockwell was grateful to be met at the dock by at least one friend, George Chappell. Chappell had found a temporary home for Kathleen and the children in New London, Connecticut, and Charles Daniel arranged for Rockwell to sleep nights in the briefly vacant New York attic apartment of the painter Middleton Manigault.

After an enervating search in obscure neighborhoods for a house he could afford, Rockwell finally found one: the old Pelton house, at 1262 Richmond Terrace, in West Brighton, on the northern shore of Staten Island. While living in New London, Kathleen had been slightly hurt in a trolley-car accident, and the $500 compensation she received was enough to pay the first month's rent and buy some furniture. The house, built before the Revolution, was uncomfortable and, when the winds were right, permeated by noxious odors from the chemical works on nearby New Jersey.

Work at Ewing & Chappell was falling off because of wartime restrictions on building; commissions for architectural renderings were few, and there was barely enough income to keep the family afloat. The sale, through Charles Daniel, of *Portrait of a Child* netted him $200; it was the only painting he had sold in a long time. Daniel finally sold two more Newfoundland paintings at low prices. Occasionally the Provident Loan Association lent five dollars on a gold pen once owned by his father.

Kent was desperate, and in April of 1917 he wrote to executives of the Northern Pacific and the Canadian Pacific railroads suggesting that he be commissioned to paint the American West for advertising purposes. He included publicity clippings and commendatory letters from Bryson Burroughs, of the Metropolitan Museum, and from the art critic Charles H. Caffin. His letters were not answered.

The Society of Independent Artists, formed in 1916 with Glackens as president, had now embarked on an ambitious program of mounting a no-jury show every year, the first one to open April 10, 1917, at the Grand Central Palace. Kent, drafted to act as full-time administrator, set up an office in the basement of the Palace early in 1917 and got busy. The constitution of the society guaranteed that every work submitted with the six-dollar fee would be included. To test the validity of the guarantee, Marcel Duchamp made art history of a sort by submitting, under the name of R. Mutt, an ordinary porcelain urinal entitled *Fountain*. Kent says that it was ruled out on a technicality: the entry card did not identify its creator. Otherwise, anything at all was accepted. There were 1,130 members exhibiting, and to avoid favoritism their work was arranged in alphabetical order, beginning with a letter chosen by lot. Understandably, the show somewhat resembled a flea market, overflowing with over two thousand works of art from good to trashy, a wild mélange of "isms" from primitive to pseudo-French abstractions. Kent showed two of his Newfoundland paintings; even his sister Dorothy entered a watercolor, and his seven-year-old son a drawing of some animals.

There were no prizes, but there was a brass band for the opening, and a huge crowd attended. The show ran through May 6 and into the red. The first act of the committee in planning the next year's show was to repudiate the debts of the first one. Kent says, "This was too much for me; I quit the Independent movement." Subsequent shows at the Waldorf-Astoria and at the Fine Arts Society, on West Fifty-seventh Street, were generally less uninhibited and played an important part in fostering acceptance of the modern movement in art. John Sloan succeeded Glackens as president the second year, and was regularly re-elected to that office until the society was disbanded during World War II.

ROCKWELL KENT

 OUR scribe has three brothers all nearly of an age and all marked by a strong resemblance to the eccentric features of their sire. Heredity has been strong with us for generations and such features as advancing culture and refinement are supposed to modify, with us have not been so affected. Take our ears, for example. A family portrait five generations old shows Round Head Thumtack painted in profile and displaying on his near side a very sail-like sound-collector. That side-face portrait gave the

45

In the years after his comfortless return from Newfoundland, economic difficulties were gradually deflecting Rockwell's energies into channels which would ultimately earn him a fame somewhat different from what he had hoped to gain from his paintings — that of the most important American illustrator of his time. It is doubtful that he anticipated or even wished for it, fired as he was with the ambition to become, more than anything else, a great painter. The process of becoming an illustrator was at first a slow one.

Back in 1906, at Tarrytown, he had amused himself and the family circle by making humorous drawings for a private, ephemeral, and little-known typewritten periodical named *The Blue Mouse*. The masthead lists as "soul" editors: James Gillespie, Blaine Ewing, and Rockwell Kent. Subscribers: Mrs. Charles Ewing and Mrs. Rockwell Kent. At this remove, it is difficult to appreciate the recondite humor of the "news" items and verse, but one can see how some of the illustrations prefigure his later satirical drawings.

Then, while at Ewing & Chappell, his friend Frederick Squires persuaded him to illustrate a book Squires had written. Working at night, Kent quickly turned out eighty-five drawings and some decorative initials. *Architectonics: The Tales of Tom Thumtack, Architect,* was published in 1914. Squires hid his identity under the name Tom Thumtack, but Kent left his drawings unsigned.

More time passed. Humorous verse written by George Chappell had been appearing occasionally in *Vanity Fair,* a chic and glossy monthly edited by Frank Crowninshield. Crowninshield, a wit and exponent of graceful living, was rapidly turning the magazine into a favorite in fashionable circles. Rockwell made a satirical drawing for one of Chappell's poems and submitted both to Crowninshield, who was delighted but insisted that the drawing be signed before he would buy it. Kent, not wishing to be identified with such frivolous work, made a tactical retreat by writing "Hogarth, Jr." at the bottom. Thereafter the team of Chappell and Hogarth, Jr., sold many more of their joint efforts to *Vanity Fair,* in the beginning netting ten or fifteen dollars apiece each time.

When architectural commissions at Ewing & Chappell came to an end, Rockwell was out of steady work. Trying to earn a living from the relative isolation of Staten Island was out of the ques-

ABOVE: A PAGE FROM ARCHITECTONICS:
THE TALES OF TOM THUMTACK, ARCHITECT, 1914

ROCKWELL KENT

tion, and in June of 1917 Kathleen and the children moved to Monhegan to occupy a cottage friends had put at their disposal, while Rockwell took a room with bath on Twelfth Street, in the Village. For some years, Rockwell's slim income came from the regular sale of Hogarth, Jr., drawings to *Vanity Fair* and to *Puck,* and from numerous small commissions of the sort.

In his Village room, still trying to augment his income, Kent made glass paintings, a form of decoration popular long ago, in which the painting, done on the reverse side of a sheet of glass, is viewed from the front. For these he worked out a number of designs consisting of single figures with decorative backgrounds of trees, flowers, birds, and the like. With a key drawing positioned under the glass, he first painted in the outlines and details; then when these were dry he would add the back-ground colors. The attraction for him was that from one design he could make innumerable replicas for sale. His friend Max Kuehne made the frames, which included a mirror. Though they were done in an Art Deco style calculated to catch public fancy, their reception was disappointing, and an exhibition of them at Wanamakers in the spring of 1918 brought only one sale.

Living alone in Greenwich Village, with his family far away on Monhegan, Rockwell had plenty of solitude for reflection and ample scope for amorous adventures in the big city. Connubial re-straint was a poor match against his thirst for life. In his autobiography, in a chapter headed "Transgression," he tells of an affair he had with a show girl he had spoken to on the street. He says it was in the summer of 1916, but it is more likely that it was the following year. His description of her does not correspond with purported photographs of her, though they are obviously theatrical prints; perhaps she did not have "golden hair and blue eyes," and no doubt "Gretchen" was a name of his own invention. In this chapter he waxes lyrical over the week they spent in New Hampshire, camping in total isolation and enjoying themselves and each other with complete abandon.

His relationship with Gretchen continued for several years, and in his room on Twelfth Street she helped him in the simpler operations of turning out glass paintings. Since Rockwell had given up all pretense of being a faithful husband, Kathleen paid with her own despair the price of his "fulfillment." As the breach between them widened, the situation was becoming so unbearably com-plicated for Rockwell that a strategic withdrawal seemed the only solution.

Improvement in finances soon made it possible. Mrs. Albert (Marie) Sterner, in charge of contemporary art at Knoedler & Co., took an interest in him and, among other things, brought him $1,500 through the sale, to Henry Frick, of his Monhegan painting, *The Seiners.* When Charles Dan-iel adamantly refused to release any of his stock of Kent paintings for inclusion in a special show at Knoedler's, Mrs. Sterner got around that by borrowing the painting *Winter, Monhegan Island,* which Rockwell had given to Robert Henri some years before. Henri generously gave it back to Rock-well, and Mrs. Sterner then sold it to the Metropolitan Museum of Art. Kent appears to have been reluctant to remember what it was sold for, but once admitted that he had received nearly twice as much as he had expected. Kent had another windfall in a mural commission from Thomas Howell, for which he received the handsome sum of $1,500. At last he had enough money to support his family for about a year and freedom to go far away. He chose Alaska.

With some misgivings, Kathleen agreed to let their son Rockwell go along; he was a sturdy boy, tall for his eight years, and would at least serve as a tenuous link between herself and her footloose husband. Late in July of 1918, the two adventurers began the long journey by train and by boat to Seward, where they learned of a place to stay on Fox Island, near Seward and less than four hundred miles below the Arctic Circle. Between the mountains and the rough waters of Resurrection Bay was a narrow strip of land owned by an old Swede named Olson, who lived there with his pet foxes and a few goats. Some distance from Olson's cabin was a small log cabin Olson had built as an additional shelter for goats. Rockwell and his son moved in after first making it at least habitable; living there in bleak isolation was a Spartan experience which both enjoyed.

Kent painted by day and drew by lamplight at night, or wrote carefully composed letters to

OPPOSITE: DRAWINGS BY "HOGARTH, JR." FOR VANITY FAIR, PUCK, AND A BASKET OF POSES, 1915–24

RIGHT: TRADEMARK FOR KENT'S GLASS AND MIRROR PAINTINGS, C. 1917

ROCKWELL KENT

his family and friends. In such a narrow terrain, for weeks made sunless by the overlooking mountains, Kent found little material for the spacious landscapes he preferred. In a mystic mood, deepened by seclusion, he turned to figure compositions in which he tried to make palpable the essential loneliness of man. Not so melancholy as his Newfoundland paintings, they reflect a cogitative man's belief in the indestructibility of the human spirit. He began to draw figures striding across dark skies studded with stars, finding in them a theme and form of pictorial expression that was to become a personal trademark.

The months passed swiftly; winter was nearly over, and father and son would have been content to stay much longer. Yet Rockwell missed the comforts of marriage; Kathleen had consistently — and sensibly — refused to leave the other children with friends and join him. Her funds were nearly depleted, and her unhappiness and resentment were only too manifest in her letters. After nearly seven months in Alaska, he and his son left Fox Island on March 18, 1919.

Back in New York, Rockwell found things going his way at last. Mrs. Sterner arranged a show of his Alaskan drawings at Knoedler's and issued an impressive illustrated catalogue; it was the beginning of Rockwell Kent's success. At the show, Mrs. Sterner introduced one of his most enthusiastic admirers to Kent. He was Egmont Arens, part owner of the Washington Square Bookshop in Greenwich Village, and editor-publisher of an art and literary magazine with the unlikely name of *Playboy,* which he printed by hand, two pages at a time, on a small press. As Kent's ink drawings were eminently suitable for printing on a hand press, Arens suggested that they cooperate in publishing them in a deluxe limited edition. They had already begun having printing plates made when George Putnam asked for permission to publish an entire book on Kent's Alaskan experience through his family's firm, G. P. Putnam's Son. The Kent-Arens project was abandoned, but some of the plates were used in Nos. 3, 6, and 7 of *Playboy.*

Soon Kent was out of debt and had over $2,000 in the bank, enough to warrant looking for a home away from New York. Through Dorothy Canfield and her husband, John Fisher, a classmate of Rockwell's at Columbia, who also loaned him some money, he was able to buy an isolated farm, known as Egypt, near Arlington, Vermont, on the southern spur of Mount Equinox, and for the fifth time found himself at hard labor rebuilding a dilapidated house to live in.

Clearly, the move to Vermont would soon leave Kent once more without a penny, and to assure an uninterrupted income that would enable him to go on painting, he and his friend George Putnam set up a novel business arrangement which made him, according to an article by Putnam in *Collier's,* June 5, 1920, "the world's first incorporated artist." Kent would receive a monthly stipend, and in return, proceeds from the sale of any and all Kent products, "be they paintings or drawings, or cordwood or potatoes from his Vermont farm," would go into the corporate treasury. Two other friends joined in the deal: Juliana Force, closely associated with Gertrude Vanderbilt Whitney in forming the Whitney Studio Club; and Caroline O'Day, an important figure in social works and feminist politics. In frequent retellings of this interesting story, including Kent's own published accounts, details vary widely, and it has often been asserted that the corporation financed Kent's trip to Alaska. Actually, according to the minutes of the first stockholders' meeting, December 19, 1919, found in Kent's papers at Asgaard, Au Sable Forks, New York, the certificate of incorporation was notarized at Rye, New York, June 26, 1919 — about three months *after* Kent's return from Alaska — and filed at Albany, New York, August 5. Rockwell Kent, Inc., began business with capital stock of $4,000, at $100 per share, with half in Kent's name; Force owned ten shares; Putnam and O'Day five each. The four constituted the board of directors, and apparently there were no other investors. Force was elected chairman, and Putnam secretary. As general manager, Kent drew something in excess of a hundred dollars per month in salary and for administrative expenses; he designed the corporate seal, a letterhead, and a handsome stock certificate.

Thereafter, events moved rapidly and happily. In March of 1920, there was a second Kent

ROCKWELL KENT

show at Knoedler's, this time of his paintings, and it attracted large crowds. Following closely on the opening was the publication, March 19, of Kent's book *Wilderness: A Journal of Quiet Adventure in Alaska,* with sixty-four drawings and a decorative map by the author. The reviewers praised it and the public bought up one edition after another. Its great success added another dimension to Kent's celebrity; his financial problems temporarily vanished, and in about two years the corporation was liquidated, the stockholders receiving a healthy dividend of 20 percent on their investment.

A fifth child, Gordon, was born October 1, 1920. Though a strict father when he was around, Rockwell took proprietary pleasure in the children, and he wrote glowingly of one happy summer at Egypt when the entire family often romped naked in the warm sun. But he was not really a family man, and he spent a good part of his time in a shack far away from the house, where he could make his own meals, even sleep some nights, and paint undisturbed by domestic concerns. From the dooryard he painted such canvases as *The Trapper* (page 272) and *Shadows of Evening* (page 270), now at the Whitney Museum, and *Mount Equinox, Winter* (page 271), now at the Art Institute of Chicago.

In 1920, the Kent children were invited to attend the Edgwood School in Greenwich, Connecticut, and the entire family to occupy the gate house of the school estate during the nine-month school term. This pleasant arrangement began in the fall of that year, and continued for two more terms. With the family comfortably and happily housed in Greenwich, Rockwell was free to do what he liked — and did. He had many occasions to travel to New York, and as a tacitly unattached male in the carefree atmosphere of the postwar decade, he succumbed to innumerable temptations to sow wild oats; "not that I *sowed* the oats," he wrote; "carried about with me, they just slipped out!" Subsequently, introduction to a madcap circle of affluent sophisticates drew him into many additional emotional alliances, including one of long duration with a lady who presented him with a specially made gold key to her apartment. The consequences of all these intimacies were predictable; in the spring of 1922, "fed up with the whole emotional mess" he had gotten himself into, Rockwell impulsively decided on escaping to South America. Feeling that no spot in the world could be worse than the one he was in at that unbearable moment, he chose one that would be an even match — Tierra del Fuego.

TIERRA DEL FUEGO is by far the largest island of the Fuegian archipelago at the extreme southern tip of South America. The western part, and most of the Chilean archipelago, consists of majestic mountains, partly submerged to form tortuous channels and thousands of bleak islands. Far down, at the very bottom of the map, and the southernmost of all, is a tiny island from which rises the promontory of Cape Horn. This region, boasting probably the world's worst climate, is buffeted incessantly by winds, swiftly alternating with rain, hail, and snow. It is the legendary graveyard of ships and sailors, and in Kent's mind was the half-formed idea of trying his mettle against the hazardous adventure of sailing "round the Horn."

Late in May, 1922, he left on a freighter bound for Punta Arenas, Chile, a port on the western shore of the Strait of Magellan. The third mate on the ship was a tough Norwegian whose name was Ole Ytterock, though everybody called him Willy. A hardened veteran of brawls and dangerous escapades, Willy was just the man to be fired by Kent's plan to round the Horn. At Punta Arenas, Kent bought a ruin of a lifeboat for a few dollars and proceeded to transform it into a sailing vessel. By the end of August, their little ship was ready for action, and Kent christened it *Kathleen.*

On the first day at sea the *Kathleen* sprung a leak and nearly foundered, but they somehow managed to get to Dawson Island, where they made extensive repairs. They continued on their journey, and for nearly five months they sailed, explored islands, and hiked through jungles and over mountains, eventually finding themselves in Beagle Channel. Kent was still obsessed by Cape Horn, but had to acknowledge the futility of venturing the frail *Kathleen* through the dangerous currents and storms that barred the way between Beagle Channel and Cape Horn. For the purpose, at Ushuaia, he borrowed a slightly more seaworthy, sloop-rigged boat with a motor, and persuaded another man, a

ROCKWELL KENT

Swede named Christopherson, to go along. Not far from their goal, terrible storms forced them to turn back, and on Bailey Island they climbed through sleet and snow to the top of a mountain for a last look southward. As if by a command from above, the storm clouds parted momentarily, giving Kent a tantalizing glimpse of the Horn, faint and far off, then closed again. The rest was anticlimactic; he sold the *Kathleen* and by January of 1923 was on a freighter bound for home.

For *Century* magazine he wrote and illustrated an account of his trip; under the title "Voyager's Log," it appeared in four parts, July – October, 1923. George Putnam also pressed him for the manuscript and drawings for a book on his adventure, and there were his Fuegian paintings to prepare for exhibition. With so much to do, it seemed most expedient to send Kathleen and the children, with a tutor, for a year's stay in the South of France, and they left in November.

Rockwell was alone again — but not for long. About this juncture in his life he wrote that he found being alone "unendurable. The biologic unit is the pair, and to divide it is to split a personality; to like it so is to confess abnormality. What were the hallucinations of St. Anthony but the warnings of human nature's safety valve?" And, quoting William Blake, "Better strangle an infant in his cradle than nurse unacted desires."

His companion that winter was an out-of-work show girl he had used as a model some years before. Kent calls her Maureen, and describes her as "that dark-haired, gray-eyed, Celtic type that is so beautiful."[2] It was a warm and useful relationship; Rockwell wrote his book and Maureen typed it.

By early spring of 1924, the text and one hundred illustrations for *Voyaging: Southward from the Strait of Magellan* had been completed, and about the same time, the Wildenstein Gallery mounted a show of twenty of his Fuegian paintings. The show was well attended but, as Kent remarked, " . . . the trend toward the so-called 'modern' schools had already alienated from realism many who, in the previous decade, might have been purchasers." *Voyaging,* however, published simultaneously in limited and trade editions in October of that year, was a signal success and was reprinted many times.

At the time of the Wildenstein show, Kent was offered an exciting proposition. Judge F. DeWitt Wells, who was planning to buy a boat in Denmark, asked Kent to accompany him there and

---

[2] "Maureen" was the same woman who came to a tragic end in the summer of 1953, when the Kents had lent her a Horn's Hill cottage on Monhegan. (This was not the Kent cottage, but one Rockwell had built originally for Mary Kelsey, a friend of his mother's. After many years of neglect, it had fallen into disrepair, and Rockwell had bought it back and refurbished it.) Maureen suffered from depression, and apparently either fell or jumped to her death into the sea one night. In 1947, the Kents had visited the island for the first time in many years and had met with hostility from some of the natives as the result of Kent's political activities. They saw Monhegan for the last time in the fall of 1953. In December of that year, Kent wrote to his friend Myron Nevelson: "Our stay on Monhegan last fall was marred by the resurrection of the alleged murder scandal and the descent on the Island and us by hordes of officials and plainclothes cops and political hoodlums and reporters. It was only a week or ten days ago when the grand jury and prosecutor announced what everybody with a grain of intelligence had known all along: that it was an accident or suicide." The cottage was taken over by friends; the house Kent had built for his mother at Lobster Cove was eventually bought by Jamie Wyeth.

ABOVE: TWO ILLUSTRATIONS FROM <u>VOYAGING</u>, 1924
LEFT: <u>KATHLEEN</u> AS SHE WAS. RIGHT: THE HOUSE AT HARBERTON

OPPOSITE, TOP: KATHLEEN KENT AND THE CHILDREN, C. 1923 – 24
BOTTOM: GILLETTE, A. M., 1925, OIL, 28 x 34", COLLECTION OF CORLISS LAMONT

ROCKWELL KENT

to act as navigator in sailing it back to America via the arctic. Kent readily agreed, as he had planned on visiting his family at Antibes that summer in any event. But his relations with the judge, whom Kent refers to as "Hizzoner," were extremely unpleasant almost from the day they left for Europe, and later that summer, when the judge peremptorily summoned Kent from Antibes to Copenhagen to take charge of the boat, Kent pronounced it unseaworthy and bowed out. The judge added a competent Danish seaman to his small crew; even so, the boat was wrecked off the coast of Nova Scotia, but without casualties.

In the middle of the summer, Kent returned to Vermont — to earn more money. Several weeks later, his son Rockwell was put aboard a Fabre liner at Marseilles to return alone in time for school. The boy had a ticket to New York, but the ship arrived there without him; he had been carelessly put ashore at New London, Connecticut, the day before. Kent was frantic. After many hours he learned that the Traveler's Aid had found the boy a bed for the night and eventually shipped him to Auntie Jo in Tarrytown. Naturally, Kent began a highly publicized legal crusade against the Fabre Line and its agents, including an order he obtained from the city marshal forbidding the departure of another Fabre liner until the company had posted a bond of $50,000. After almost two years of litigation, Kent permitted his lawyer Philip Lowry to settle the suit and keep the proceeds as his fee.

With his family still at Antibes, Kent was alone during the winter of 1924 – 25. By now, it was abundantly clear to Kathleen that her attachment to her husband hung on the slenderest of threads, and when she wrote to him suggesting a divorce whenever either one wished it, Rockwell not too reluctantly accepted the idea and from then on held himself to be free. He lost no time finding a second "other half"; a woman of independent means and artistic pretensions. She was rather dramatically neurotic as well, but Kent fancied himself more capable of handling her than her psychiatrist; they became engaged and his bride-to-be bought a house in the mountains and he set about enlarging it.

Rockwell informed Kathleen of his intentions to marry again, and in June of 1925 he sailed for France. At Bonson, in the Maritime Alps, Kent painted all summer, spending weekends with his family at Juan-les-Pins. The Kents were divorced at Nice that summer and Kathleen received the Vermont place as settlement. In view of his fluctuating income, the decree specified no exact amount of alimony payments other than tacit provision of adequate funds for his family.

Kathleen and the children returned to New York at the end of summer, Rockwell soon after. She helped him establish an apartment in Greenwich Village, and he also rented a studio nearby on Perry Street. Little Kathleen (they called her Kay) was to live with Rockwell so she could study the violin with David Mannes. Kay, at fourteen a beautiful girl, tall for her age, was happy to play the young lady romantically squired around the Village by her father, for whom she had deep affection that seldom wavered. Several years later, when he was in Greenland, she wrote, "I am only interested in telling you how much I love you, even though you are a terrible Father. . . . I am not married yet, and am expecting you to live up to your promise and become my husband when you get back."

Rockwell fared less well with his ex-wife; without consulting him she sold the Vermont place, which he would have wanted to buy, and for a long time Rockwell could communicate with her only indirectly, through Kay or Philip Lowry. Eventually, Kathleen accepted the situation; Kent's relations with their children through the years were to vary individually from warm to perfunctory.

When, in January of 1926, he received a cable from his unstable fiancé calling off their marriage because she had fallen in love with someone else, Rockwell characteristically took it all in his stride. In his studio on Perry Street, besides working on his paintings, he systematically took up wood engraving, lithography, and commercial illustration as the most direct and reliable means of earning money for his increasing expenses. A lucrative commission from the advertising firm of N. W. Ayer & Son to make a series of advertising drawings for Marcus & Co., the New York jewelers, brought in a handsome check every month.

But financial success and an active social life were not enough for Rockwell; he wanted most of all to get married and move again to the country. For the attractively affluent and impulsive man to begin the process was a matter of weeks. At a house party in Manhasset, Long Island, he met Frances, a recently divorced member of the Lee family of Virginia. Rockwell promptly fell in love with the charming blue-eyed blonde, eighteen years younger than himself, and proposed to her the following evening. After sixteen successive evenings together, she accepted, and they were married on the fifth of April.

Frances, with her social background, had many personal connections in common with Rockwell; also in common was a taste for the gay and free life of the "roaring twenties." That she also shared his penchant for rigorous living is doubtful. Their honeymoon in the Adirondacks, alone in the cold and snowbound summer house of the Ralph Pulitzers, gave her broad hints of what life with her new husband would be.

The four months they spent in Ireland that summer were at least less strenuous, though not very comfortable. They found an ancient, typically Irish, low-slung stone house overlooking Donegal Bay. The house was in ruins, and all that remained fairly intact was a single room at one end, which had lately been used as a cowshed. It was very small and without a door, but it had a fireplace to cook in, and overhead a decent thatched roof. Rockwell cleaned out the dung, laid a cement floor, put in a door and a wider window, built a bedstead and other furnishings. Like their poor peasant neighbors, they baked bread over a peat fire, ate potatoes, cabbage, oatmeal, and other wholesome Irish fare, drank poteen from a neighbor's clandestine still.

Rockwell was bent on staying there until he had accumulated enough paintings for an exhibition, so Frances agreed, not a bit reluctantly, to return to New York to find an apartment. She found a pleasant six-room flat at 3 Washington Square North, and also rented a studio for Rockwell on the top floor. They were joined by Kay and by Frances's small son Dick. The new Mr. and Mrs. Rockwell Kent now had the means and the place to participate fully in Manhattan's gay life; they entertained lavishly — bohemians as well as financiers; moved freely in the rarefied precincts of the Pulitzers, the Whitneys, the Gordon Abbotts, the Watson Webbs, and were frequent guests at social affairs on suburban estates. Despite such pleasant distractions, Kent was enormously productive in his studio.

In the spring of 1927, Wildenstein's exhibited thirty-six paintings Kent had made in Ireland, and the Weyhe Gallery showed his Irish watercolors and drawings. The two shows were successful, and the Kents celebrated with a huge housewarming.

ABOVE: DRAWING FOR AN ADVERTISEMENT FOR MARCUS & CO., JEWELERS, C. 1927–29

ROCKWELL KENT

Actually, Kent's burgeoning prosperity was to come more directly from his success as a graphic artist and printmaker. When he went to Alaska in 1918, his friend Carl Zigrosser had given him material for wood engraving to experiment with, and after his return he took up the medium in earnest. His first large print, *Blue Bird*, was included in a deluxe portfolio, *Twelve Prints by Contemporary Artists*, prepared by Carl Zigrosser as director of the new Weyhe Gallery, and it was also selected by the American Institute of Graphic Art for its book *Fifty Prints*, 1926.

For Kent, the transition from rendering drawings in ink with pen or brush to the more formal disciplines of engraving on wood was smooth and perfectly natural. And his pen drawings began to assume the superficial character of metal engravings, with their firm outlines and their clear tones made up of uniformly spaced parallel lines. To these he often added areas of solid black with dramatic effect. Thus his pen drawings and wood engravings complemented each other, together creating a graphically potent style that was new and distinctive, not easily overlooked. In less than ten years, Kent was to gain international recognition for his engravings and to be pronounced the most widely known and successful illustrator and graphic artist in America. His illustrations, treated as works of art by well-known corporations, conferred on their advertisements a cachet which set them far above the usual run of publicity. Kent was fortunate in being one of the first artists to reflect the growing concern for elegance in printing.

Interest in finely designed and printed books as subjects for collecting reached a high pitch during the prosperous twenties. The swelling market for high-priced limited editions created a favorable climate in which gifted designers and quality printers flourished. One of the most distinguished entrepreneurs of fine bookmaking was Elmer Adler, who in 1922 had established his Pynson Printers in New York with the avowed purpose of producing the very best work regardless of time or cost. And in 1929, George Macy founded the Limited Editions Club, offering to 1,500 yearly subscribers one new fine edition of a literary classic per month at fifteen dollars each. His venture was such a success that he later began publishing less expensive editions under the imprint of the Heritage Press. Renewed interest in good book design had a salutary effect on trade-book publishing as well.

Rockwell Kent was admirably equipped to profit from this trend by virtue of an informed interest in all aspects of book production and the remarkable affinity of his illustrations to the printed page. Some of his finest books were made at Pynson Printers; the Limited Editions Club and other discriminating publishers gave him ample scope for his genius. In 1926, the Lakeside Press of Chicago commissioned him to design and make the drawings for a fine edition of Herman Melville's masterpiece, *Moby Dick*, a project which took nearly four years to complete. Also, Bennett Cerf and Donald Klopfer, publishers of the highly successful Modern Library series, had decided to issue other types of books "at random," using the name Random House as imprint. They chose Kent to illustrate the first title, Voltaire's *Candide*. During a discussion in Cerf's office, Kent casually drew for them a trademark they adopted for use in various forms ever since.

ABOVE: CHILD AND LAMB, 1926, WOOD ENGRAVING ON MAPLE, 2-5/8 x 2-1/2″

OPPOSITE, TOP: WHEN THE SUN SHINES (IRELAND), 1926
BOTTOM: BLUE BIRD, 1919, WOOD ENGRAVING ON MAPLE, 6-1/16 x 6-1/16″

ROCKWELL KENT

K. MCMXIX

For the *Moby Dick*, Kent put in many weeks of intensive research on whaling lore before starting the drawings. In June of 1927, he sent the first completed drawings to William Kittredge, design director of the Lakeside Press, who wrote, "These are magnificent and exceed our fondest expectations. Your great genius as a thinker, painter, and draughtsman was never more successfully demonstrated."

The Kents spent the summer of 1927 at Woodstock, New York, the art colony in the Catskills, where they occupied the big Shotwell house, former home of a professor at Columbia University. As usual, Kent's days and nights were crammed with social activities and work. From Kaj Klitgaard, a retired Danish master mariner, he took lessons in the science of navigation; young John Carroll, already noted for the elegance of his dreamlike, opalescent paintings of women, made a portrait of Frances.

In August, the nationwide controversy over the seven-year-old Sacco-Vanzetti case came to a boil when a Massachusetts court condemned the two men to death. Like thousands of others, Kent had pronounced the trial a travesty, and had joined in appeals for clemency. When Governor Fuller's refusal to grant it was supported by his three specially appointed advisers, one, president of Harvard, and another, president of the Massachusetts Institute of Technology, Kent wrote later that he was shocked that any university, thought to be "above all a means of deepening and enriching the humanity of man," should acquiesce in such a "deep offense to justice, humanity, and common decency," calling it "a crystallization of class prejudice." The execution of Sacco and Vanzetti, more than anything else, crystallized Kent's growing commitment to social causes, for which he was to become an obstinate and untiring champion. For a start, in his "deep loathing of a state whose courts, whose leading citizens, whose governor, whose people had promoted, perpetrated, and condoned so hideous a crime," he wrote to the Worcester Museum canceling the show of his paintings scheduled for the fall. Vowing to "have no relations of any public nature" with Massachusetts, he added, "I can unfortunately attach no public importance to my resolution: it is merely necessary to my own integrity."

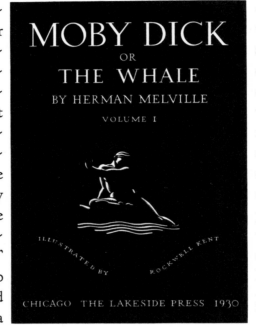

In September, the Kents bought an abandoned farm on 257 acres near Au Sable Forks, New York. Surrounded by sloping pine forests and with a splendid view of Whiteface Mountain and the Adirondack Range, was a large level area of farmland and meadows. Within six weeks, Rockwell's plans for a sprawling two-story house had been drawn and construction begun. Meanwhile he was busier than ever. That year, in addition to painting, printmaking, advertising work, and preliminaries on the *Moby Dick* project, he completed the illustrations for *Candide* and two decorative paintings for Steinway & Sons. He was also appointed editor of *Creative Art,* the American edition of the British monthly *Studio,* a position he held from November to the following April, when he resigned because of the pressure of other work.

Kent needed to earn plenty of money to support his new life style; that he managed to be so productive may be laid to his natural pertinacity and boundless energy. A normal working day for him was from five in the morning to about ten at night, with a half hour for lunch and perhaps a little longer for dinner. With so much to do, he saw no reason as a practical man for wasting his valuable time doing work that could be done just as well by an assistant. Andrée Ruellan, a gifted young artist he had met in Saint-Tropez, worked for him for a short time before pursuing her own successful career. Another assistant was Ione Robinson, a romantically beautiful and talented girl he had met in Woodstock. In New York City he saw her again and offered her a steady job at forty dollars a week,

ABOVE: TITLE PAGE FROM <u>MOBY DICK</u>, 1930

OPPOSITE: THE BATTERING-RAM ILLUSTRATION FROM <u>MOBY DICK</u>, 1930

**THE STORE FOR MEN
MARSHALL FIELD
& COMPANY**

which she readily accepted, coming to work in December of 1927. The character of Kent's designs required utmost precision and clarity for their successful translation into print or for engraving on wood; every line and detail was carefully worked out on tissue before being transferred to drawing paper or the woodblock. Ione had to learn to draw exactly as he did, to follow his lead in cutting on hardwood blocks, for which a magnifying glass was usually necessary. She adapted quickly, but soon learned that her employer was, as she put it, "a bit of a Prussian when it comes to making people work." Like Kent, she worked long hours; the steady pace made her think of a factory, and she said that there was always so much going on at the Kent house that it was like a three-ring circus.

The *Candide* illustrations occupied Kent off and on for many months. The book, produced by Pynson Printers under the direction of Elmer Adler, was published by Random House in an edition of 1,470 numbered and signed copies in April, 1928. Its flawless format, with complete harmony between type, paper, and illustrations — almost silvery in tone — brought instant recognition as a masterpiece. The edition was sold out before publication date; stray copies changed hands at greatly advanced prices. In addition there were ninety-five copies in a special linen and leather binding, offered at seventy-five dollars. For these copies the illustrations were colored by hand, an egregious example of gilding the lily but indicative of the current infatuation with bibliophilic rarities. To Ione and to as many assistants as Kent could muster fell the grinding task of coloring the thousands of individual illustrations. The following year, Kent's *Candide* illustrations were published in trade editions — one for the Literary Guild, whose wide distribution brought his work to the attention of many who perhaps had never before seen a fine book. Grateful for the success, Random House threw a spectacular cocktail party in the artist's honor.

Kent christened his new house in the Adirondacks "Asgaard," after the mythological Nordic "home of the gods." It proved to be his final home — or, rather, one should say that he made it into a permanent base of operations from which he was to sally forth time and again on further adventures. A rousing housewarming in August of 1928 was the starting point for his next adventure. At the festivities, Kent's friend Arthur Allen announced that his son Sam was going to sail to Greenland in a small boat. To Kent, already steeped in heroic Nordic sagas, the instant permission he got to go along was a dream come true. On June 17, 1929, the sturdy thirty-three-foot cutter *Direction* sailed from Baddeck, Nova Scotia, with three men on board: Sam Allen, Lucian Carey, Jr., both experienced sailors, and Kent, who was chosen navigator. *Direction* carried them without serious mishap around Newfoundland and along the coast of Labrador, then across the treacherous ice-filled currents of Davis

ABOVE: COVER FOR MARSHALL FIELD CATALOG, 1928

OPPOSITE, TOP: COLOPHON FOR RANDOM HOUSE

CENTER: INVITATION TO "A SO-CALLED TEA"
FOR ROCKWELL KENT GIVEN BY RANDOM HOUSE, 1930

BENNETT CERF
DONALD KLOPFER
HAVE THE HONOR TO INVITE YOU
TO A SO-CALLED TEA
OR INSPIRATIONAL ORGY
FOR THE SPIRITUAL BENEFIT
OF
ROCKWELL KENT
FRIDAY, JANUARY TWENTY-FOURTH
FROM FIVE O'CLOCK TO ELEVEN
RANDOM HOUSE
20 EAST FIFTY-SEVENTH STREET
R · S · V · P

THIS EDITION, PRIVATELY PRINTED,
LIMITED TO 99 COPIES, OF WHICH THIS IS NO. 1

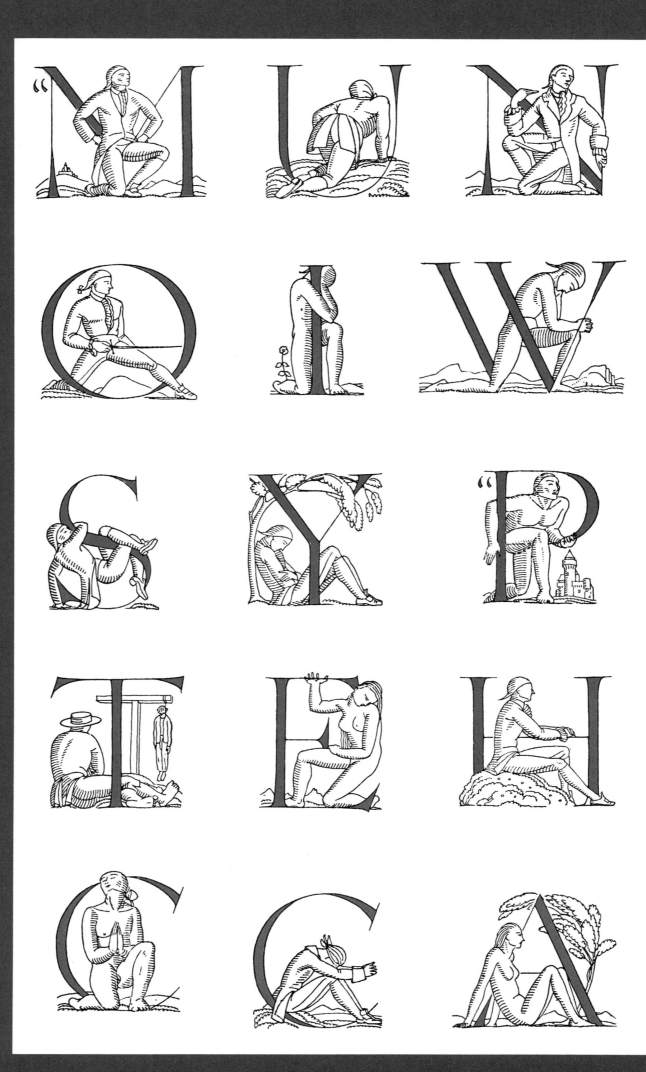

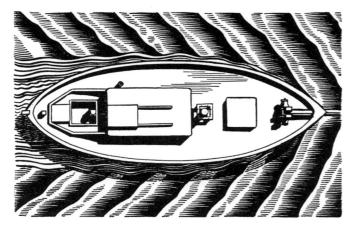

Strait, only to be wrecked July 15 on the western coast of Greenland. Most of Greenland, the world's largest island, lies within the Arctic Circle. It resembles a huge ice-covered bowl, the weight of which has depressed the ground surface to 1,200 feet below sea level. Toward the sea it presents an unfriendly fringe of icebergs and high-walled fjords. The people, mostly Eskimos barely subsisting on fishing and seal hunting, live in isolated communities along this narrow edge, hardly an ideal place to be stranded in a small boat with a hole in its side.

With the help of the natives, most of the supplies on board were salvaged and the boat was towed to Godthaab for repairs. Sam and Lucian left for home on the next ship, but Kent stayed on. After all, he had come to see Greenland and to paint. Decked out in Eskimo clothing and as a partly assimilated but endlessly fascinating visitor, Kent was soon on easy terms with the Greenlanders, and the regional doctor took him along on his rounds to other settlements in search of subjects to paint. But time was running out and there were still the *Moby Dick* illustrations to complete. Confident that he could do this work just as well abroad as at home, he radioed Frances to gather up all the material and meet him in Denmark. In September, he took the steamer *Disko,* bound for Copenhagen. On board he met Peter Freuchen, the arctic explorer, and Knud Rasmussen, another explorer and a noted recorder of Eskimo life and folklore, who offered the Kents the hospitality of his home near Copenhagen. At Rasmussen's house, Kent completed the *Moby Dick* illustrations, sending the final batch of 157 drawings to Lakeside Press on November 5, 1929. As he already had a contract to illustrate *The Canterbury Tales,* he spent the remainder of his time in Copenhagen researching the life and dress of Chaucer's time.

Kent's combative instincts, which seldom lay dormant very long, were notably exercised immediately after his return from Denmark, this time against the Delaware & Hudson Railroad. When the Kents alighted from the train at Plattsburgh, New York, they learned that train service from there to Au Sable Forks had been discontinued during their absence on the perhaps reasonable grounds that few people ever used it. It was a typical Adirondacks winter; laden down as they were with luggage, paintings, and six frisky Great Dane puppies given to them by Freuchen, the only way they could get home was by taxi, over thirty miles of miserable roads. To Kent, this was a blatant example of the "public be damned" attitude of what he asserted was a "hydra-headed beast" that controlled not only the railroad but the lives of virtually all the people of the region through its ownership of the newspaper, the bank, and most of the business and industry — and that its "alter ego was the Republican Party." Kent, calling in his lawyer friend, Philip Lowry, started a personal crusade against the railroad. After many months of litigation, the railroad was ordered to restore service on the Au Sable branch, but succeeded in engineering a reversal of the order a year or two later. Kent was disgusted, but at least he had wet his feet in the murky pool of local politics.

When the Kents transferred their household to Au Sable Forks, they also brought along their "three-ring circus," where on those broad acres it was to have much greater scope. If one may be permitted to disregard strict chronology for a moment, perhaps this would be the best place to insert some accounts of Asgaard's social life during its livelier seasons. Through the years, Kent had a succession of secretaries and assistants on the place when his work required it, and there was always plenty of

OPPOSITE: ORNAMENTAL INITIAL LETTERS FROM <u>CANDIDE</u>, 1928

ABOVE: TWO ILLUSTRATIONS FROM <u>N BY E</u>, 1930

RIGHT: DEDICATION PAGE ILLUSTRATION FROM <u>N BY E</u>

ROCKWELL KENT

household help to deal with the crowds of visitors and overnight guests that descended on the farm to play golf, bathe in the swimming hole, ride the horses, or gather in Asgaard's popular "Joe's Bar." At one time, partly for fun but also out of practical necessity, Kent managed their accommodations by issuing a handsomely printed reservation certificate ("All trains met — no charge. Parking space and Garage. Landing field on premises"), with a stub for prospective guests to fill in and return beforehand. One of the high points of one summer in the thirties was the wedding of Rockwell's daughter Barbara to Alan Carter, a musician and professor at Middlebury College. Contingents of guests arrived at all hours for two days; by all accounts it was an affair nobody would forget.

Nearby, in the early fifties, were both Angus Cameron and Albert Kahn, at that time partners in publishing; Donald Ogden Stewart bought a neighboring farm. At most parties there had always been impromptu musicals, parlor games, and merry pranks.

Despite high jinks and late hours, Kent generally maintained his habit of rising at five in the morning and, after breakfast and perhaps a swim, disappearing into his studio for a good day's work. It is said that he could compete with the hardest drinker, yet show no effects.

In late summer of 1930, the Asgaard establishment acquired a courtly major-domo in the exalted person of one "Prince Michael Romanoff." The short, dark man's brilliant conversation was his stock in trade; his "implied" claim to Russian nobility, however, had been compromised by frequent sojourns in jail as a vagrant and rubber-check artist. Though Kent had not been taken in by the spurious nobleman's pretensions, it amused him to have him around. Mike could cook and, among other chores, perform as a ceremonial flunky; when the Kents were away, he suavely bore the mantle of gracious host to chance visitors. The arrangement lasted but a few months. Later, Mike traveled extensively as the famous Rockwell Kent, granting interviews and signing Kent's name to books — and checks. He even sailed to France in his new incarnation, emerging in evening clothes from his tiny corner below decks to mingle with the first-class passengers. The Paris police sent him back to America. In July, 1933, faced by deportation to Russia by a New York court, Mike admitted that he was born in the United States and not in the Winter Palace. After several months of detention, he was released on probation with the condition that he drop a vaudeville contract through which his troubles were to be exploited. In April, 1935, he was again in jail, and was nominated "Vagrant No. 1 of New York City." Whoever or whatever he was, Mike eventually found a haven in Hollywood, where he operated a restaurant; Romanoff's became fashionable and was often mentioned in gossip columns.

For Rockwell Kent the illustrator, 1930 was a banner year. The *Moby Dick,* in a superb edition of a thousand three-volume sets boxed in aluminum slipcases, was universally acclaimed a masterpiece. Lakeside Press also printed a chunky one-volume trade edition for Random House, where in the excitement over Kent's illustrations they forget to include Melville's name on the binding and jacket. Also that year, Kent's *The Canterbury Tales of Geoffrey Chaucer* was published by Covici, Friede in limited and trade editions, and *N by E,* Kent's journal of his Greenland adventure, was published by Brewer & Warren, also in limited and trade editions. His *N by E* was extremely popular and was reprinted many times.

The books just mentioned represent a total of 473 separate drawings in addition to work on the formats and other details, and while they were being printed, Kent was already preparing three other books, entailing another 156 separate drawings, for publication in 1931. In 1930 alone, Kent also made jackets, frontispieces, and/or minor illustrations for eighteen additional books, besides numerous advertising drawings and prints. He wound up the busy year of 1930 with two additional projects. One was to design and draw the plans for a country mansion for his friends Mr. and Mrs. J. Cheever Cowdin. Kent was delighted to have them for neighbors, and he generously did the work without charge. It was to Cowdin, a Wall Street broker, that Kent had entrusted, for investment, the $50,000 he had inherited from a relative in 1927. Now, Kent was making money so fast that he didn't even bother to ask Cowdin for an accounting.

OPPOSITE, TOP: POST ARRIVAL, 1935, O/C, THE PUSHKIN MUSEUM OF FINE ARTS

BOTTOM: MIRRORED MOUNTAIN, SOUTH GREENLAND, 1929, O/C MOUNTED ON WOOD, 33-1/2 x 44-7/8, THE HERMITAGE

The second project posed a problem; Kent had been commissioned by Raymond Moore, founder of the Cape Playhouse, to design and execute a large mural for The Cape Cinema, on the Playhouse grounds in Dennis, on Cape Cod. After agreeing to do the work, he remembered his vow not to have anything to do with the Commonwealth of Massachusetts. Rather than break his word, he adopted the subterfuge of creating the design in his own studio and got the scenic artist Jo Mielziner to paint and install the mural and collect the $5,000 fee for himself.

With Asgaard and his bank account well established and all his various projects completed, Kent inevitably turned his thoughts to Greenland again, eager to experience an entire winter there and to share the rigorous life of the natives as intimately as possible. On the advice of Peter Freuchen, he went to Igdlorssuit, a small settlement on Ubekendt Ejland (Unknown Island) on the west coast of Greenland, about 225 miles north of the Arctic Circle; he arrived there in July of 1931. At a polite distance from the other Eskimo houses he built one for himself, similar in most respects, except that he used all wood for the siding, not knowing that turf is much warmer. The construction of his house was, for the Eskimos, a prolonged social event, every day from dawn to dusk, not to be missed except out of urgent personal necessity, for the festive spirit blurred distinctions between those working for hire and those who were not. The house was finally finished in August; at last he was "at home" in Greenland. Now he needed a housekeeper, one who would administer to his creature comforts and see that he was warmly clothed in the approved Eskimo style. He also needed a dog team to carry him and his equipment on painting expeditions.

idea of privacy never entered her head; she saw no reason why she should have a room of her own or, as her employer's kifak, object to sleeping on the floor. She took pride in her housework, but also considered it her duty and privilege to monitor her employer's social life as well. Under the Kent-Salamina regime, the household flourished; Kent entertained in the approved Eskimo style and was in turn invited to other houses. Using her prestige as mistress of the house, Salamina winnowed out the freeloaders and helped to assemble a select circle of

Enter Salamina, as Kent named her: "a handsome, well-built woman of perhaps thirty, dark-haired but as light-complexioned as a swarthy European. She had great poise and dignity." She was a widow, and the youngest of her three children lived with them. As an Eskimo, the Eskimo friends congenial to herself and her master. Fiercely possessive, she tried by her sharp looks to intimidate any pretty young girl who dared to become too familiar with her "Mr. Kinte," but with little success.

David, an Eskimo friend, helped care for Kent's dog team and safely guided him over the treacherous ice on painting expeditions. During the long winter, Kent was obliged to work indoors by lamplight because he had to complete nine double-page illustrations for a Random House edition of Goethe's *Faust,* which he had promised to send to the printer in Germany on the first southbound mail sledge in the spring. Back in New York, in 1933, he was dismayed to learn that the printer had failed and the project had been abandoned. It took six months to retrieve the drawings, which he eventually sold to New Directions for an edition they published in 1941.

From Frances he received a few letters at first, and in early winter one or two brief messages in their private code by the Godhavn radio station; then nothing at all — and she had promised to join him in the spring! It was the end of March before he finally heard from her; she would be on the first steamer from Denmark.

ABOVE: BINDING DESIGN FOR MOBY DICK (VOLUME TWO),
THE LAKESIDE PRESS, 1930, BLACK CLOTH STAMPED IN SILVER, 4TO.

OPPOSITE: DETAIL OF MURAL ON THE CEILING OF THE CAPE CINEMA
IN DENNIS, MASS., 1930, 6,400 SQUARE FEET

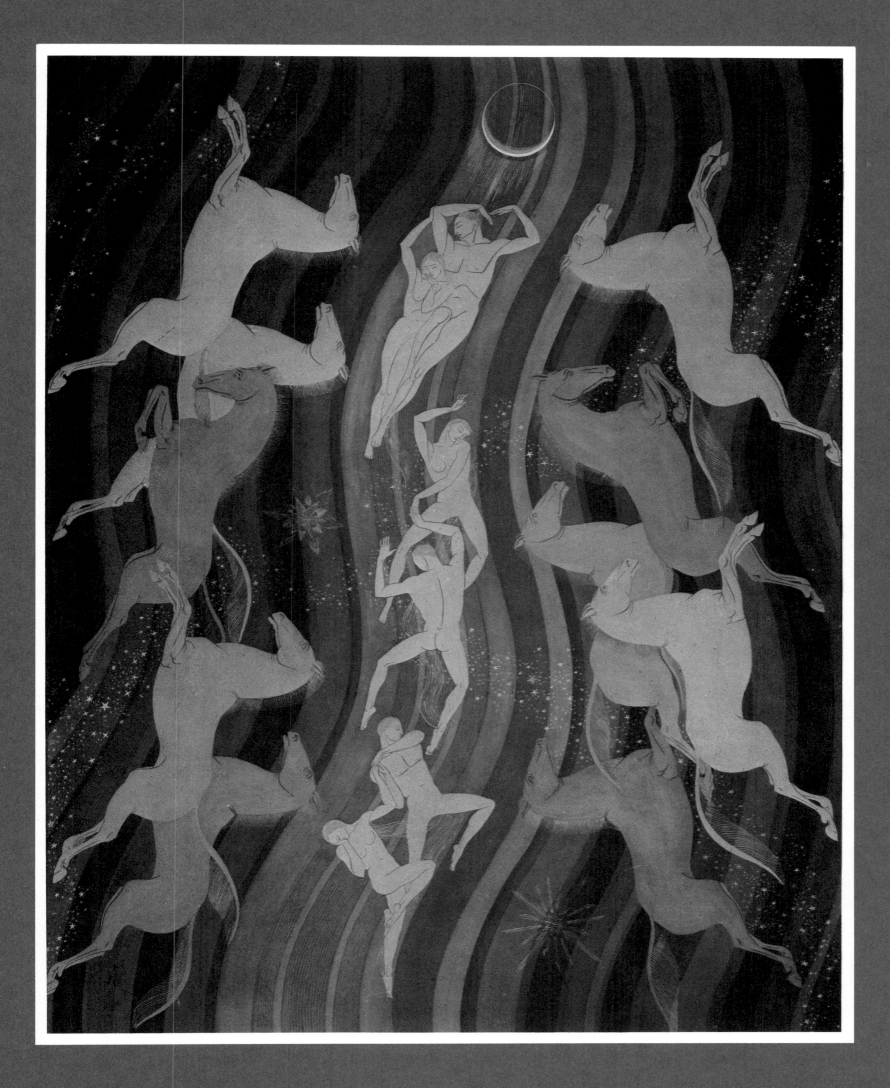

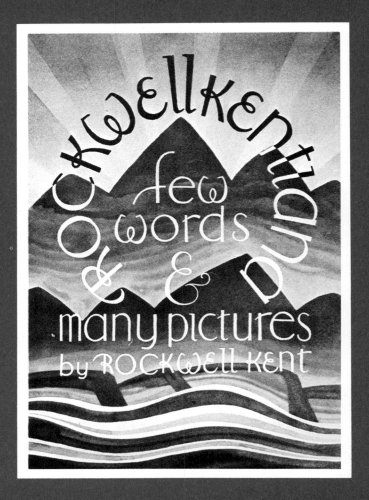

Immediately, Rockwell and David, with a team of fourteen dogs, started southward to meet her when the ship docked at Holsteinsborg. It was an arduous trip over treacherous terrain, and when they reached Godhavn sixteen days later they could go no farther and had to wait another ten days for Frances to be brought up by motor launch.

On the arrival of Frances at Igdlorssuit early in May, Salamina politely vacated her steward-ship of the Kent household and went to live with a neighbor. And to the legal wife, without bitter-ness, she relinquished also the more interesting perquisites attached to it, all except her vigilance over "Mr. Kinte's" doings. What Frances thought of all this is conjectural. What is perhaps more certain is that by October, when she and Rockwell left for home, the additional experience in rigorous living had not improved her taste for it or made it an acceptable alternative to being periodically neglected.

It was from Frances that Rockwell first learned that the $50,000 he had so impulsively en-trusted to Cowdin to invest for him had been lost in the great Wall Street crash, but he was not par-ticularly disturbed; at fifty-one and in the fullness of his powers, he could easily compensate for the loss of even that much money. From Greenland he was returning with many paintings, his journal would furnish material for more books, and the royalties on previous books were impressive. Back home at Asgaard he immediately found plenty of commissions, and in addition, during 1933 he made and published five wood engravings and seven lithographs. And in his own backyard he discovered another windmill to tilt at.

Though he had no trouble paying for extensive improvements on his farm, he saw that many of the Adirondacks people, suffering from the current Depression, were in danger of losing their prop-erty by foreclosure; their plight was aggravated by the shady dealings of the controlling political clique, whose tax assessments were as much as a third lower than those of the farmers, including his own. Since he was the most vocal agitator for local reform, it was only natural that the newly formed Jay Taxpayers Association should appoint him its chairman. Their grievances were amply justified, but all their efforts came to nothing; they were defeated by their own ineptitude and ignorance of political realities. Reflecting on their failure, for a moment Kent regretted allowing himself to be involved — af-ter all, he was an artist and should have stuck to his painting — but as a human being and a citizen he had made a commitment just as important to himself. And for him the smell of battle was an irresistible intoxicant to which he was destined to succumb over and over. (At seventy, licking his wounds from so many battles, he pointed out that from his youth he had been subject to this "congenital failing," for which he offered no apology.)[3]

Though auguries for Kent's success in politics were not encouraging, his stature as an artist was notably heightened by the publication, in October, 1933, by Harcourt, Brace & Co., of *Rock-wellkentiana,* an impressive survey with many reproductions of his work, a random selection of his articles on art, a bibliography, and a list of his prints by Carl Zigrosser. Also in October of that year, Kent made his début as a professional speaker on a lecture circuit. Beginning in Cincinnati, he made forty-four public appearances; except for the Christmas holidays, he was away from home and Frances for six months.

Soon after his return to Asgaard, weary and unsettled in mind, and feeling the urge to get away from it all, he mortgaged the farm to raise additional money, and in June he set out again for Greenland, with his son Gordon in tow, after first extracting from Frances a halfhearted promise to join them in the spring.

Kent's return to Igdlorssuit was all he had fervently hoped for. Ecstatically he wrote, "It was an escape from discord into harmony. Nothing had changed: the settlement, its friendly people crowded on the shore to welcome me; and Salamina — tears of ineffable happiness flooding her eyes." She forthwith retrieved her exalted station, and Kent acquired another dog team for painting trips.

[3] Even later, in 1961, Kent wrote to an unidentified American author: "People have often asked me why I, an artist and writer, put aside that proper work to engage in political activities. I have answered that if the Adirondack woods are on fire it is only a question of how close to my studio and home the fire gets before I stop painting and become a fire fighter. We must all, I believe, become fire fighters now. . . . "

OPPOSITE, TOP: HILLTOP GRAVES, NORTH GREENLAND, 1932 – 33, O/C ON PLYWOOD,
25-3/4 x 46-3/8", KIEV MUSEUM OF WESTERN AND EASTERN ART
BOTTOM, LEFT: PROMETHEUS, 1931, ENGRAVING ON COPPER, 3-15/16 x 2-3/4"
RIGHT: JACKET FOR <u>ROCKWELLKENTIANA</u>, HARCOURT, BRACE AND COMPANY, 1933

ROCKWELL KENT

He was far away from Igdlorssuit frequently, camping alone for several days and nights at a time. There, in the silent wastes of North Greenland, he made intimate contact with himself, shucking off the ordinary routines of communal life, doing whatever he felt like doing, without regard to time or anything else. In his earlier years, he had given expression to mystic moods in paintings with figural compositions, but had eventually abandoned such themes, having found ample scope for them in his prints and illustrations. Figures do not usually inhabit his landscapes, and then they are often incidental. And though he was a lover of nature, capable of faithfully recording it in its infinite diversity, he seldom painted it from close up. In his paintings he preferred the all-encompassing sweep of massive forms — limitless skies, undulating hills and mountains, spacious foregrounds of earth and sea. In this respect he was a master, creating space and distance in even the smallest drawing. This characteristic sense of remoteness perhaps reflects the element in his nature which periodically drove him to the edges of the world, and one is tempted to surmise that, despite his frequent and manifold commitments to love, friendship, and his fellowman, Kent was essentially a loner.

At the settlement he made many drawings, mainly as material for illustrating projected books and articles. He appears not to have been moved to paint portraits of his Eskimo friends, even of Salamina, though in his home still hangs a strongly painted small canvas of another young Eskimo woman, Pauline, in a somber mood. Soon after their arrival, Kent had hastily built a small turf hut especially for Gordon, but he shortly pre-empted it as a refuge from the bustle and clatter of domestic life. There, in seclusion, he slept, mostly cooked for himself, and worked through the winter. There he wrote *Salamina,* one of his most charming books, and drew the illustrations for it. He also made the illustrations for *The Saga of Gisli, Son of Sour.* In early March of 1935, all this work was completed and shipped to Harcourt, Brace.

Rockwell had not heard from Frances since the previous fall; then in March he received word that she was living in Arizona and would not come to Greenland. He was bitterly disappointed, having hoped to remain there another year. In desperation he considered shipping his son home and going to Europe, where he would make the illustrations for a new edition of Shakespeare's plays commissioned by Doubleday, Doran; at least he would earn a much needed twenty-five hundred dollars, and the work would distract him from his intolerable sense of rejection. However, en route to Copenhagen, a cable informed him that Frances, victim of an auto accident, was in a Tucson hospital. The only thing to do was to go to her at once. Besides, waiting for him at the Copenhagen post office was a letter from Carl Zigrosser telling him that he had been chosen by the Public Works Administration to execute two murals for the new Post Office Building in Washington, and sketches had to be submitted by September 15.

Kent was relieved to find Frances well on the mend, but he was highly indignant over her having rented Asgaard to a Mrs. Blair. This was a desecration he could not tolerate, but Mrs. Blair stubbornly insisted on strict observance of all terms of the lease, and when he returned to New York he was obliged to stay in the apartment of his sister-in-law Mrs. Kendall Lee Glaenzer, on East Fifty-seventh Street. What galled him perhaps even more was that Philip Lowry, recently banished from his list of friends, was the monster who had assisted Frances in the transaction. In answer to a furious letter from Kent, Lowry reminded him that he had willingly deeded the property to Frances some time before, and she therefore had the right to rent it; furthermore, she had been left on her own for an entire year and was running short of funds. Also, the lease specifically exempted use of his studio. Kent wrote a long note in the margin of Lowry's letter and sent it to Frances. It reads, in part: "I trusted you in my absence with the property . . . and you hired it out to strangers. Must I believe you are completely false? I require that the cur Lowry be completely and forever dismissed. . . . I need the Ausable property made over to me. You may trust *me* not to rent *your* things to the highest bidder. . . . God end my life for me! R. K."

Kent was in no mood to be temperate, even with Frances, for whom he nevertheless continued to profess great love, forgetting that he had been consistently neglectful of her and openly hostile to her son. Apparently, for him love was still something to be celebrated on his own terms. Though the attraction between them was to endure for some time, the bonds of matrimony were unraveling.

The four months' rental of Asgaard came to eight hundred dollars. Kent felt that using the money for himself would be to acquiesce in the violation of his high principles; and, coming from what he described as "a notoriously wealthy family," the money represented evil by association with that class of society that enriches itself with callous indifference to the public weal; it must be turned against them. He "wiped the stain" from his domain by sending the money to the New York headquarters of the Communist Party of America.

As always, Kent's work and his own concerns came first. There were the forty-two Shakespeare drawings to complete; well over a hundred decorations to make for a Limited Editions Club's edition of Whitman's *Leaves of Grass;* and the Post Office Building murals to do. The subject chosen for Kent's two panels was "Mail Service in the Tropic and Arctic Territories of the United States," and would require research trips to both Alaska and Puerto Rico. Leaving Frances to return to Asgaard at her leisure (he directed that she immediately fumigate the house), he flew to Alaska.

Salamina, published in October of 1935, was widely praised and reviewed. The London *Times* pointed out that it was "the first book about Greenland and the Greenlanders to be written by an artist . . . the men, the women and children who crowd into the pages of this rich book are human beings first and Greenlanders afterwards." Kent's frank revelations of his amorous encounters with Eskimo girls provoked considerable comment and inspired a number of cartoons in national magazines. His friend Louis Untermeyer wrote a limerick and typed it on a greeting card to Kent:

> *A vigorous painter named KENT*
> *Said, "I figure my time is well spent*
> *In rubbing the noses*
> *of She-Esquimauxes*
> *To further my evil intent."*

With Kent's return from Greenland in 1935, his arctic adventures came to an end. Emerging from the twilight remoteness of a primitive land, he was only partially prepared for what he found at home: the terrible effects of the Great Depression, which at one point left twelve million without jobs and sent hundreds of thousands wandering around the country desperately seeking any kind of subsistence. From the shifting sands of economic disintegration in the thirties, protest groups were sprout-

ROCKWELL KENT

ing like weeds all over America; labor's attempts to obtain relief by organizing mass industries were being met with fierce resistance.

Inevitably, Kent's empathy with the underdog drew him into one controversial movement after another. In November of that year, he got himself deeply involved in the strike of six hundred workers at a marble quarry in neighboring Vermont, and went to their meetings and solicited funds for their support. To raise additional money, the sculptor Paul Manship offered to buy a large block of marble from another quarry, with the idea of cutting it up for sale to sculptors and architects. Kent drafted and sent a circular letter of appeal with the whimsical suggestion: "Buy Your Tombstone Now . . . Pay Before You Enter." Response was bitterly disappointing, and by February of 1936 the strikers were in such desperate straits that they had to give up the fight.

The Depression had been particularly hard on the world of art. Many artists barely survived on the small checks received for work done on various Federal Art Projects; others had been unsuccessful in finding alternate means of earning a living. In New York, a group of prominent artists organized the American Artists' Congress and invited Kent, among several other notables, to speak at its first meeting, held on St. Valentine's Day, 1936. The congress, a broad coalition of diverse talents with views ranging from non-political to extreme radicalism, had more than six hundred members by the end of the year. Later it came under suspicion as a Communist front.

In one respect the Artists' Congress did some good. A suggestion for the cooperative production of anti-war and anti-fascism posters came to nothing, but a call for art prints in any medium brought submissions from artists all over the country. From these a jury selected a hundred (each by a different artist) and duplicate prints were exhibited simultaneously in thirty different cities during the month of December, 1936. Not surprisingly, most of the artists chose themes reflective of the Depression or their deep concern with social and labor problems. The exhibitions and publication of a completely illustrated catalogue did much to further public interest in the print as a popular art form and as a source of income for many artists.

In July of 1936, Kent spent a week in Puerto Rico prospecting for material for his Post Office Building mural. There he saw that under the tropical luxuriance of the beautiful island lay a morass of administrative corruption and systematic exploitation of the peasants, who lived in unimaginable poverty and squalor. He talked with numerous agitators for Puerto Rican independence as the only cure for the island's ills, and identified himself with their cause in a way that made headlines. The completed murals were mounted on the walls of the Post Office Building in September of 1937 (pages 328 – 29). One panel depicted the departure of a U.S. mail plane from Alaska; the other a group of dark-skinned Puerto Rican women receiving letters from a mailman on horseback. The murals were approved readily enough, but a Washington newspaperwoman took a second look at what seemed to be an insignificant detail: held in the hand of one of the women was an unfolded letter written in a mysterious language which defeated all the local scholars but was eventually identified by Vilhjalmur Stefansson, the arctic authority, as Kuskokwims, an obscure Eskimo dialect. Translated it read: "To the people of Puerto Rico, our friends: Go ahead, let us change chiefs. That alone can make us equal and free." Though the offending message caused a minor tempest in Washington, the murals were accepted and Kent duly received his $3,000 fee for the work.

ABOVE: TWO DRAWINGS FROM WILDERNESS, 1920
OPPOSITE, TOP, LEFT TO RIGHT: JACKET DESIGN FOR THIS IS MY OWN, DUELL,
SLOAN & PEARCE, 1940; JACKET DESIGN FOR N BY E, RANDOM HOUSE, 1930
BOTTOM: POSTER FOR SPANISH AID WEEK, 1937; ADVERTISEMENT FOR KENT'S
ASGAARD DAIRY, SILK SCREEN POSTER IN SIX COLORS, C. 1935

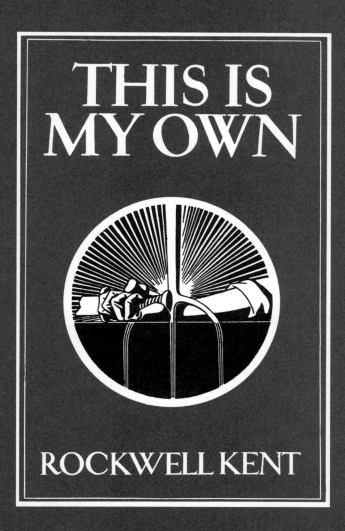

THIS IS MY OWN

ROCKWELL KENT

N by E

ROCKWELL KENT

THAT SPAIN'S CHILDREN
MAY   LIVE

GIVE! SPANISH AID WEEK
MAY 30TH TO JUNE 9TH

NORTH AMERICAN COMMITTEE
TO AID SPANISH DEMOCRACY
NATIONAL OFFICE: 381 FOURTH AVENUE, NEW YORK

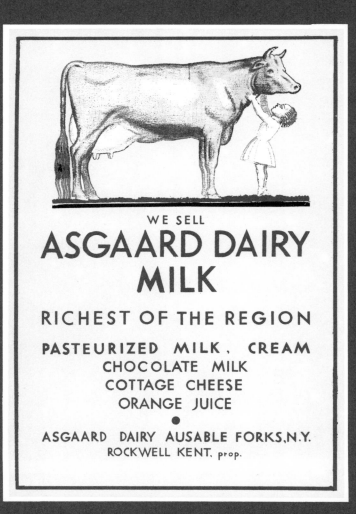

WE SELL
ASGAARD DAIRY MILK

RICHEST OF THE REGION

PASTEURIZED MILK, CREAM
CHOCOLATE MILK
COTTAGE CHEESE
ORANGE JUICE

•

ASGAARD DAIRY AUSABLE FORKS, N.Y.
ROCKWELL KENT, prop.

While some sections of the public began to look askance upon Kent's well-publicized political activities, his popularity as an illustrator increased. Not very willingly, he had agreed that Frances take a leave of absence from her duties as secretary and wife for six months of every year. She suffered from bronchial troubles for which she found some relief by living in Arizona. In 1936, he had "fled the emptiness of the big house" to hole up in his studio for the winter, where he lived like a hermit, seeing no one and having his mail forwarded to Frances to answer. Then, in early January of 1937, he broke away from his isolation by going on a three-month lecture tour which took him from Massachusetts all the way to Oregon. Later in the year, as the newly elected vice-president of the National Committee for People's Rights, he flew to Brazil as a political observer, stopping briefly on the way at Puerto Rico where, he asserted, he was welcomed by the *people* with open arms. Kent was rapidly becoming a VIP; in 1938, he was nominated vice-president of the International Workers Order (IWO), and in May of that year he addressed the American League for Peace and Democracy. His speech, "The Enemies of Democracy," was broadcast by a New York radio station.

Kent was commissioned by the General Electric Company to create a mural for their projected exhibition building at the New York World's Fair, scheduled to open on April 30, 1939. Since he would have to do the work in New York the winter before, Frances was persuaded to stay with him there instead of going as usual to Arizona. But she was left to herself most of the time, as Rockwell worked long hours daily in a rented downtown loft with his two assistants and he attended meetings four evenings a week. The following summer at Asgaard, he was again too deeply involved in his own concerns to be companionable. Being a useful supernumerary in her husband's busy life, an ornament to his rare moments of relaxation, was too small a return for her devotion, and when she left for Arizona in the fall of 1939, both had the premonition that it was for good.

For Rockwell, marriage to a beautiful young woman may have been indispensable to the enlargement of his life, but fidelity on his part was superfluous. He had amply demonstrated to his first wife, and later to Frances, that he expected his sexual antics to be accepted as a matter of course; but there were also too many instances of indifference and neglect even less likely to be forgiven. Despite the warmth and generosity he displayed on various occasions, a deep current of self-involvement inevitably carried him away from any emotional attachment that had become inconvenient. And, as subsequent events were to prove, the impending defection of Frances at this time was for Rockwell less traumatic than inconvenient.

Frances was not only usually available as a secretary, among other things, but over the years she had become marvelously proficient at deciphering his minute handwriting and finding her way through his complicated rough drafts to produce a neat typescript. Kent was planning to write another book, and now that she was gone, he badly needed a replacement with similar qualifications. When a friend offered his help in finding a new secretary, Rockwell made it plain that, besides a willingness to share his solitude at Asgaard, she should be "lovely to look at, lovely to listen to, lovely to have about day in, day out."

Kent was very much impressed with a letter he received a few weeks later from a Miss Shirley Johnstone; she had heard of the job and was interested. On his next trip to Manhattan he went to see her at Brentano's, where she was employed. He took her to lunch, was delighted with her, and promptly engaged her. Very soon Rockwell took to calling her "Sally," as a variation on his mother's name, Sara, and henceforth Shirley was known to everyone as Sally. (In Greenland, Rockwell had also paid tribute to his mother's memory by calling his Eskimo housekeeper "Salamina.")

Sally's first day at Asgaard was the second of January, in 1940. She was born in England but raised in Canada, so the cold northern winter was no shock to her, and she handled herself on skis and snowshoes like a native. Kent was enchanted with the lovely young woman, no older than his youngest daughter, Barbara, and in no time at all declared his love. Surprised, and unwilling to be instrumental in breaking up his marriage, Sally packed her bags and left the following morning. But Rockwell pursued her to New York, explained the situation, and she was finally persuaded to return. Frances came to Asgaard to meet her and give her blessings; obligingly she obtained a divorce in Las Vegas, leaving the terms of support and maintenance to Rockwell's judgment. Sally was warmly approved by the family. Frances wrote to Rockwell, "Darling, our lives are too entwined to ever be untangled. We both know that . . . Sally *must not* feel that Ausable is not all hers, with me as just a sort of member of the family." The wedding took place on the tenth of May at the home of Barbara and Alan Carter in Vermont.

It was the beginning of a warm and sympathetic union which, despite a few early "digressions" on Rockwell's part, flourished all the rest of the artist's life. After a two-week honeymoon, the new partnership began in earnest. Sally handled the huge correspondence; Rockwell painted and drew, and wrote a book about his twelve years at Asgaard, mailing the manuscript pages in batches to Frances to type. *This Is My Own,* with illustrations by the author, was published by Duell, Sloan & Pearce in November, 1940. The title, taken from Walter Scott's famous poem beginning "Breathes there a man with soul so dead, / Who never to himself hath said, / This is my own, my native land!" accurately epitomizes Kent's abiding love for America, but he did not stick at expressing himself uncompromisingly on political and social issues that disturbed him. The book had good reviews, but as a consequence of subsequent adverse publicity about Kent it was allowed to go out of print, and in June of 1943 excerpts from it were read into the *Congressional Record* as being allegedly subversive.

That Kent's name should be mentioned in Congress is not surprising; since the marble-workers' strike of 1935 he had been drawn into one liberal crusade after another. He wrote articles and innumerable letters, joined committees, traveled great distances to attend meetings of various unions or any other groups with which he was in sympathy. His affiliations were diverse, and more extensive than it seems possible for any one man to find time for; during the years, their number ran to more than fourscore. Among them were: American Artists' Congress, vice-chairman; League of American Writers; American Youth Congress; United Office and Professional Workers of America; National Committee for People's Rights, chairman; International Longshoremen's and Warehousemen's Union, lifetime honorary member; International Workers Order, vice-president and, for several years, president; Committee for Fair Play to Puerto Rico; United Scenic Artists; Brotherhood of Painters, Decorators and Paperhangers; American League for Peace and Democracy, member of its national committee; International Labor Defense; American Committee for Democracy and Intellectual Freedom; Artists' League of America, president; National Council of American-Soviet Friendship, chairman.

Kent seldom declined an invitation to make a speech and, being by the famous Rockwell Kent, his utterances were invariably quoted in the press. Though he declared that his radical views

OPPOSITE, TOP, LEFT TO RIGHT: MAN AND SNAKE, 1942, STUDY FOR A POSTER, 11-3/8 x 12";
SUGGESTION FOR A FLOAT IN THE WOMAN'S SUFFRAGE PARADE, C. 1913, PENCIL, 10-1/2 x 12-1/2,
COLLECTION OF JOSEPH M. ERDELAC
BOTTOM: GET THE HELL OUT!, 1940, POSTER, 20-7/8 x 15-1/8", COLLECTION OF JOSEPH M. ERDELAC;
STUDY FOR A WAR POSTER, 1941, PENCIL ON PAPER, 14-1/2 x 11-3/4", COLLECTION OF SALLY KENT GORTON

ROCKWELL KENT

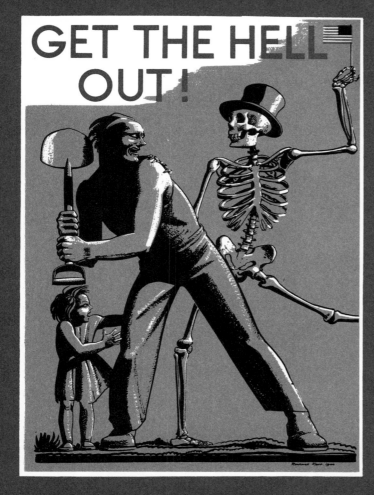

GET THE HELL OUT!

were not inconsistent with American democracy and love for his country, he nevertheless laid himself open to suspicion by his open support of many organizations generally believed to be under control from abroad. Moreover, on principle he often disdained to answer loose charges that he was a rabid Communist, though when, as early as October of 1936, an investigator told the Dies Committee that he *was* one, Kent took the trouble to send a letter of denial to Martin Dies, to which he received no reply. Many who knew Kent intimately confidently assert that he was never a card-carrying member of the Communist Party; however, there were too many newspaper readers in the country who were convinced of the contrary, and with the rise of hostility against him during the following decades came a corresponding decline in his popularity as an artist and writer.

Kent's exhibition "Know and Defend America," an impressive showing of forty of his paintings which opened at Wildenstein's in New York on February 4, 1942, and then went on to Pittsburgh and Los Angeles, was the last important display of his paintings for a long time. And Kent finally gave up his lecture tours as well; in 1958 he wrote to a correspondent, ". . . although my lectures were ostensibly on art and life in Greenland the urgency of national and world affairs forced me to so recognize them in my lectures that I became at last unpalatable."

He also found himself unpalatable to some of his best clients. When he openly supported the efforts of the International Typographical Union to organize employees of the Lakeside Press and R. R. Donnelley & Sons in 1942, the management turned against him; despite the huge success of his *Moby Dick* illustrations, they later refused to have anything to do with him, and a projected new edition of the Bible, to be illustrated by him and distributed by Sears, Roebuck, was abandoned. Though his relations with General Electric had become both cordial and lucrative, he did not permit such considerations to dilute his pro-labor principles, and when the workers at G.E.'s Schenectady plant went on strike in January of 1946, he made a token appearance on the picket line, dramatically garbed as an Eskimo in an expression of sympathy for the regular pickets, who, he said, "must man the lines continually in rugged weather." As he already had a signed commission from G.E. for a 1947 calendar painting, the firm was obliged to accept and pay for it, but that was the last job he was ever to get from them. Other doors were shut to him, but he seldom lacked for commissions, and at Asgaard he painted, adding continually to what he called his Rockwell Kent Collection, and established a thriving dairy business from his herd of purebred Jerseys. In 1948, Kent ran for Congress on the American Labor Party ticket; even though he knew he hadn't the slightest chance of being elected, he said he did so because as a candidate for office he would have a chance "to say things publicly that ought to be said; and of being listened to."

In 1948, Henry Wallace, Franklin Roosevelt's first wartime Vice-President and chief exponent of the New Deal, was the Progressive Party's candidate for President. Wallace's liberal policies attracted extreme leftists to his support, inevitably giving rise to allegations that the Progressive Party was actually controlled by the Communist Party. Kent was therefore severely criticized by his neighbors for stumping for Wallace. Cantankerous as usual, Kent's response was to have "Vote for Wallace" printed on the Asgaard Dairy's bottle caps. Local animosity toward Kent climaxed in a crippling boycott of his dairy soon after he mailed five hundred reprints of a pro-Wallace article he had written for *Fraternal Outlook,* official publication of the IWO, which was promptly printed as a news story in the *Essex County Republican* of February 27. Two dairy employees quit, and Kent then made an outright gift of the dairy and all its equipment to the two that remained.

Newspaper stories of the boycott and of Kent's support of Wallace aggravated anti-Kent sentiment all over the country, though sometimes it was turned against an innocent bystander: Norman Rockwell, painter of the hugely popular *Saturday Evening Post* covers. The May 22 issue of the *Post* carried a letter from an irate Virginia woman who would no longer buy *any* magazine containing pictures by Norman Rockwell because of his Communist leanings. In his printed reply, the editor set her straight, remarking, "People have been mixing up the two Rockwells for years," and in all fairness quoted Kent's assertion: "I am not a member of the Communist Party and never have been." Very often both artists were alternately embarrassed or amused at having their identities confused, even by the literate.

It must be remembered that in 1948 the world was far from recovered from the shocks of the Second World War, which had come to an end only three years before, and our relations with Soviet Russia had already begun to cool — especially after Stalin had mounted his blockade of Berlin. Fears that the Soviets were bent on the indefinite expansion of their power and of Communist doctrines were alarmingly substantiated by the Communist takeover of Czechoslovakia in February of 1948. The threat of another war hung in the air.

In May, 1949, Kent with longtime friend Albert E. Kahn and about forty other Americans attended the World Congress for Peace, in Paris, though without the blessing of the United States government. In the spring of 1950, he again attended the congress, this time serving on a committee to persuade France to join with other nations in outlawing atomic warfare. At Paris he made a speech before the Chamber of Deputies; then, at the invitation of Soviet officials, he joined a delegation for his first visit to Russia. From Russia he flew to Stockholm, where he was met by Sally, and took part in framing a peace petition publicized as the Stockholm Appeal. The Premier of Sweden strongly objected to the title, affirming that neither Sweden nor its capital had endorsed it, and in this country Secretary of State Dean Acheson characterized it as part of the Soviet Union's "spurious peace offensive." Nevertheless, in the United States more than a million people signed the petition, which was circulated and promoted allegedly under the direction of the American Communist Party.

On his return from Stockholm, Kent crossed the country speaking for the Appeal; on occasion he also gave glowing accounts of his visit to Russia. Kent's double-barreled assault on the accepted American opinion of the Soviets and their aims was widely reported in the press. In translation from the Tass news agency, *The New York Times* quoted a typically truculent statement he had made in Moscow: "It is only fair to state that, in speaking for peace, I am not speaking as the official representative of the American government. I must add, in honesty to myself, that the American government is not representative of me."

In July of 1950, Kent applied for a passport to Prague as a member of an international jury for the awarding of prizes for painting, literature, and the cinema in outstanding service to the cause of peace. His request was denied. To Kent, the message was loud and clear; however, the following year he optimistically applied for what he considered a routine renewal of his passport to go to Ireland, stating that his sole purpose was to go there and paint. He had already booked passages for himself and Sally when he received a letter from the Department of State's passport division notifying him that it was unwilling to grant him a passport for travel to any countries for any purpose. This was too much; with the help of the Emergency Civil Liberties Union and its general counsel, Leonard Boudin, he brought suit against the State Department on the grounds that the denial was unconstitutional. To raise funds for legal expenses, an exhibition of Kent's work was staged at the old Great Northern Hotel in New York and lottery tickets were sold for his prints.

The mood in America at that time was grim, marked by deep and largely hysterical fear of Communism, fertile ground for sowing seeds of suspicion and prejudice against fellow Americans. And it was in February of 1950 that Joseph McCarthy, the undistinguished Senator from Wisconsin, badly in need of a stratagem to assure his re-election, made his famous claim that he had in his pocket "a list of 205 known Communist Party members working in the State Department." For several years McCarthy usurped the national spotlight like a wild man, hurling unfounded charges against government agencies, institutions, and organizations, against countless individuals in public and private life, smearing reputations right and left. Contributions in support of McCarthy's crusade poured in, and the press had a prolonged field day reporting his every accusation in screaming headlines. In one of his cartoons, Herbert Block, of the Washington *Post*, labeled the national paranoia "McCarthyism,"

ROCKWELL KENT

a name that stuck and eventually became identified in the dictionary with the most blatant kind of political hooliganism.

Kent was subpoenaed to appear before McCarthy's committee on July 1, 1953. The encounter ended in a draw, since Kent actually had nothing to conceal. Indignantly he refused to answer McCarthy's stock question: "Are you or have you ever been a member of the Communist Party?" Later Kent regretted invoking the Fifth Amendment; on the basis of his refusal to answer the question he was not allowed to read into the court record a prepared statement charging that the Senator was the leader in a Fascist conspiracy. Copies of Kent's statement were distributed to reporters, but only one newspaper printed the complete text.

One fallout from the McCarthy hearing was particularly galling to Kent. The Farnsworth Art Museum of Rockland, Maine, canceled a comprehensive exhibition of his paintings scheduled for the summer of 1954. Kent's complaint to the Artists Equity Association drew a tepid response. His chagrin had another dimension: getting on in years, he had been concerned about final disposition of his growing Kent Collection, and the Farnsworth Museum had already made tentative plans to accept it and to build an annex to house it. The museum's board of directors peremptorily forbade it.

Somewhat subdued, Kent retired to Asgaard and wrote his autobiography, *It's Me O Lord*. A big book of 617 pages and many illustrations, it was published by Dodd, Mead in May

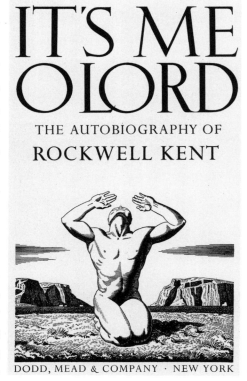

IT'S ME
O LORD

THE AUTOBIOGRAPHY OF
ROCKWELL KENT

DODD, MEAD & COMPANY · NEW YORK

of 1955. Prolix and chronologically vague, it is nevertheless a complete and circumstantial projection of the entire man and a fascinating mixture of self-revelation and evasion. Like most autobiographers, Kent was not above self-praise or a little fancy embroidery to improve his image. From the book emerges a not unsympathetic conception of a willful and passionately obstinate human being, self-sufficient yet generous and gregarious, worldly and practical yet stubbornly naïve in his ideals of social justice. The book and its reviewers did much to put Kent in a more realistic and sympathetic perspective.

Even at the relatively high price of ten dollars it sold quite well; the *Daily Worker* offered it to new subscribers at a discount.

For lack of a passport, in 1957 he had been obliged to decline an invitation to celebrate his seventy-fifth birthday in the Soviet Union. What rankled him even more was that when he was invited to exhibit his work in Russia, his requests to borrow his best paintings from American museums and most collectors were turned down. The final collection assembled for shipment included about thirty-six of his paintings and sixty prints. The exhibition, which opened in December of that year at the Pushkin Museum of Fine Arts in Moscow, and in March of 1958 at the Hermitage in Leningrad, was the first major show of an American artist's work to be seen in Russia. It created a sensation, with posters, radio programs, and extensive newspaper coverage. The director of the Pushkin Museum sent photographs of large crowds waiting in line to see the show. Fuming at the unjustified abrogation of his right as an American to be present at his own exhibition, Kent put all the blame on Secretary of State John Foster Dulles.

Never one to hold his fire when aroused, Kent shot a verbal volley at Dulles that made considerable noise. In early October, 1957, the world had been electrified by news of the successful launching by Soviet scientists of Sputnik I, the first satellite to be sent into orbit round the earth, and thirty days later, of Sputnik II, this time with a live dog as passenger. Speaking on television in Chicago, Kent deplored "the miserable spirit in which we received news of the great Russian achieve-

ABOVE: TITLE PAGE FROM IT'S ME O LORD, 1955

OPPOSITE: KENT AT WORK IN HIS STUDIO AT ASGAARD, C. 1941

ment," adding, "We will launch a better and bigger rocket, putting into it not a harmless little puppy but John Foster Dulles — equipped, of course, with a passport — far into the heavens into permanent orbit, as near to God as Dulles likes us to believe that he deserves to be." Kent was very proud of this gibe, repeating it with variations on subsequent broadcasts and in letters to friends.

Kent was but one of thousands of American citizens who were at that time denied passports because of their political associations. To passport applications had been added a questionnaire as to past or present membership in the Communist Party. Kent had steadfastly refused to submit such an affidavit as irrelevant, and when he brought suit in the district court for the District of Columbia he was joined in the suit by Dr. Walter Briehl, a psychiatrist who had also refused to submit such an affidavit. The suit went from the district court to the court of appeals, and finally to the United States Supreme Court.

On June 16, 1958, the Supreme Court ruled in favor of Kent and Briehl. The vote in that landmark decision was a close one: five to four, the majority represented by Chief Justice Earl Warren and Justices William O. Douglas, Hugo L. Black, Felix Frankfurter, and William J. Brennan, Jr. In Justice Douglas's opinion he wrote that "freedom to travel is an important aspect of the citizen's 'liberty,' guaranteed by the Fifth Amendment provision against depriving a person of his liberty or property without due process of law." Its effect was henceforth to permit all American citizens (barring those engaged in criminal activities) to travel abroad for whatever purpose they chose. In an interview, Kent remarked that it gave him "grim satisfaction to win a case of law against John Foster Dulles," adding that "I fought for this as a matter of principle and spent almost my last cent."

Whether the Kents could afford to travel at that time is an academic question inasmuch as during the summer of 1959 they were the official guests of the Soviet Union, to stay as long as they would like and with all expenses paid. They were feted in Moscow, Leningrad, and other cities, toured Bulgaria and Rumania, and returned home in August laden with gifts and lively memories of lavish Russian hospitality.

Kent's love affair with the Russian people blossomed under the warmth of their ministrations and praise. Collectively they became surrogates for the many Americans who had turned their backs on him. No institution in his own country had shown any interest in accepting his large Kent Collection on any terms; like an unrequited lover, and perhaps also out of spite, in 1960 he offered his gift to someone else — the Soviet Union. Writing to his friend Andrei Chegodaev, a member of the U.S.S.R. Academy of the Arts, he said, "I want my pictures to be seen and loved; and that could only happen in the Soviet Union."

It was a prodigal gesture, a gift of more than eighty of his paintings, some dating back to his Monhegan days, and some eight hundred drawings, prints, and other graphic works, including books and bound copies of his handwritten manuscripts. The gift was celebrated by a widely publicized exhibition in Moscow, with the Kents attending the opening November 19, 1960.

In 1962 the Kents were again in Moscow, for a reception in honor of Kent's eightieth birthday; members of the United States Embassy declined to attend. Premier Khrushchev sent a congratulatory letter. The Kents no doubt enjoyed more privileges and had a closer look at that country than any ordinary visitors. Kent was a celebrity wherever he appeared; receptions, speeches, banquets, entertainments, and guided tours were the order of the day, even in the most remote Soviet states. On a state farm on the lower border of Kazakh, they were invited to stay for "a cup of tea," which consisted of soups, salads, legs of chicken, legs of duck, raspberries, apricots, followed by sheep's head — eyes for the guest of honor, ears for his wife and the hostess — then roast lamb, regional dishes, and

ABOVE: EMBLEM FOR NATIONAL COUNCIL OF AMERICAN-SOVIET FRIENDSHIP, INC.

72   ROCKWELL KENT

huge pastries, all washed down with wine, vodka, cognac, and champagne, and finally, the "tea." Gifts to the Kents were equally lavish: an alabaster box containing five topazes, a balalaika, a landscape painting, a Kazakhstanian rug with Kent's name woven into it. In lieu of the traditional gift of a horse, Kent was presented with a native horseman's outfit, a six-foot, long-sleeved green velvet robe, with a hat of fur and velvet. At Tashkent, in Uzbek, still farther south, Kent collapsed and was flown back to Moscow, where he was met by a Red Cross ambulance and taken to a hospital for observation and rest. The Kents, with fifteen pieces of luggage and innumerable crates and boxes, arrived home by ship in September; they had been away four months.

On November 3 of the same year, Kent suffered a stroke while painting alone in his isolated studio. Though his left arm and leg were unusable, he managed to hop into his old Chevy and drive to the house. On November 29, he wrote to his friend Dan Burne Jones, "Though I am making steady but slow recovery, my speech is still so impaired that I dictate with considerable difficulty." Reports of Kent's poor health brought an invitation to return to Russia for a good rest. On the arrival of the Kents in Moscow early in March of 1964, they were given a suite in the luxurious sanatorium at Barvikha, but the inevitable round of entertainments and tours ensued, and when Rockwell and Sally boarded the Polish ship *Batory* for home early in July they were both worn out. Ruefully, Sally appraises their "vacation" in her diary: "From the health point of view little has been accomplished . . . and oh, the dinners and the endless toasts! Now I think only of home." Kent still suffered from an abnormally slow heartbeat, and in December, in a Montreal hospital, an electric cardiac stimulator was inserted into his chest. The operation was successful and Kent carried a pacemaker through the rest of his life.

In April of 1967, Kent was awarded the International Lenin Peace Prize in recognition of his services to the Communist-sponsored peace campaign. As honored guests on the *Alexander Pushkin,* the Kents sailed from Montreal on April 28, 1967. At Leningrad, they were met by representatives of the Lenin Prize Committee and conducted to Moscow for the presentation ceremonies. Kent received a diploma, a gold medal bearing the portrait of Lenin, and 25,000 rubles, which in American money amounted to exactly $27,687.80. In his acceptance speech, Kent condemned the intervention of the United States in Vietnam, and on June 8 he sent to the Vietnamese Ambassador in Moscow the following letter:

"Dear Sir: Being a citizen of the United States of America, I am deeply outraged at the unprovoked and utterly illegal invasion of the territories of the people of Vietnam by my country's armed forces; and, as a citizen, conscience-stricken at my own *de facto* involvement in my country's shameful acts.

"I beg your honor, therefore, to transmit to the suffering women and children of Vietnam's Liberation Front the enclosed sum of ten thousand dollars ($10,000), it being but a token of my shame and sorrow. I am, sir, Yours most respectfully, Rockwell Kent."

In due course he received a telegram: "Dear Mr. Rockwell Kent, Artist of the People and International Well-Known Public-Man: I beg to convey to you the warmest sympathies and the most heartfelt thanks of the Vietnamese People. Thanks for your generous support to our just and invincible struggle. The Vietnamese People are fighting for their national and sacred interests and at the same time for the high dignity of human being and for friendship between peoples. Wish you good health. Respectfully, Pham Van Dong."

Coming as it did amidst growing American sentiment against the war, and especially on the heels of anti-war demonstrations in New York City and San Francisco on April 15 — the largest to that date — Kent's grand gesture received not nearly the adverse publicity it would have provoked at any other time. The Kents left for home after three months; it was their last visit to the Soviet Union.

Regardless of frequent interruptions and the indifference of American collectors to his paintings during these years, Kent remained productive. In 1960, he had written to his friend Chegodaev,

"For twenty years I have been painting, as it were, in a vacuum." And to another friend he wrote that for many years he had abstained from exhibiting his work or offering it for sale because of the general hostility toward him. He did, however, have one patron of considerable importance.

In 1950, through a New York dealer, Kent had shipped three of his paintings on approval to James J. Ryan, a wealthy sportsman and flying enthusiast of Virginia. Ryan promptly bought all three and asked to see more. In 1952, Ryan commissioned Kent to go to the Canadian Rockies and paint a picture of Mount Assiniboine. Ryan continually bought paintings from Kent and for a number of years was his principal source of income. Ryan was very likely to send one of his planes up to Au Sable Forks to pick up a few paintings for consideration. In a letter of July 15, 1959, to Leonard Boudin, Kent wrote, "Late Saturday afternoon, Jim Ryan sent one of his planes for me. I flew to New York, was a guest of his at the Pierre, had dinner with him . . . was handed a check for two paintings, went to bed; and the next morning, without seeing him again, was conveyed in his limo to LaGuardia Field, whence again in one of his four planes I was flown back to Plattsburgh." And again, on May 25, 1965, he wrote, "Jim Ryan was here, thank God, left some of his money, for which I am to send four small Alaska sketches which were hanging on the wall of my studio."

The Kents also visited Oak Ridge, Ryan's huge country estate in Nelson County, Virginia. In October of 1961, they were there for two weeks. Their host was with them for only a day or two; the rest of the time Kent painted outdoors from dawn to dusk. He and Sally took special delight in touring the great manor house: ". . . its foyers, hallways, reception rooms, studies, libraries, living rooms — is virtually a great gallery of Kent paintings. I have never seen my work displayed in such quantities, so beautifully framed and hung!" Kent returned to Asgaard with "perhaps a dozen canvases, well begun," which he finished during the winter; Ryan bought several of them.

Kent always thought of his paintings as expressions of his interest in living, and his own style "the embodiment of economy, precision, and dignity." He saw no reason for change, and he had no use for the rising crop of young artists who followed slavishly the latest fashions in modern art. There is little difference between his earliest canvases and his later ones except for an early departure from the free-flowing brushwork he had learned from Chase and Henri. His approach to painting was largely dictated by methods acquired while turning out thousands of illustrations and wood engravings; these, by their nature and his own preferences, required a foundation of careful drawing and explicit design quite alien to the new generation's taste for uninhibited expression.

In his twilight years, with the bleak patterns of the icy North no longer accessible to him, he still sought at Asgaard to capture the silent magic of snow, but he found equal satisfaction in recording the verdancy of the gentler seasons and the glow of autumn. From his own doorstep he painted, over and over, from season to season, the view looking across the broad expanse of the meadow to the simple shapes of the Asgaard dairy barns and the undulating hills and mountains beyond, with the skies above them suggestive of limitless space and an almost palpable silence so congenial to his nature.

Sloping down in another direction were groves of trees merging into a dark forest of pines. In the summer of 1961, before his vacation at Oak Ridge, he wrote to Ryan, "I have been painting constantly — trying, for a change, to paint trees — in preparation, as it were, for painting that lovely Virginia countryside of yours." It was a new challenge, this striving for what Walt Kuhn in his own last years had asserted was "the ultimate accomplishment — to paint trees as they really are."

After many delays, Kent's last important book, *Greenland Journal,* appeared February 5, 1963, though the limited and trade editions carry the date 1962. While it is one of his most charming works, the paucity of reviews made it much less successful than it deserved to be. However, the clouds over his name had begun to disperse, and his paintings and prints were once more in demand. In the summer of 1964, the *American Book Collector* issued a special Rockwell Kent number, with an extensive bibliography, indicating a lively interest in his books. And in 1966 Richard Larcada, a

OPPOSITE: ON EARTH PEACE, 1962, LITHOGRAPH ON STONE, 8-1/16 x 5-3/32"

OPPOSITE, LEFT AND RIGHT, AND RIGHT: INK DRAWINGS FROM GREENLAND JOURNAL, 1963

New York dealer, began regularly to display and sell his work.

A much more significant harbinger of Kent's return to favor was the important exhibition "Rockwell Kent: The Early Years," held during the month of August, 1969, at the Bowdoin College Museum of Art, Brunswick, Maine. The museums and collectors that had refused to lend their Kent paintings to the 1957 exhibition in the Soviet Union now willingly sent them to Curator Richard V. West for the Bowdoin show. It was a superb retrospective: sixty of Kent's finest paintings made between 1903 and 1935, lent by seventeen museums and ten private collections. A large eighty-page catalogue with fifty-three full-page reproductions was issued. As guest of honor at the opening, he was so surrounded by crowds that he was unable to have more than a glance at his paintings. Sadly aware that he was not likely ever to see most of them again, he and Sally left for home the next morning; matters at Asgaard were much more pressing.

On the night of April 19, 1969, the house had been struck by lightning while the Kents were asleep, and though volunteer firemen swarmed in from all directions, equipment for pumping water from the pond came too late to be of much good and the house burned to the ground. Nearly everything inside had been destroyed, including a library of ten thousand books. However, from the cellar of the smoldering house file boxes containing about fifty thousand letters and other papers were rescued and stacked on the lawn. In describing the catastrophe, Sally wrote, "Next day, as though in penitence for the deed, the heavens laid a funeral pall of snow upon the blackened ruin." The water-soaked and partially charred papers were later shipped to the Archives of American Art, then based in Detroit. The Detroit Institute of Arts made a large, warm room in the basement available for the drying out and restoration of the papers, and they were eventually deposited in the new quarters of the Archives of American Art in Washington, D.C.

Undaunted, the day after the fire Kent was already at work in his nearby studio drawing the plans for a new house, to be built on the old foundations but minus a second floor. On July 11, he wrote to his friends Victor and Ellen Perlo that the roof was already shingled, the sides of the house enclosed, and he and Sally might be able to move in by Labor Day. "But, gee, things cost an awful lot of money! And if we do move in then we may not have chairs to sit in, beds to sleep in, or tables to eat from. But lots of pots and pans and dishes and miscellaneous useful articles were saved, so we will actually *not* be starting again from scratch."

Once more the house was open to visitors, but Rockwell was not the lively host he once was; he had trouble talking, his hearing was badly impaired, and he was full of sleep. Gradually, he became withdrawn and saw only a few close friends. In Sally — constant companion and faithful partner in all his endeavors — he knew that he had at last found the perfect mate. In a moment of remarkable prescience, he told his good friend and neighbor John Gorton that he expected him to take good care of her. (John and Sally were married December 28, 1973.)

Realizing that his time was running out, Kent began to dismantle his studio and put his effects in order for the final dissolution — signing prints, identifying photographs; oddly enough, adding figures to some of his paintings. For some time he had been trying to bring his autobiography up to date, patching it together from files of papers and a detailed chronology assembled by Sally. Much of it deals with his experiences in the Soviet Union and his gratitude for the friendship of that country's people.

Rockwell Kent died March 13, 1971, in a Plattsburgh hospital, eleven days after he had suffered another stroke, and within three months of his eighty-ninth birthday. A private memorial service, conducted by his old friend Corliss Lamont, was held at Asgaard on the fifteenth. His final resting place, not far from his old studio cabin, has over it a large gray marble slab. Its chaste design, suggestive of one of Kent's own title pages, bears his name and dates and a bird-and-olive-branch device, and above them the fitting words THIS IS MY OWN.

ROCKWELL KENT

Rockwell Kent once remarked that he had always loved adventure and reflecting on it; that as a result he had always needed to paint, and because painting alone was inadequate, to write; that he always had ideas for pictures, and ideas to be expressed in words. "Everywhere that I have been I have had enthusiasm and excitements; I have had the excitements of certain little risks that I have run, the enthusiasm of being where nature was immense, where skies were clear at night, where lands were virginal. I have stood in spots where I have known that I was the first white man who had ever seen that country, that I was the supreme consciousness that came to it. I have liked the thought that maybe there was no existence but in consciousness, and that I was in a sense the creator of that place. And because I have been alone so much and have been moved by what I have seen, I have had to paint it and write about it."

The compulsion to write surfaced early; in boarding school the intricacies of English composition intrigued him and provided the initial stimulus to express in words the same speculations about the unknowable infinite that were to suffuse so much of his earliest paintings and prints. The instruments for writing therefore became as necessary to him as pencils and brushes. He considered himself as much a writer as a painter because he thought in terms of literature as often as in terms of art.

Kent was no scribbler; hardly ever does one find among his papers even a note or a list which has not been neatly indited. His bound manuscripts and the letters he wrote in his own hand are a pleasure to look at, with their widely spaced lines and ample margins. The extremely regular, minuscule script reflects the precision of an engraver, but the modesty of its size gives no hint of the strong personality behind it.

In his writing he took considerable pains when time permitted his making a rough draft; reconsidered phrases are frequent and carefully revised, entire paragraphs crossed out and begun anew. He constructed his sentences with care, his satisfaction in getting them just right heightened by the contemplation of seeing them later transmuted into print; his journals and the letters sent from far away to family and friends were actually rehearsals for what he wanted to say in his books. He habitually read aloud what he had just written, revising and polishing until he had achieved what he considered would be pleasing to the ear as well as to the mind. He said that he wanted his writing, with all its digressions and asides, to appear perfectly natural and to read like verbatim records of his conversation.

Perhaps he sometimes overdid it. Yet this indirect approach to what he had to say is just as characteristic of him as the efficient directness with which he applied himself to his art. And because of it, he reveals much more of himself in his writing than in his art, unconsciously uncovering the mainsprings of those strong convictions which so often alienated him from people with opposing views. To understand him, one must read his own words; these selections from his autobiography, his travel books, and his letters will speak for themselves.

ABOVE: FRONTISPIECE FROM <u>VENUS AND ADONIS</u>, 1931

ROCKWELL KENT

THE EARLY YEARS

CHILDHOOD

Of the effect of my father's death upon my mother I know nothing but the sorrow that is apparent in the pictures of her that were taken at the time and later. Schooled by the character of her upbringing to the stern suppression of all her emotions, particularly when these were of an unhappy nature, and forever silent as to my father and their marriage and my father's death, it required my own maturity to bring me to any realization of how utterly devastating to her that loss must have been. Even at the time, every precaution seems to have been taken to conceal his illness from my little brother and me and, I must assume, to explain his death as but another of those departures and long absences to which we were accustomed. And while the consequences to the family were serious — the loss to us children of a father's discipline and guidance, and to all of us of a security which once had seemed to be assured — they led to no such sudden changes in our way of life as children could have felt. It was, in fact, as though the work upon a structure well begun had been halted, leaving it for the ravages of time to disclose the temporary nature of its foundations. Abandoning our New York residence, we returned to Tarrytown where, disposing of the dogs and horses, my mother began the practice of those economies that throughout the following fifteen years were to become ever more stringent. My mother's mother, Grosmama we called her, now came to live with us and to share in the care and upbringing of the children, of whom — it is now the winter of 1887 — there were soon to be three.

I can recall something of the great blizzard of early March [of 1888], the vast amount of snow, the drifts a story high. No doubt we children loved it. But as the snow had come, so, swiftly under the warm March sun, it departed. And when, on March twenty-first, Mother told my brother and me that the children of friends living a mile away would like us to spend the whole day with them, away we went afoot over the almost snow-free road. I can barely remember the wonderful time we had that day. And I do remember that when, that evening, we got home we found that a stork had been there and had brought us a little sister. Rockwell, Douglas, and Dorothy; and Mother and Grosmama: that was now our household.

The Great Mogul James Banker having, as we have noted, died, friendly relations had been re-established with his widow, my great-aunt — Aunt Josie as we called her — although throughout the years she was to reveal herself more as a niggardly patroness of poor relations than a woman reunited to a niece who had for years been as a daughter. For periods, during which our own house may have been rented, we lived with Aunt Josie in the great Irvington house. She cannot have been one to love small children, for such love would have engendered in them a responsive emotion of which some memory would remain to me. She had none of her sister's, my Grosmama's, great warmth and tenderness, at least not toward us; remaining, to use my mother's borrowed expression, an "Olympian," to be as much as possible avoided. And for that object what setting could have served us better than that great house of many rooms and the, to us, limitless estate with all its varied natural and landscaped features: lawns to roll on; meadows of long grass to hide in; the ravine and the stone bridge that spanned it, a low, arched bridge that hid a glamorous, cool, dark, robbers' cave beneath. The fountain that had in its center a statue of a man with a pitchfork sitting on a big fish that squirted water; the smaller fountain with a statue of somebody else and that, mostly out of order, always had a lot of fascinatingly horrible dead toads on the bottom; the iron deer in the meadow that we used to ride — that came to have a wasps' nest under its tail; the box-hedged garden and its grapevines that the old gardener, William Morrison, was always chasing us away from; and the bowling alley where we could roll the balls and make all the noise we wanted to, for it was far from the house; and, for rainy days, the great verandah around three sides of the house; and, on the verandah, wonderful games like quoits and beanbags, and a big affair with holes on top to throw metal disks into, and numbered compart-

OPPOSITE: MADONNA OF THE VALLEYS, ILLUSTRATION FOR A POEM BY WORDSWORTH, VANITY FAIR, 1922

ROCKWELL KENT

ments into which by subterranean passages they slid; oh, it was a wonderful place, Irvington, for kids to get away from an old aunt and from the old uncles who visited her, none of whom seemed to like children very much, to get away and have a wonderful time.

And the house itself, indoors, was a glamorous and largely mysterious place! It was traversed by a broad hallway that divided it into two parts: the used part, whereof the dining room had come to serve Aunt Josie and the family as an all-day living room, the adjacent pantry and closets and the broad, dark, walnut stairway; and across the hall the far larger and forbidden half. It was that part of the house, entered through either of two great doorways with silent easy-swinging doors, and trodden noiselessly on the deep-piled carpets, that was to me a realm of inexhaustible wonders. I would first enter either of two large-windowed intercommunicating drawing rooms, or parlors, both no doubt in their reality of shining brass and porcelain and lacquer, plush and satin, truly elegant, but possessing to my eyes an untouchable throne-room elegance that I could literally hardly endure. It was the great library, entered from either of the parlors, the library with its shelves upon shelves of beautiful books, its albums upon the tables; its paintings on the walls; its great statues in the deep reveals of the windows; its wonderful music box with polished bells and cymbals and I've forgotten what more wonderful orchestral instruments *visible* but — such was my fear of discovery — not to be touched and played; and there was the big cabinet into which

ROCKWELL
ALASKA MCMXVIII

R. K.

I'd peer and, against the light, look at one after another great colored transparencies of the world's wonders — of which, incidentally, Mount Vesuvius in eruption was the most thrilling; yes, it was the library that I most lingered in and loved. And it was amid the treasures of the library that, gazing ardently at the big painting of the lovely half-clothed Lorelei playing her siren's harp at sunset on her cliff above the Rhine, or stroking the sleek, bare, bronze limbs of the lady on the panther, there came to me the first premonition of future ecstasy and shame.

And there was another statue that held me, this one life-sized and of marble. A woman — oh, so beautiful and sad! — a poor woman, in "unwomanly rags," sat stitching, forever wearily stitching, on a garment that could never be finished. *The Song of the Shirt:* I believe that my first questioning of why and how such tragedy could be, stemmed from the compelling sorrow of this figure. Yes, it was in the library at Irvington that I experienced the first spiritual stirrings that I can recall.

It was, if at Irvington at all, at any rate not at church. Aunt Josie was a devout Episcopalian and regularly attended Sunday service at St. Barnabas Church. Punctually, as the victoria with liveried coachman and footman on the box would appear before the house, Aunt Josie would emerge attired, I suppose properly enough, in a dress of rustling black taffeta and jet and lace but wearing a bonnet of such preposterous proportions and eccentric shape as to mark her for astonishment and covert laughter wherever she might be seen. Not the solemnity of church, nor the peals of the organ, nor the treble voices of the choir, nor the people in their Sunday best: not anything touched me but my own silly humiliation at how Aunt Josie looked.

No: if we are looking for an early religious experience of our young hero, church, in Irvington, with Aunt Josie, is not the place. Nor was my first school — again in Irvington — significant as the nursery of a budding mind. I must have been very small at the time, for it was to Miss Bennett's School for Girls that I was sent or, rather, taken mornings and brought home from. Of Miss Bennett's

ABOVE: FRONTISPIECE FROM <u>WILDERNESS</u>, 1920

ROCKWELL KENT

I remember nothing but the great number of little girls and some little boys, of all of whom I was tragically shy. I mainly remember the agony of sitting in the classroom and wiggling my legs and trying so desperately hard to keep from doing it; and the immense relief and greater shame of at last having to wet my drawers. Over and over again I did it, until at last it was decided that something was wrong with me and I must therefore not go to Miss Bennett's school any more. Yet not a thing was wrong — and I tried so hard to tell them so — but that nobody had ever told me where the bathroom was; and I was much too ashamed and shy to ask.

You see, we children were everywhere very much alone, both in that great Irvington place where we only occasionally met the children of our only neighbors, the Jaffrays and McVickers, and in Tarrytown where of nearby neighbors, but for one boy of my age, Al Grant, we had none at all. The village, to be sure, was not too far away for us to have made friends but — and this must now be told — it was nevertheless, in the most disparaging English-Victorian sense of the term, "the Village," and consequently out of bounds for children of the Gentry, however decaying or decayed their economic status may have been. One *just didn't play* with *village kids;* and that — either by force of moral suasion or of law — was that.

School once begun, and regardless of the humiliating reason for its temporary discontinuance, had to be pursued. So upon our return to Tarrytown I was entered at a little private school in the village conducted in his own home by a most genial and kindly, bearded man, a Professor Richardson. That he taught us the rudiments of the three R's I have no doubt; and that he taught us history, American history, my memory of fighting the Revolutionary War with snowballs every winter recess-time and after school is the clearest evidence. But it was in the second of the three Rs, wRiting, and as a brilliant disciple of the American school of calligraphy plagiarized and popularized by "Professor" Spencer, and forever to be remembered as "Spencerian," that Professor Richardson excelled. A development of Eighteenth Century English penmanship, its basic principle of execution was the use of the forearm or, as it proves in practice, of the entire arm from the shoulder down — instead of the fingers; these, apart from the little finger, which rested on the paper, serving merely to hold the pen. Both the extreme slope of the Spencerian hand and the exaggeratedly shaded downstrokes called for a special type of penholder, an implement that, with its cantilevered pen support and finger-fitting holder, is as curious to modern eyes as, to the eyes of future generations, will no doubt be the "functional" back-and-bottom-fitting sitting machines that some deluded mortals of today are fancying. But anyhow, just like the chairs, they worked; and the marvelous beauty of the Professor's Spencerian birds of paradise is as memorable to me today as, in its time, it was inspiring. I loved to write; and, as the copybook text no doubt instructed me, I so improved each shining hour that at the school commencement in June I was awarded "for excellence in penmanship" not only a Spencerian penholder but a gold medal. It was the only gold medal — *real* gold medal rather than a certificate of award entitling me to go to Tiffany's and *buy* myself a medal — that I was ever in my life to receive. Perhaps that's just as well.

[IT'S ME O LORD]

CHILDHOOD, DRAWING FROM "THE SEVEN AGES OF MAN," 1918

ROCKWELL KENT

" " M Y   B E T T E R   S E L F " "

I read a lot, and reading was encouraged. First of all, in early childhood, there were the German books: *Struwwelpeter,* and *Koenig Nobel,* and *Robinson Crusoe,* and *Der Ritter in die Not;* and *Aesop's Fables* in German, and Andersen's and Grimm's fairy tales. Then came my father's and an uncle's boyhood books, their Oliver Optics: *Little Bobtail, Work and Win, The Sailor Boy;* and the whole eight volumes of the Blue and Gray Series. And the "Frank" books by Harry Castlemon: *Frank on a Gunboat, Frank Before Vicksburg,* six of them in all. And Henty! One after another I read them, and learned history with far more pleasure, if less truth, than I had ever learned it in school. I loved to read. And I was no sooner earning money for myself than I began, one volume at a time, to buy the authors I liked best. The first of these was Scott.

Since in all the books — at least from Optic up to Scott — the heroes were invariably youths or men of incorruptible virtue and dauntless courage, and their villains uniformly bad, the notions of good and evil, which my elders at home had been at unremitting pains to implant, assumed corporeal form; what had been mere moral abstractions were now transmuted into the flesh and blood of heroes, heroes to worship and to emulate, and bad men to detest. To be like them, my heroes: how deeply I aspired to! How — in my thoughts, at least — I tried!

And, now that we have come to heroes, the moment has arrived — and how reluctantly I welcome it! — to introduce a hitherto unmentioned member of our household, a young companion of exactly my own age and so closely resembling me in outward appearance that, but for the sort of "holier than thou" expression which distinguished him, we might have been — although we never were — mistaken for each other. I give you — as by my elders he had been introduced to me: my Better Self.

Writing at a period almost two-thirds of a long lifetime distant from the memorable year in which at long last I came to a satisfactory working agreement with him, I find it difficult to recall either the time or the exact circumstances of his entry into my life. It would be consistent with his character, as I subsequently came to know it, that he chose as the occasion to be introduced some such embarrassing moment as that of my detection in the stealing and consuming of a can of Eagle Brand condensed milk. That I there and then accepted him, in a sense admitting him to my heart and councils, is evidence enough of my early unsophistication and of a real desire, through such virtuous companionship, to better myself. Your Better Self: remember him, they'd say. Heed him. Be like him if you can.

At first, and for some years, I accepted him as, morally, the living counterpart of the heroes of my books; yet his persistent intrusions upon me at all moments of pleasant and illicit self-indulgence, his admonitory upraised finger, that placid, goody-goody look with which he regarded me, led me through gradually increasing exasperation to despise him as an obnoxious prig, and finally to that treaty or settlement to which, in the previous paragraph, I have alluded, and the details of which I will in due time relate.

Yes; looking back upon him now, he was in many respects singularly like my heroes: like Little Bobtail, like Frank; perhaps, even, like Ivanhoe and Quentin Durward. Would they, had they lived close to me, have proved such prigs?

[IT'S ME O LORD]

ROCKWELL DISCOVERS THE POOR

The time had been when I would feel a little troubled, now and then, at our having less money than a lot of other people; and now, believe it or not, I began to be troubled at having more. We now had servants, and their lot began to trouble me.

Christmas was always a great festival to us, to all our friends in Tarrytown. At the initiative of the Ewings, a dozen or more of us would begin, weeks before Christmas, rehearsing carols, employing as our coach or director a certain Englishman, Professor Walker, a violinist, a teacher of music, and a resident of Tarrytown. His method was the Tonic Sol Fa System, and his Cockney pronunciation of the vowels was a constant source of amusement to us. "Dao is dao," he would say, "just as a tyble is a tyble." Thus, laughing a lot and having a general good time, we'd meet and practice; so that on Christmas Eve we'd be in shape to carol quite prettily under the windows of our friends. And, after such caroling in the late December cold, be in good shape for my mother's welcome to her Christmas tree.

The trimming of the tree was to us all a labor of love, and in particular to me, for, as the artist of the family's younger set, the chief responsibility was mine. One Christmas Eve, having completed the trimming and lighted the candles to judge of the effect, I suddenly became aware of our maid, a Polish girl, standing in the doorway and gazing at the tree with eyes of such awe and wonder that for a moment she seemed not to be aware of having been observed. Then, as though startled from a trance, she gasped: "It is so beautiful!" And all at once I knew that to none who should see the tree that night would it mean so much, and that in this girl's wonder the tree had found its fulfillment. Yet she who loved it most would not be there. The thought was not a happy one.

Months later this girl fell ill, so ill that an ambulance had to be sent for to take her to the hospital. She was in great pain, and it was decided that rather than attempt to maneuver the stretcher down the stairs she should be carried down, and that I should do it. So I did; and laid her on the stretcher. Her back was toward me; and it was painful for her to turn, as she then did, so that she might without discourtesy say "Thank you, sir." I was ashamed.

And I was ashamed when Taka, a Japanese whom we later employed and who, unhappily, had also to be hospitalized, refused to let me help him on with his coat because a master might not do that for a servant.

It was a happening of no particular importance to come across an old man, an old Frenchman, crawling about in a mosquito-infested swamp catching frogs with his hands. He sold them, so he told me, as food for snakes in the New York zoo. Or, on another painting ramble, to talk with an old old woman, a veritable hag, living alone in a dilapidated house in an isolated patch of Westchester wilderness, and learn from her in what fear she lived. She told me of a tramp who had molested her. "What did he want?" I innocently asked. She fairly spat her answer. "Woman," she said.

The poverty of so many people, the dire, hopeless poverty of some, came to be more and more a burden to my mind. That, in general, it was in no remote way related to what of themselves, as individual men and women, they were, became increasingly apparent. Oh yes; I'd heard all about the dirty Irish, and about the greasy Wops and Dagos, and the stupid Polacks, and the depraved and sinister Chinamen; and how if you gave them clean places to live in they'd turn them into sties, and if you trusted them they'd betray you. I knew all that, I knew the lie of it. And for the lie, for what it rested on and for its consequences, I knew I must accept my share of blame. But what I didn't know — not yet — was what to do.

[IT'S ME O LORD]

OPPOSITE: SEATED NUDE, 1931, LITHOGRAPH ON STONE, 8-1/4 x 7-7/16"

ROCKWELL KENT

HORACE MANN SCHOOL

Manual training as an adjunct to book learning was basic to Horace Mann's principles of education; and the manual training I received at the school proved of basic importance to me. It enlarged the horizon of my life, opening channels of activity that were subsequently to lead me, on one hand, into the ranks of labor and, on the other, to that *respect* for craftsmanship which, regardless of my own work's shortcomings, I hold to be fundamental to the practice of all art. What joy there is in *making* things. In beating red-hot iron into useful, often lovely, shapes; in making patterns, molding them in sand, in casting them with molten metal, in turning them on a lathe to the precision that their use demands; in fashioning from a stick of wood a penholder, itself a means toward the fashioning of words to give substantial form to thought; to transmute paint to mountains, seas, and depths of space; to flesh and blood. What joy, what pride one takes, in making things!

Mechanical drawing was important in our curriculum; and, again, the high degree of craftsmanship that it demanded — of accuracy of measurement, of sheer draftsmanship in terms of utmost precision — not only served, however unsuspectedly by me, to incline me toward my eventual profession, but to train my hand for service to it. But of even greater importance was the stark, material realism of which such drawing is the expression. Our concern was not with what things *looked* like but with what, in all their three dimensions, they essentially were. And, since we were in part required to design and prepare working drawings of what we'd later make in the shop, some were of things as they at last should be. In that respect they were projections of our imaginations upon paper in terms as simple, real, and accurate as we could devise, and differed from art in no respect but that, inviting a practical rather than an emotional response, they served an exclusively material end.

If, at Horace Mann School, I received training in Fine Art (that pretentious term for pictures), I have forgotten it. If I did receive it, it was doubtless of the utterly stultifying nature that has characterized pre-college art teaching until quite recent years. It is therefore well forgotten. At any rate, I, and all my generation, were happily spared all the silly, sensual indulgence in irresponsible self-expression that, from messy "finger painting" to often messier abstractionism, characterizes much of the therapeutic school art of today. Not living in the great atomic age, we didn't need it.

[IT'S ME O LORD]

ABOVE AND OPPOSITE: MEDALLION DEVICES FOR A. B. DICK CO., C. 1934

RUFUS WEEKS

It happened, it just happened, that at this revolutionary period of my life when I most needed — even more than I needed books — the active companionship of a mind cut closely to the pattern of my own, and instruction directly applicable to America of the moment and to the problems of a particular young American, it just so happened that I met that friend in need in the person of an old family ac-quaintance and not far distant neighbor, Rufus W. Weeks.

Mr. Weeks was a man of advanced years who enjoyed the wealth and comfort of living to which his brilliant mind in lifelong service to big business entitled him. He was the actuary and vice-president of a major insurance company. He was also a devout Christian conforming his life to Chris-tian standards. He was also — or, as he would have said, in consequence — a Socialist and a member of the Socialist Party.

I had first come to know of Rufus Weeks when as a boy I had occasionally attended the "so-ciables" held in the community house and library which he had established in the nearby village of Pocantico Hills. Open all day and evening to everyone, regardless of his color, social status, or religion, it had featured a weekly get-together, with dancing and good things to eat, which *all* classes — the masters and their servants, the bosses and their employees, the rich, the poor — were urged to attend, that they might mingle in good fellowship. For at least some years these get-togethers were continued with success, only to be eventually abandoned by Rufus Weeks himself on the ground, as he later ex-plained to me, that they served only to lend a false and misleading façade to the ugly reality of the class struggle, a struggle that was only to be resolved by the action of the working class itself.

And now with Rufus Weeks I could discuss the many aspects of life that had come to trou-ble me: the origin and existence of privilege and its transmission to unworthy heirs; the concentration of great wealth in hands which had not labored to create it; the existence of poverty in a land of plenty; of unemployment — with always so much crying to be done! Loving the world — our earth;

ABOVE: STEEL PUDDLING OPERATION, 1945, PEN DRAWING FOR CHARLES BRUNING CO.

ROCKWELL KENT

loving America, "its rocks and rills and templed hills," as perhaps only a painter could perceive and love them — I had indulged myself with Utopian thoughts of how happily people could live and work together, cooperating rather than contending. Why couldn't they? These were all problems that had troubled Rufus Weeks in his own youth; and to their better understanding and, perhaps, their solution in my own mind he brought the wisdom of his everlasting youth. Through what he told me, and through what my fortified awareness prompted me to procure and read, I came to realize that only through such vast upheaval and change as is termed revolution could social equity at last come to prevail.

"No man may be termed 'intelligent,' " said Rufus Weeks, "who is not a revolutionist." . . .

It was on an evening of early fall, in 1904, that Rufus Weeks in his coupé, his Negro coachman driving, stopped to pick me up and take me to my first Socialist meeting. The meeting was a small affair — no more than six or eight persons, including Mr. Weeks's coachman, attending — and was held in the apartment over the store of a local druggist named Sokol. I can recall no details of the meeting save that at the close of an hour or more of political discussion I was admitted as a member of the party, given a card to which a month's-dues stamp was affixed, and that I paid my twenty-five cents dues. But I do remember the warmth of those good-hearted people, and of our foreign-born hosts in particular; and the marvelous goodness of the Russian sourdough corn bread that they served us — then, and every evening of the many that I came to visit them.

The issues that concerned us in those days did not include today's transcendent issue, war or peace. They were in the main purely domestic, and concerned such matters as full employment, child labor, the eight-hour day, and labor's right to organize. They included the problem of recurrent depressions and the growing power of the trusts — with, for us of Tarrytown, a living example in a fellow citizen, the elder John D. Rockefeller. We knew, as half the world now does, that Socialism offered the only final solution to our domestic ills, and we agitated for the present adoption of remedial legislation. They were, of course, right who then denounced our program as "Socialistic"; and we, it has been proven, were right in our conviction that it would prevail. For to a large extent the measures we then fought for have been woven into the pattern of the American way of life.

I had not read the letter that, in 1897, the militant labor leader Eugene V. Debs had written to our next-door neighbor in Tarrytown, John D. Rockefeller. Touchingly expressive of his own political adolescence at that period, it is also, in its naïve belief in the inherent goodness of mankind, as the voice of adolescent youth in general and of me as, at the age of twenty-one, I might have spoken. Writing of the wholly Utopian dream of a cooperative commonwealth, he said:

> The purpose of the organization, briefly speaking, is to establish in place of the present cruel, immoral and decadent system, a cooperative commonwealth, where millionaires and beggars . . . will completely disappear, and human brotherhood will be inaugurated to bless and make the world more beautiful. . . . In this movement there are no class distinctions. Rich and poor are equally welcome to help dethrone Gold and elevate humanity. Then the strong will help the weak, the weak will love the strong, and the Human Brotherhood will transform the days to come into a virtual Paradise.

Romantic? Fatuous? Of course. Yet let's not laugh; rather than for laughter there is cause for tears that mankind is unworthy of such faith.

On the morning of the first Tuesday after the first Monday of November, 1904, our maid announced to "Mr. Rockwell," that a carriage was at the door for him. It proved to be one of the victoria hacks of the period. "Who sent you?" I asked the driver. "The Republican Party," he answered. "Please thank them," I said, "and tell them that I'm walking down. I'm voting Socialist."

My first vote was for Debs.

[IT'S ME O LORD]

WILLIAM M. CHASE

William M. Chase was, in his day, a famous painter and a famous teacher. His work in landscape, por-traiture, and still life has the enduring virtue of absolute and forthright honesty; and the weaknesses of his own somewhat superficial nature. A respecter of Frans Hals and Sargent — more, it must be said, for their manner than their content — he was a brilliant technician; and, as is too often the case, showed himself more discerning of surface appearances than of deeper and more essential values. Rather to point this comment than to be flippant, I may say that in his work he showed less under-standing of people than of codfish; for it is mainly for his paintings of fish that he is remembered. In reaction to the messy, tobacco-fingered Barbizon school and the "greenery yallery Grosvenor Gallery" stuff, Chase was an exponent of the *plein air* school. He went to nature, stood before nature, and painted it as his eyes beheld it. And if he didn't *kneel* before nature, that, as a matter of religion, was his own concern. More interested in *impressions* of the subject than in deeper and more labored prob-ing, the work of his students consisted mainly of pictures swiftly painted at one sitting. And valuing facility or fluency of brushwork, he favored large canvases as offering a larger opportunity for its dis-play.

The output of his class was prodigious, each student turning in from six to a dozen canvases for the master's Saturday-morning public criticisms. The studio where these criticisms were held was of ample size to accommodate the fifty to one hundred people who, as students or as visitors, attended. The pictures were displayed on a three-tiered reversible screen, its rear being loaded while the pictures on the front were under criticism. When all was ready — the audience in its place, the pictures mounted to be shown — the master would appear. Chase was a little man, dapper in dress to the point of foppishness, spatted, batwing-collared, his cravat drawn through a priceless jeweled ring. He in-variably wore a carnation in his buttonhole. Gray-haired, gray-bearded, and mustachioed, he was a handsome and distinguished-looking man. Black-ribboned pince-nez completed — shall we say his makeup? No, it all was natural to him — completed William M. Chase.

In his criticisms Chase was insistent upon one thing: truth. Go before nature, use your eyes, and then paint what you see. Respecting nature's variety and unexpectedness he urged new points of vision, what now we call the "candid camera shot." He called them "queers," and offered prizes for the queerest. Fair and impartial in his criticisms, understanding and considerate of others' points of view, he was nevertheless intolerant of affectation and of those aberrations of "self-expression" into which, even in those days of normal extraversion, some students strayed. A good world, it was then; and, compared to subsequent periods that I have known, an almost unbelievable world. For it was a world that people loved even more than they loved themselves.

But Chase respected truth and craftmanship not as in themselves an end but rather as the means essential to the attainment of, to him, the final end: success and money. Art was a commodity that must find a market and, through its own excellence, hold it. Art was an achievement honored by mankind, and to deserve that honor Art must be good.

"Look at me," he would say. "Beginning as a shoe clerk trying on ladies' shoes, I have come to be the guest of kings."

In some respects Chase and his students might have been of those Florentine days referred to by the poet Dechartre, in a novel by Anatole France:

> Happy days, when no one dreamed of that originality to which today we so eagerly aspire. The apprentice was content to follow his master. His sole ambition was to resemble him, and it was quite involuntarily that he appeared different from the others. They worked not to win fame, but to earn a livelihood.

Chase was a realist; and his impatience with unrealism and with all straining for effect is expressed in a happening at one of his public criticisms.

As the screen was turned around to bring another lot of pictures into view, the master found himself confronted by an array of dismal daubs whose subject matter, if they had any, was lost in the murk of black paint with which the canvases appeared to have been smeared. For a long time he contemplated the works, turning at last to ask who had done them.

"I did, Mr. Chase" came the cheerful response from a female newcomer in his audience.

Again he looked at the pictures, long and earnestly, only to turn with the admission that he didn't understand them.

"Oh, but I felt that way, Mr. Chase," said their creator.

Chase took off his pince-nez and looked at the lady. "Madam," he said, speaking ever so earnestly, "the next time you feel that way, DON'T PAINT."

The Shinnecock "Art Village" was the evidence and the reward of Chase's renown as a teacher and of the devotion of his followers. Designed in the main by the well-known architect Grosvenor Atterbury and his associate Katharine Budd, it consisted of the large studio as its dominating feature and a street of ten or twenty cottages, the largest of which served as a boardinghouse for students, and one or two others as lodging houses. The majority of the cottages were owned by such as we may term "Friends of Art." And among these were my mother and aunt.

[IT'S ME O LORD]

ABOVE: CENTRAL PARK, 1904, PENCIL ON PAPER, 3-5/8 x 5-7/8",
COLLECTION OF JOSEPH M. ERDELAC

ROCKWELL KENT

ROBERT HENRI

The New York School of Art was not a school in the accepted sense of providing its students with instruction in all that was needed as a basis for the pursuance of their prospective careers. Established as a commercial enterprise by a onetime painter, Douglas John Connah, it enlisted as instructors such painters as by their individual reputation or achievement were most certain to attract students. Chief among its teachers, of whom there were three, was William M. Chase; and next to him in the order of their featured importance were two younger men: Robert Henri, recently returned from successes abroad, and the still younger Kenneth Hayes Miller. It was the night class that I joined; and Henri was its instructor.

Henri as an instructor, Henri as a leader of revolt against Academic sterility, Henri as an inspirational influence in American art, is possibly the most important figure of our cultural history. Personally he was a striking figure, though his physical distinction, aside from his tall, lean stature, was of an utterly unorthodox nature. His small head, his excessively wide and well-fleshed cheekbones, his little, low-bridged nose and narrow eyes, the sharply tapering oval of his face lent his shallow countenance a distinctly Eurasian character that was somehow confirmed by the marks of smallpox which it bore. I have termed Chase distinguished; he unquestionably was. Yet his distinction was that of the Napoleon-complexed little man who, in compensation for that littleness, had contrived a role, and studied it, and dressed and groomed for it, and come to live it so that it came at last to be himself, the sometimes dinner guest of kings. Henri's distinction, on the other hand, was as the emanation of his warmth of heart and of the richness of his mind. It was the aura of his personal integrity.

Henri's criticisms made no pretense to such showmanship as Chase delighted in. They were earnest and, at times, impassioned; and being almost invariably personal — that is, directed to one student at a time and while at work, and to none but such as might be working near at hand or who had grouped themselves to listen — they were mainly in the tones of quiet conversation.

Henri was in a very deep and true sense a man of the people. His dominating interest was humanity. And the early poverty which, to Chase, had been the taking-off point for his flight to fame and affluence continued with Henri as the mother earth of his spirit. Henri never took off. He was a democrat, not by compulsion of a philosophic mind, but naturally and from his heart. His people were mankind. To them — their joys and sorrows, their hopes and their despairs, their world in its material and emotional entirety — art should give utterance. Art was a means of speech and not of picture making. And, implying the essential identity of the artist with mankind in general, how make this utterance at once more poignant and authentic than by constituting art, to each of us in the most personal sense, a means of self-expression?

To students of that day, accustomed to the critical evaluation of art by standards that had come to be closely identified with the current Academic sterility, this view of art was as a proclamation of freedom, of *freedom with responsibility*. It remained for the artists and psychiatrists of subsequent decades to discover and exalt its therapeutic values, and reduce it to its inevitable grotesque absurdity.

That emphasis on human values which Henri sought for in his students' work was of a qualitative rather than objective nature. Disregarding the works of the great masters of the Renaissance, he shared the current disrespect for "storytelling" art; and if he showed a greater interest in labor, underprivilege, and dilapidation as the subject or background for a picture it was merely because, to him, man at this level was most revealing of his own humanity. But it was *quality* he sought: the weight, the warmth, the loveliness of flesh; the grace of movement, gesture; the whole imponderable dignity of man. Less what our eyes could see than what we *felt*: and if the expression of such feeling appeared, in what we did, as undisciplined and sometimes chaotic as feelings essentially are; if knowledge was discounted and craftsmanship contemned, these were but casualties in a greater cause, their loss the means toward a noble end.

I have come to realize, in looking back upon my student days, that a factor quite equal in importance to instruction may be one's school associates. My associates, my fellow students in Henri's night life-class, were men and women who, almost without exception, either worked and earned their livings elsewhere, or, like myself, pursued other studies during the day. Art was to them, as it had become to me, a matter of fundamental necessity proven, as it were, by the sacrifice of leisure, recreation, and, by many, of hard-earned money. The apparent qualities of Shinnecock — those of its master, of his students' work, and, socially speaking, of the students themselves — were of the surface. Mannered was Chase; well mannered were we all. Contrary to that, we of the night class were, in both our work and our behavior, if not ill mannered, lacking all manners but those which stemmed from our good hearts and natural sensibilities.

Having joined the night class immediately upon my decision to abandon architecture, I resumed it following the ensuing summer vacation, continuing with it until, at midyear, I gave up college. My days now free to study art, I enrolled — on a continued scholarship — in Robert Henri's morning life-class and in the afternoon class taught by Miller. I now began to *paint* from the living model or, as we say, from "Life."

As Chase had taught us just to use our eyes, and Henri to enlist our hearts, now Miller called on us to use our heads. Utterly disregardful of the emotional values which Henri was so insistent upon, and contemptuous of both the surface realism and virtuosity of Chase, Miller, an Artist in a far more precious sense than either, exacted a recognition of the tactile qualities of paint and of the elements of composition — line and mass — not as a means toward the re-creation of life but as the fulfillment of an end, aesthetic pleasure. To translate this into terms of literature, he stressed the *sound* of words, the *cadence* and the *rhythm* of a line, as though regardless of their meaning or their truth. He showed himself the mystic in his attribution of supra-values to material elements which the subjects of his later paintings would confirm. Yet the importance of style as intrinsic to the expression of thought is undeniable; and Miller's emphasis upon some of its elements was of value to me if for no reason but as a corrective of Henri's disregard of it. . . .

Of even greater value was, to begin with, my contact with his earnestness and, later, as our friendship ripened, his companionship in playing baseball, a sport that we both persisted in for more years than was properly consistent with our growing professional dignity.

The freedom of self-expression which, under Henri, sounded the keynote of the school was confined during working hours, and by our own absorption, to the limits of paper and canvas; and before and after work and during intermissions was confined by nothing. The very dilapidation of the premises freed us from any consideration of what damage we might do to them. We painted up the walls, we smeared the woodwork; and in the extraordinary spirit of camaraderie which then prevailed converted the studios into gymnasiums for athletic sports or noontime forums for mock oratory. The entry of a new student to the class was invariably the occasion of a beer and cheese "setup," for the cost of which the new man, solemnly informed that it was an entry requirement, was the victim. And, from those whom we suspected of wealth, we extorted plenty.

But this was not the poor devil's only ordeal. There was a certain older man among us, named, as I recall it, Toft. He was a large, a portly man; and, contrasted to the character of the mob with which he had cast his lot, extremely dignified. Carefully keeping Toft out of sight until the newcomer, together with the rest of us, had got to work, we'd have him make his entry wearing hat and coat. "Good-morning, Mr. Henri," we would say; and while our monitor, Guy du Bois, assisted the mock master with his duds, we'd all, seemingly — and the new man in the most deadly earnest — apply ourselves to our work with the concentration proper to the master's presence. Then Toft would stage his act — and it was good!

After a leisurely survey of all that was being done, he would, in the manner of Henri, begin his man-to-man circuit of criticism: some students' work he'd find quite passable, some not so good; and at last he would arrive at the newcomer. Long, as though raptly, he would look at the beginner's sad performance; then "You've studied a long time?" he'd say.

"Why, no," the incredulous victim would reply. "This is my first day."

"What?" cries our Henri-Toft. "I can't believe it! Class, come here!"

And as we'd gather around him he'd proceed to tell the poor devil that he was unquestionably the greatest natural genius of his age, a Rembrandt, Michelangelo, and Rubens rolled in one. "Congratulations! Bravo!" And he would pass to the next student in line, say Edward Hopper who as the John Singer Sargent of the class would have already produced an obviously brilliant drawing.

One look at Hopper's drawing, and Henri-Toft would fly into a rage. Denouncing Hopper, denouncing his work, he'd reach for the drawing to destroy it. Hopper then would strike him; and the whole class, taking sides, would fall into an uproar.

But who is this who now jumps to the master's side? Who calls upon himself the brunt of Hopper's wrath? Who is this champion? One guess.

The routine never failed.

[IT'S ME O LORD]

A YEAR, BY "HOGARTH, JR.," C. 1919, PEN ON PAPER,
5-13/16 x 12-1/2", COLLECTION OF JOSEPH M. ERDELAC

MILLER AND HARTLEY

My acquaintance with Kenneth Hayes Miller, begun as a master-pupil relationship during my student days at the New York School of Art and made significant to me by his authoritative support of certain reservations I had felt as to Henri's teaching, had grown into a close friendship founded, curiously, less on our common profession than on our very common, thoroughly plebeian love of baseball. In fact, as Miller's work inclined toward mysticism my interest in it waned; and when in addition to this tendency he began to ferret out what he alleged to be erotic symbolism in the work of the greater masters of the past and, among those of the present, in the paintings and drawings of Cézanne, and, influenced no doubt by Freud, to attach basic significance to it, I felt not only disagreement but disgust. But baseball was another matter; and, with a number of our younger confrères and such of the architectural draftsmen as I could corral, we played a lot of sandlot baseball in the early spring.

Marsden Hartley, whom I had come to know in the course of the Beaux Arts Gallery show, became a constant visitor, dining with us as an accepted member of our little family several times a week. Hardly if at all familiar with his work before that show, I had promptly recognized him as a painter of rare distinction, if not of genius. I must identify his work at that period as the now well known Maine series. Objective without being realistic, it preceded his unfortunate Berlin residence and the lasting influence upon him of the morals, pageantry, and art of a decadent imperial capital. Hartley's was one of the most sensitive minds I have ever encountered, but a mind so subtly, even preciously discriminating as to defeat the very thought of action as a desecration of man's higher sensibilities. The normalcy of our household, two parents and their children, the normalcy of our outlook upon life, of our beliefs, our hopes, our interests, appeared to hold for him, to whom such living was denied, a perverse fascination; almost at times it seemed to torture him, so unutterably sad would his mood be. Writing to me, he said : "I have risen to great and beautiful spiritual heights with you and love all that it means to me — the loveliness of your own spirit and the exquisite beauty of those spirits around you which complete you. Kathleen and the sweet babies: I have read no lovelier poem, I have heard no lovelier song, I have seen no lovelier picture than that which you have offered me so generously with open heart."

Hartley, in his strange way, adopted us. He made our house his home; and it was somehow consistent with his adoption, and with himself as we had come to know and care for him, that when he'd complacently direct Kathleen as to what, because he liked it, we should all have for dinner and how it should be seasoned, we could only be amused.

[IT'S ME O LORD]

ABOVE: MAN UNDER WATERFALL, 1920,
WOOD ENGRAVING ON MAPLE, 2-3/4 x 1-3/8″

ROCKWELL KENT

DARWIN

How I could have gone through four years of high school — let alone preparatory school — and four years of college without even having heard of the theory of evolution or of Charles Darwin, I cannot guess. Nor can I now recall through whose indiscretion or in what forbidden book they were revealed to me. Ever since, as a little boy, it had dawned upon me to question the concept of a being, God, as the originator and ruler of mankind, his world and universe, I had felt a vague, critical dissatisfaction with the accepted answers, a dissatisfaction which I had lacked the intellectual initiative to even at- tempt to clarify. Yet the questions, importunate as all unanswered problems are, remained; and although relegated, as they doubtless came to be, to the plane of the unconscious, they smoldered, gathering heat that needed but the match's touch to set aflame. And Darwin, his *Origin of Species,* was the match.

To assert that I read the book painstakingly from cover to cover, only to be at last con- vinced, would be to attribute to myself the nature and character proper to a scholar or a scientist. And I am neither. I've used the symbol of a match: I was as tinder to that match; as tinder heated to the near-combusion point. A touch of flame, and I exploded. How far I read, I don't recall. Not far. "Of course!" I cried; for suddenly it was as though a great light, a new sun, had risen on a world of darkness.

My family — my aunt and mother — were not religious in the word's narrowest sense. Yes, they believed in God; they sometimes, though not often, went to church. I doubt they ever prayed. They were women of good education; they had read a lot. And they were liberal in many of their views. Yet when at Christmas a little stuffed monkey was hung on the Christmas tree for me, and la- beled "Rockwell's Cousin," I was a bit ashamed and sorry for them.

[IT'S ME O LORD]

ABOVE: SUPERMAN, ILLUSTRATION FROM WILDERNESS, 1920

ROCKWELL KENT

ART AND TOLSTOI

The occasional discussion of books that I listened in on at the Henri school was a bit beyond the depth of a reader of Sir Walter Scott and George Eliot. That Eugène Sue, Verlaine and Baudelaire, and the French Decadents in general were read and admired, I realized, but only in retrospect, to be somewhat in keeping with a slightly morbid overtone of Henri's influence. They were but names to me, and they remained but names. But one day another writer was mentioned: Tolstoi. Someone had just read a little book of his called *What Is Art?* It was a joke: they laughed at it. Yet something made me want that book. I bought a copy. I didn't read it all, just glanced through it; for I found it to be just as silly as the others had. How ridiculous to deride, as Tolstoi did, those writers and musicians whom everybody knew to be great. Tolstoi was funny. But I kept the book.

One day, it can hardly have been more than two or three years later, I picked up *What Is Art?* again, began to read it. And suddenly it was as though my whole being had achieved the power of utterance, as though a God within me spoke, resolving the chaos that was me — my mind, my heart, my conscience — into an integrated man, aware and purposeful.

It has never been my custom to mark books, but marked is the book I read that day. Marked is its last passage.* It is this:

> *The destiny of art in our times consists in this: To translate from the region of reason to the region of feeling the truth that the well-being of people consists in their union, and to substitute for the present kingdom of force, the kingdom of heaven, that is, love, which presents itself to us all as the highest aim of human life.*
>
> *It may be that in the future science will discover for art new and higher ideals, and that art will realize them; but in our time the destiny of art is clear and definite. The problem of Christian art is the realization of the brotherly union of mankind.*

[IT'S ME O LORD]

---

*Kent marked one other passage:

Whatever absurdities may arise in art, once they are accepted among the higher classes of our society, theories are forthwith elaborated to explain and authorize these absurdities, as if there was never an epoch in history in which in certain exclusive circles of people, false, formless, and meaningless art, which left no trace and was perfectly forgotten by posterity, was not accepted and admitted. [Trans. Charles Johnston. Philadelphia, 1898.]

This became one of Kent's favorite books. In the Asgaard fire of 1969 the binding was badly damaged, and Sally had it rebound in leather for her husband. — ED.

ABOVE: GET UP!, ILLUSTRATION FROM <u>WILDERNESS</u>, 1920

ROCKWELL KENT

Published monthly by The Condé Nast Publications, Inc., Boston Post Road, Greenwich, Conn.—
Executive and Publishing Offices at Greenwich, Conn. Editorial Offices, 19 W. 44th St., New York.
Cable address, Vonork. Condé Nast, President; Francis L. Wurzburg, Vice-President; W. E. Beckerle,
Treasurer; M. E. Moore, Secretary; Philippe Ortiz, European Director, 2 rue Edouard VII, Paris.
Subscription $3.50 a year in the United States and Colonies, Mexico and Canada, $4.50 in Foreign
Countries. Single copies 35c. Address all correspondence relating to subscriptions to Vanity Fair,
Greenwich, Connecticut. Entered as second class matter at the Post Office at Greenwich, Conn., under
the act of March 3, 1879. Printed in the U. S. A. by The Condé Nast Press. Copyright 1926 by The
Condé Nast Publications, Inc., Reg. U. S. Patent Office.

Vol. 27 No. 5   *Subscribers are notified that no change of address can be effected in less than one month*   35c a Copy $3.50 a Year

ABOVE: CONTENTS PAGE FROM <u>VANITY FAIR</u>, JANUARY 1927

OPPOSITE: DRAWINGS BY "HOGARTH, JR.," FOR THE <u>NEW YORK TRIBUNE</u>, 1922 (TOP ROW, LEFT AND CENTER);
FROM <u>PUCK</u> (TOP ROW, RIGHT; SECOND ROW, LEFT AND RIGHT; BOTTOM ROW, RIGHT);
FROM <u>VANITY FAIR</u>, 1924 (BOTTOM ROW, LEFT); INITIAL LETTER DRAWINGS FROM
<u>ARCHITECTONICS: THE TALES OF TOM THUMTACK, ARCHITECT</u>, 1914

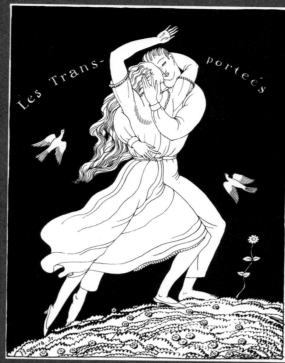

Winters on the east coast of Newfoundland are long and, with the shortened days of that high altitude and the dampness and the frequent storms of an Atlantic rampart, dreary or not as one contrives to make them. They are not cold as we had known winter cold in northern New England and in Minnesota. And the winter of 1914—15 was to us neither a season of discomfort nor of tedium. We had our many friends; we had our music and our books; Kathleen had all of us to care for; and I had my work. Yet to any pretense that my prevailing mood in wartime Newfoundland was one of cheer, my paintings give the lie. Compelled, by the nature of the weather and the difficulty of going far afoot, to work indoors and in the narrow confines of my studio, forced to reflect and, by reflection, thrown upon the harsh realities of a war-time world, my work was in no degree an outpouring of delight in visible nature but, rather, a continuous wail of lamentation of man's tragic, solitary lot in the vast and soulless cosmos. The war, the senseless sacrifice of lives, the hatreds war engendered; and, on us, the foul suspicions so at variance with our true, innate integrity: these facts oppressed me to a degree to which I only let my work give utterance. *Ruin and Eternity, The Voyager Beyond Life, Newfoundland Dirge, Man the Abyss, The House of Dread:* such were my titles when I later showed the work. And they were justified. . . .

The most successful of the pictures, to my mind — if the conveyance of a mood of despair may be termed success — was *The House of Dread.* Upon a bleak and lofty cliff's edge, land's end, stands a house; against its corner and facing seawards leans a man, naked even as the land, and sea, and house; his head is bowed as though in utter dejection; and from an upper window leans a weeping woman. It is our cliff, our sea, our house stripped bare and stark, its loneliness intensified. It is ourselves in Newfoundland, our hidden but prevailing misery revealed.

Nor was my reading in that period well calculated to relieve my sense of tragedy: *Wilhelm Meister* read again, its passages of poignant sadness moving me again to tears; the Greek tragedies as translated by Andrew Lang, the sorrowing of *The Trojan Women* so close, it seemed, to that of the women of Newfoundland for sons and husbands lost at sea and in the war. Of these wives of fishermen Kingsley's verses told the story:

For men must work, and women must weep —
And the sooner it's over, the sooner to sleep —

Happening, during the five anxious weeks that, following the assassination at Sarajevo, preceded England's declaration of war, to be reading Thucydides' *History of the Peloponnesian War,* I was struck by his account of how the armies of Athens and Sparta were drawn up facing each other across their border, each waiting for the other to commit an overt act that might be held up to the people as a ground for action. It shed a light on what was going on in Europe. It points to what is going on today.

[IT'S ME O LORD]

ROCKWELL KENT

At last we come to a happening that for more than half a century the Kents have thought of (and with some nostalgia) as the concluding act of what has been to them *The Tragedy of Newfoundland*. The stage is the unfenced portion of our Brigus house-yard not visible from the windows of the little house itself; the time a lovely day in mid-July of 1915. The sky is blue, the windblown water of the bay, reflecting the zenith, sparkles with tiny whitecaps; the hills are flooded by morning sun, while across the harbor the little settlement of Frog Marsh with its white-washed walls and picket fences seems to our eyes — as must our house to theirs — the very home of peace and happiness. The "hero" — or the villain, I — stands splitting kindling.

And now appear two men approaching down the road: one is the Brigus constable, I know him well; the other, a big man dressed in plain-clothes? Who? Clearly there's something up: be nonchalant. And sure enough, as — after a few introductory pleasantries — I am to learn, there is.

"You, Mr. Kent," says the big one somewhat pompously. "You and your entire family are to leave Newfoundland at once!"

"And by whose orders?"

"The Inspector General's."

"And you? Your papers please?" I glance at them and hand them back.

"Well," says the deputy at last, "I guess we'll go."

"So soon? On such a day? Well, anyhow, goodbye."

I lift my axe and go on chopping wood.

FAR FROM "at once" but when the children (four by now) have all recovered from the whooping cough — a generous period of grace having been granted by the friendly Governor — we leave exultantly for home. On board the steamer at St. John's there joins us at the rail our little bowler-hatted friend, the sleuth.

"Come to make sure?" I ask. He has. He counts us.

The siren blows; hawsers are slackened, drawn on board. We're off. And as the gap of seething water widens in our wake we, sadly, have no hope or thought of ever seeing Newfoundland again.

[AFTER LONG YEARS]

ROCKWELL KENT

TRANSGRESSION

One summer day in 1916 — a day so fair, its sky so blue, its sun so bright and warm that it invited thoughts of meadows starred with buttercups and daisies, of babbling brooks and singing birds — I found myself at the torn-up corner of Forty-first Street and Seventh Avenue, and about to step upon the plank that bridged the mud pond at the curb, when I observed a young woman about to cross it from the other end. I stood aside. And as, with downcast eyes to watch her step, she crossed, I looked at her. And what with its being the month of June and all that I have said about the day, what with her being so prettily dressed in white and its so well becoming her golden hair, red lips, blue eyes; what with my being me, it suddenly came over me that never in all my life had I seen so entrancingly lovely a creature. She crossed, and went demurely on her way. And that — had I been Little Bobtail or any of my Oliver Optic heroes, had I been one of those characters that in my youth I had striven so hard to emulate; in fact, had I but been the late-lamented Better Self of mine — that would have been the end of our little story. But I wasn't. Suddenly it flashed upon me what a boob I was to stand and watch her walking off, never again, no doubt, to cross the pathway of my life. A few long steps and I had overtaken her. I touched her arm. "You are so beautiful," I blurted out, "I've got to speak to you." She had stopped still: "What do you want to say?" she asked. "There is so much I want to say," I answered her, "that we should go some-place to talk." We went someplace. And the upshot of our talk, and of many meetings and more talk, was that hardly two weeks later we alighted together from the train at Peterboro, New Hampshire, and with two packsacks — a small one, and one so big and heavy that I could hardly lift it from the ground — were driven as near as possible to the base of Mount Monadnock. Instructing the driver to meet us at that spot one week later, we were left alone. And now — not against the background of New York, its torn-up muddy crossing, its littered streets, its din of traffic, but in the calm and sweet environment of the New Hampshire forest — let us look at Gretchen.

Yes, she had golden hair and light blue eyes, and red, inviting lips; and in her face this day there shone the anticipation of such a mad adventure in happiness as she had never known and doubt-less never dreamed of. All was so new to her, a city girl, a dancer in the Follies! All was, somehow, so right for her. She, with her sturdy limbs, her trained agility, her strength and grace, was right for what we planned to do: to climb the mountain, on its high ridge pitch our tent, and, for a whole week, live there. So, no sooner had our conveyance passed from sight than we, eager to reach our goal, shoul-dered our packs and set out on the trail.

To that one week I could devote a book, so vivid is my memory of it; not as a part of life but as an experience so utterly remote from that mainstream current upon which most of us, from the cra-dle to the grave, are borne along as to appear an interlude of living in another world. Time, they say, marches on: "Hold it!" we said to Time. "In one week we'll be back." Alone at so serene an altitude that mankind far below could no longer be distinguished, his villages appearing as mere specks, their mightiest steeples, emblems of morality, quite impotent to prick the lower atmospheric shell of our ethereal universe, aloof and far removed from obligations, duties, custom, law, and all the fabric of so-ciety, we had no sense of guilt; and, like Eve and Adam following their fall, could abandon ourselves to the enjoyment of every pleasure that the body and the soul of man might crave. Naked we'd roam that treeless ridge, climbing its ledges, leaping their fissures, bathing from time to time in its warm rainwater pools. We burned, and then grew brown as primitives; and when toward evening the shadow of the rocks that sheltered our campsite fell upon us, we would sit before our fire, cook and eat our evening meal, and watch the shadow of the mountain creep and enfold the land in its dark mantle. We'd watch the tiny house lights of the plain come on, and marvel at the stars. Then, tired by all the day had brought, we'd sleep.

ABOVE: DECORATIVE INITIAL LETTER FOR THE MODERN SCHOOL, 1922

ROCKWELL KENT

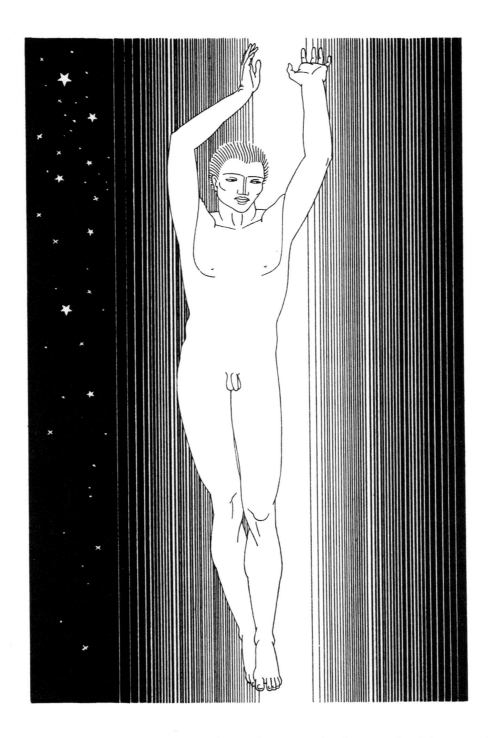

THAT A RELATIONSHIP so strangely and intimately begun should, even in the mundane lower world, continue was inevitable; but not more so than that its consequences upon others should be serious and, as the years should prove, enduring. I believe that it was Shaw who stated that if the transports of love at its beginning should be maintained, lovers would perish. But one might add, and I, in obvious rationalization of myself, do add that, conceding Shaw's observation to be true, life without such love's recurrence would be desolate. To how, in the best interests of, on the one hand, the family and society and, on the other, of the countless individuals who are, by nature inflammable and avid for experience, the contradiction can be solved, I have no answer; nor should one whose marriage was, through his own actions, to suffer continuous deterioration, presume to offer a solution. One life — but *one!* — we have; and what a world, how varied and how vast!

[IT'S ME O LORD]

ABOVE: FRONTISPIECE FROM LEAVES OF GRASS, 1937

ROCKWELL KENT

MONHEGAN

Monhegan! We've reached the harbor's mouth; we've entered it; we've reached the wharf; we're moored; I've jumped ashore. My bag in hand, I race up the hill, and race along the road to the old Brackett House. Two minutes in my room to get out of — what did Miss Libbey call it? — my "stylish suit," and into an unstylish one; and like a puppy let out of his pen I'm off at a run to see, to climb, to touch and feel this wonder island that I've come to.

Hugging the harbor shore, I reached the island's southwest end where the surf makes suds around the Washerwoman Rock or breaks on Norman's Ledge; then on to the gully of Gull Rock, and over it to climb the smooth, bald, winter-surf-washed rock itself; and on again to Burnt Head; and then down and over a broad waste of boulder-strewn, bare granite ledges to climb the headland, Whitehead, and from its hundred-and-fifty-foot height look far out to sea toward Africa and England. It was so vast, so beautiful that clear blue day, with the green grass and dandelions at my feet! And Blackhead, its twin headland seen from there in all its mass and dignity of form, Blackhead, its dark face splotched with gleaming guano! Then on again over the intervening minor headlands and the gullies tangled with the debris of fire and storm, and through such tangles up and over Blackhead; and down again — real climbing now to pass the rocky gorges — to the massive giant granite cube of Pulpit Rock. And then at last, like a quiet passage in a tumultuous symphony, a sheltered harbor after storm, the gentle, grassy slopes of Green Point, still thickly starred with the blossoms of strawberries to be. And the seal ledges and their happy denizens — sunning themselves or slithering and diving off the rocks as though in sport, the water dotted with their almost human heads. Then on to Deadman's Cove and its lone fish-house outpost of the settlement. And always, looking inland from the shore, there was the dark spruce forest, another world, a deeply solemn world that I should come to know.

UNLIKE MOST New England villages, Monhegan had no plan, no straight, broad, elm-bordered avenue faced by the houses in their white-fenced yards; there was no avenue, there were no trees, there were no picket fences. No one had ever "laid out" Monhegan; it just grew. And past the random houses wandered a narrow road, a track first worn there by the oxen of other days and now kept open by the one-horse, drop-axle wagon that was the island's sole conveyance.

The harbor of Monhegan was formed by an adjacent smaller island, stark, treeless, whaleback-shaped Manana, and lay open to the southwest wind and seas. On the Monhegan shore of the harbor, and mainly clustered around the wharf and two small beaches, stood the fish houses, most of them two-storied structures with runways leading to their lofts. Unpainted and weather-beaten, they proclaimed to eyes — and *nose!* — the island's industry. So too did every foot of intervening ground occupied, as it was in summer, by drying-flakes for cod, and by the pyramids of lobster traps and heaps of painted buoys withdrawn for the season.

Monhegan: its rockbound shores, its towering headlands, the thundering surf with gleaming crests and emerald eddies, its forest and its flowering meadowlands; the village, quaint and picturesque; the fish houses, evoking in their dilapidation those sad thoughts on the passage of time and the transitoriness of all things human so dear to the artistic soul; and the *people,* those hardy fisherfolk, those men garbed in their sea boots and their black or yellow oilskins, those horny-handed sons of toil — shall I go on? No, that's enough. It was enough for me, enough for all my fellow artists, for all of us who sought "material" for art. It was enough to start me off to such feverish activity in painting as I had never known.

From breakfast until noon, from after lunch until suppertime, here, overlooking the village or the harbor, there, on the rocks or headlands; on fair days — how I loved them in their sharp, clear rev-

elation of infinitude! —and on those so "artistic" days when fog made mystery mysterious, all day of every day I painted. And at night —I slept? At first I did, who wouldn't? —in that clean sea air, those ocean-tempered, summer nights, after the day's hard work! And then suddenly —for no reason that I or anyone else could ever fathom —I didn't sleep; I couldn't. I shall never forget those nights, those interminable sleepless nights; the unrhythmic grunting of the buoy on the distant shoal, the blaring of the Manana foghorn on thick nights: wide-eyed, I'd lie there until the sky was gray with the approaching dawn. Then only could I sleep. And in the daytime from sheer sleeplessness, and even as I worked, I'd drop to sleep again.

STANDING UPON A HEADLAND, I'd look down at lobstermen at work, their dories almost in the backwash of the surf. God, how I envied them their power to row! To pull their heavy traps! I'd see my own thin wrists, my artist's hands. As though for the first time, I saw my work in true perspective and felt its triviality. It is easier to do a job of work, said Oscar Wilde (I think he said, to dig a ditch), than to write about it. What rot! Why, Oscar never worked in all his life.

With these thoughts, this envy, agitating me, those social and political convictions which had hitherto existed as figments of my mind and heart began to acquire substance. Not just from Whitehead, but from empyrean heights had I *looked down* on life, *down* at the masses, and not with them, *up*. Was I as a painter to constitute myself an *onlooker* at the doing of the fundamental jobs of life, or be one doing them? What would I do, I thought, should workingmen not work for me? The answer shamed me.

Speaking of the "inferiority complex," a friend of mine, Chester Aldrich, once said to me, "But what is a fellow with an inferiority complex to do about it if he really is inferior?" Well, I had the complex, and I was inferior. But quite definitely there was something I *could* do about it: get to work. So as fall drew upon us and the island's migratory visitors began to take their flight, I stayed. And moving from the hotel to the little house of Ben Davis and his wife —old white-bearded Uncle Ben and younger, motherly Aunt Annie —I got a job as assistant teamster, longshoreman, and well-driller to Hiram Cazallis, who was all these things in one. I got to work.

[IT'S ME O LORD]

ABOVE AND LEFT: TWO ILLUSTRATIONS FROM MOBY DICK, 1930

ROCKWELL KENT

happened.

"You have done well, Sir Bedevere," said the king. "Now carry me to the shore for there is a boat that is waiting for me."

Sir Bedevere did as his king commanded. There waiting was a brass boat and in it was the Lady of the Lake, Nymue, who had come for Arthur.

When King Arthur was placed in the boat, Sir Bedevere wept.

"My king, you are dying and I will be all alone."

King Arthur opened his eyes and said:

"Know that I shall not die at this place. For the Lady of the Lake has come to take me to the valley of Avalon where I shall yet live for many years. But the day will come when I shall return to England. And with my return will come peace, and war shall be no more. Take back this message and farewell."

With these words the great King Arthur disappeared.

War Shall Be No More.

It is June of the year 1906 and the subject of our story, the man we have occasionally presumed to term "our hero," has just turned twenty-four. The story is ostensibly the autobiography of an artist and writer; and yet of art and literature we have thus far heard so little, and of other matters so relatively much, that the art-loving reader may well cry out in his exasperation: "Shoemaker, stick to your last." Believe me, dear art lover, I am sticking to it. Or should I say, more truthfully, I'm getting to it.

Although Apelles, in Pliny's classic story, is given the last word, the shoemaker might well have replied: "The leg, for my criticism of which you have rebuked me, is indeed my concern; for could there be a foot and shoe without it? And could there be a leg without a body? A body without a heart and mind? Could there be man without society? And is not all mankind my proper, true concern?" But the artist Apelles would doubtless not have stayed to listen.

The fact is that there on Monhegan Island, between and after days of work with maul and drill, with hammer and nails or at the oars, on days it blew too hard at sea, on Sundays, I was painting; painting with a fervor born, as I have said, of my close contact with the sea and soil, and deepened by the reverence that the whole universe imposed. What though my artist friends felt true concern at what they thought my waste of time. Just let the man grow up: his art will follow. And art being properly a by-product of living, how little would a man love life who loved art more! How little can the graven-image worshippers love God!

At any rate, life — not just as looked at but as lived — was to me so exhilarating and so infinitely beautiful that I could strive for nothing but, through experience, a greater share of it. If I could only re-create the world as I beheld and sensed or, even in some measure, understood it, let what I did be art or not, it was enough.

Art is not art until it has effaced itself. Only when the blue paint of a sky ceases to be just color — becoming as it were the depths of space — is that blue right, and truly beautiful. Only when green becomes the growing grass, or the earth colors land and rocks, when indigo becomes the ocean, and the colors of a figure become flesh and blood; only when words become ideas; when the sounds of music becomes images; only when every medium of the arts becomes transmuted into a portion of our living universe, only then is art consistent with the dignity of man.

Truly I loved that little world, Monhegan. Small, seagirt island that it was, a seeming floating speck in the infinitude of sea and sky, one was as though driven to seek refuge from the impendent cosmic immensity in a closer relationship to people and to every living thing. I came to know each individual flower and bright-colored mushroom and toadstool that grew beside the woodland paths. I would watch them bud and blossom and be saddened when at last their petals fell; and be infuriated by some vandal's having trampled them. I won't say that I loved the rocks; I just respected them. And when I'd find some fellow's, some brother artist's, palette scrapings on them, I'd read it as the measure of his miserable soul.

Often in writing, often in speech, I use the name of God. Yet it is neither as a "believer" that I use it, nor in vain: God had become to me the symbol of the life-force of our world and universe; a name for the immense unknown. Imponderable, yet immanent in man, in beasts and birds and bugs, in trees and flowers and toadstools, in the earth, sun, moon, and stars. It — I choose the impersonal pronoun as alone consistent with my faith — it was to me a force as unmoral as such manifestations of itself as storms or earthquakes, and for that very reason greatly to be feared. It was as unmoral and impersonal and splendid as its sunset's light on land and sea — and for that reason to be reverenced. I feared and reverenced God. In fear and reverence I painted. That mood forbids defining art as self-expression.

It is true that a man's every act is to some degree a revelation of himself — even, or most of all, those acts of greatest self-forgetfulness. This is true of every gesture that he makes, of every utterance; it is most true when it is most forgotten, least true when striven for. It is as vain to strive for individuality as to attempt to lift oneself by one's own bootstraps; and it is self-defeating, in that to reach those bootstraps one must stoop. It is, after all, a consoling thought that with the one absolute virtue that art can have, integrity, we need not, indeed we must not, concern ourselves. We can, each for himself, but echo Martin Luther: *"Ich kann nicht anders."*

Man as a part of nature, a product of its alchemy, and minutely conditioned by the terrestrial and cosmic environment, exemplifies its laws and principles; while in that act of re-creation, which is art, he copies God. What is the artist's striving for good craftsmanship but reverent emulation of God's work? What is his vaunted stock in trade, aesthetics, but what his senses apprehend of universal law — what nature's laws in operation look like, sound like, how they feel? What are they but the countenance of life; their converse, ugliness, the face of death.

Fundamental to all consideration of art is its purpose. To be entitled to the honor that society bestows upon it, it must unquestionably have a social value; that is, as a potential means of communication it must be addressed, and in comprehensible terms, to the understanding of mankind. In fact, good manners should forbid our listening in on art not meant for us.

Art as a social force has grave responsibilities and will be judged by its discharge of them. It can enliven or depress us, foster our hopes or deepen our despair; it can build our faith or destroy it. By awakening us to the beauty of our world and to the dignity of man, it can be a powerful factor in human progress; or it can lure us apart from this world into the sterile, loveless solitudes of never-never land. Whatever course a man's art takes depends upon himself. And, now that we have devoted a few pages to talking about art, we may add that it is as futile to discuss art and define it as it is to discuss and define love: for it is one of those things that take care of themselves. *Culture (Sociol.): the sum total of ways of living built up by a group of human beings.* We shall have no art but what our cultural soil will yield.

[IT'S ME O LORD]

ABOVE: ILLUSTRATION FROM MOBY DICK, 1930

OPPOSITE, TOP: ISLAND VILLAGE, COAST OF MAINE, 1909,
O/C, 41-3/4 x 55-3/8", THE HERMITAGE

BOTTOM: SORROW, MONHEGAN, 1907, PENCIL AND CHINESE WHITE,
9-1/2 x 8", COLLECTION OF JAMIE WYETH

Far the most profitable hours of my spare time were my nights at home. Seated in my rocker, my feet at the open oven door, the lamp at my elbow, my curtains drawn to shut out the night's immensity, my purring cat for living company, I'd read. And, reading only the books I had sought out as offering companionship in my thoughts and light along the way my thoughts and life had taken, their authors, giving me as all true writers do the utmost of themselves, became as friends of mine, friends in a more intimate and personal sense than any flesh-and-blood friends I had known. Books, as the living speech of intimates, as, frequently, their most soul-searching utterances, had come to mean too much to me to ever be deserving of so little as to be loved as books. I was too young, too lusty, lustful, lonely, too starved for intimate companionship and love, to stoop to book-loving.

We were a choice group who lived together in my little house on Monhegan. We were Tolstoi, who, as we know, had been my friend for years; and with him, Jesus. And Turgenev, a new friend but a loved one — though I could never quite forgive his hero's being a sportsman, could never reconcile the shooting of living creatures for the fun of it with his great tenderness toward humankind. There was Ernst Haeckel, that fiercely opinionated, uncompromising, crusty, fearless old German; he really laid it on the line. *Hier steh ich Haeckel!* I stood with him. And there was Thoreau: I knew him at that time only through *Walden* and his miscellaneous essays and addresses. Through his experiences in living at Walden Pond, the frugality of his living, the conservation of his slender means for  freedom to reflect and write, and perhaps above all by his deep and courageous concern with freedom and justice, I came to love him as a far warmer nature than history has given him credit for. There was another crusty old German in our group, a man introduced to us rather frighteningly as a philosopher: Schopenhauer. But we found him quite a simple soul — testy, at times, and always outspoken — but fundamentally a man of shrewd and sometimes devastating common sense. (Of *common* sense, Henry Thoreau, if you remember, said we had too much. We needed more *un*common sense. But Henry always had a way of playing with words.)

Then there was Ruskin. None of us cared so very much for him. He struck us as a bit ladylike. Maybe it was just his watercolors. Tolstoi, and I too, liked his identifying *beauty* with *life,* and *ugliness* with *death.* (I probably got that idea from him.) But working hard at manual labor, as I did, it always amused me that he made so much of having done a good watercolor sketch on the same day that he had swept the steps of the Town Hall of Brussels from top to bottom. And why in the world, we'd wonder, should *he* be sweeping those Town Hall steps?

Henri Frédéric Amiel, his *Journal* having just been warmly introduced to the American people by Mrs. Humphry Ward, was introduced to us by my friend Mary Kelsey. I was moved by the exquisite beauty of his reflections but found myself far too sympathetic to the materialism of Ernst Haeckel, and to the practical, down-to-earth ethics of Tolstoi's religion, to be tolerant of Amiel's mysticism. We were, as a whole, a group of extraverts, finding in life outside ourselves so much to occupy our thoughts that we inclined to be intolerant of introspection. The still uncut pages of Amiel's *Journal* are the most telling evidence of how little we inclined to listen to him.

Thomas Jefferson, who knew both friendship and wine, found them alike, raw when new, and ripening with age. My own friendship for the Victorian poets, for Shelley, Byron, Keats, Coleridge, and Wordsworth, had ripened with the years. They, happily, were of a vintage to endure; I hope I am. At any rate, the Victorians' and my own essentially emotional response to life formed the sound basis of a close and lasting friendship.

[IT'S ME O LORD]

ABOVE: ILLUSTRATION FROM <u>MOBY DICK</u>, 1930

ROCKWELL KENT

CODIFIED VIRTUE

The one redeeming feature of the bleak December day I left Monhegan was the northeast wind; it cut two hours from the *Effort*'s trip and landed me in Boothbay Harbor in time to catch the mailman to Wiscasset. But the misery of that horse-and-buggy ride I shall never forget: those fourteen endless miles with stops at every other letterbox! The alternating snow and freezing sleet! And I in city clothes! But then how good it was to reach the warm Wiscasset railroad station; to have three hours' wait to dry my clothes and thaw my bones; and then, the weather clearing, to walk about that sweet New England town reflecting on the goodness of its people's simple lives. There had been a heavy snowfall at Wiscasset and the sound of sleigh bells gladdened the air.

And now a big sleigh with prancing team and jingling bells drives to the station door, and stops. The door bursts open and a man comes in carrying two heavy paper suitcases. He is followed by a young woman who goes quickly to the big central radiator. She is cold. Putting down the cases, the man leaves without a word to the girl; the sleigh drives off. And now in come a half-dozen young sub-teenagers. They range themselves on a set along the wall, whisper among themselves, look at the girl, and laugh derisively. What can be wrong? The girl, seemingly about twenty years of age, is nice enough looking in a colorless and unpretentious way; a working girl, one would judge. Quite obviously, she is pregnant.

More passengers come in. They too stare at the girl, whisper and stare. At the sound of the train whistle the passengers and the kids pour out onto the station platform, leaving the girl to struggle with her heavy bags. "Let me have those," I say to her. "Take mine, it's lighter." Boarding the train, I stow the bags and sit down with the girl. This is of such interest to her fellow townsfolk, who have eagerly sought seats near us, that it takes a bit of hard staring on my part to enforce at least a semblance of propriety. "And now, young lady, let's have it: what's this all about?" Reluctantly at first, and then as though the sluice gates of her heart had burst, she tells her story.

Yes, she was born in Wiscasset, raised there. Her father had died when she was fifteen; at her mother's remarriage she had been thrown upon her own resources. Waitress in local restaurants, and then cook, she had gotten employment a year ago as resident cook for the proprietors of a small lumber mill, a father and his son. She became the son's mistress. In sordid detail she told of the father's assault upon her during the son's absence, of fighting off the old man with everything that she could lay her hands upon. Her pregnancy becoming manifest, she told of her mother's utter repudiation of her, of the scorn of her fellow townsfolk, of the youngsters' jeers. Now, fired from her job, with little in her purse and all she owned besides in those two bags, she was headed for Portland, a city where she knew no one and nobody knew her.

When the train reached Portland, it was raining. I carried out her bags and put them beside her on the station platform. And as I shook her hand goodbye I passed her whatever money I could spare. It was very little.

As the train drew out, I saw her struggling with her heavy bags. Her fellow townsfolk, who had also left the train at Portland, had paused on the platform and were watching her. One or two of them were men. None moved to help.

I have remembered this little story, this vignette of life in a sweet, pretty little New England town, because the sudden rush of shame that overcame me as the train moved out, the shame and consequent remorse that I was back on board the train, has never left me. And I have *told* the story here because it is New England.

Being New England, it might have been New York; it might have been America—east, west, north, south—small-town America. Wherever virtue has been codified and criterions of respectability have supplanted the innate goodness of the human heart—it might have been. And so, of course, it might have been Tarrytown—only how was I to know! And so, not knowing, I was glad to head for home again—so wildly glad that as the miles grew less my heart burned and I found it hard to breathe. How good, how infinitely good, is home!

[IT'S ME O LORD]

ROCKWELL KENT

MONHEGAN, 1909

That summer I had determined to paint; so paint I did. Every fair day and almost every daylight hour of every day I was at work. The fairest, clearest, sharpest days I loved the most; the northwest days when the windblown ocean plain stretched dark as indigo to a horizon knife-sharp against the golden lower sky; when the sky from gold became by imperceptible gradations emerald, and the emerald became cobalt; and the cobalt, a deep purple at the zenith — often so dark, that zenith sky, that one could see the moon by day and almost, one imagined, stars. What in the world has happened to mankind that *soft* — soft lines, soft colors, soft effects — means excellence? What's wrong with artists that they're ravished by the world in fog? Are good eyes a misfortune, and good ears a handicap? And clear perception and an unbewildered mind a sin? What is art's function but to make life clearer to us? Should artists not be seers? Should seers not see? I ask these questions: let some normal being — let the reader — answer them.

[IT'S ME O LORD]

ABOVE: DRAWING FOR EMBLEM FOR JUNIOR ART PATRONS, 1921

ROCKWELL KENT

ALASKA
DISCOVERY, 1918

We must have been rowing for an hour across that seeming mile-wide stretch of water.

The air is so clear in the North that one new to it is lost in the crowding of great heights and spaces. Distant peaks had risen over the lower mountains of the shore astern. Steep spruce-clad slopes confronted us. All around was the wilderness, a no-man's-land of mountains or of cragged islands, and southward the wide, the limitless, Pacific Ocean.

A calm, blue summer's day — and on we rowed upon our search. Somewhere there must stand awaiting us, as we had pictured it, a little forgotten cabin, one that some prospector or fisherman had built; the cabin, the grove, the sheltered beach, the spring or stream of fresh, cold water — we could have drawn it even to the view that it must overlook, the sea, and mountains, and the glorious West. We came to this new land, a boy and a man, entirely on a dreamer's search; having had vision of a Northern Paradise, we came to find it.

With less faith it might have seemed to us a hopeless thing exploring the unknown for what you've only dreamed was there. Doubt never crossed our minds. To sail uncharted waters and follow virgin shores — what a life for men! As the new coast unfolds itself, the imagination leaps into full vision of the human drama that there is immanent. The grandeur of the ocean cliff is terrible with threat of shipwreck. To that high ledge the wave may lift you; there, where that storm-dwarfed spruce has found a hold for half a century, you perhaps could cling. A hundred times a day you think of death or of escaping it by might and courage. Then, at the first softening of the coast toward a cove or inlet, you imagine all the mild beauties of a safe harbor, the quiet water and the beach to land upon, the house-site, a homestead of your own, cleared land, and pastures that look seaward.

Now, having crossed the bay, thick-wooded coast confronted us, and we worked eastward toward a wide-mouthed inlet of that shore. But all at once there appeared as if from nowhere a little, motor-driven dory coming toward us. We hailed and drew together to converse. It was an old man alone. We told him frankly what we were and what we sought.

"Come with me," he cried heartily, "come and I show you the place to live." And he pointed oceanward where, straight in the path of the sun, stood the huge, dark, mountain mass of an island. Then, seizing upon our line, he towed us with him to the south.

The gentle breeze came up. With prow high in the air we spanked the wavelets, and the glistening spray flew over us. On we went straight at the dazzling sun, and we laughed to think that we were being carried we knew not where. And all the while the strange old man spoke never a word nor turned his head, driving us on as if he feared we might demand to be unloosed. At last his island towered above us. It was truly sheer-sided and immense, and for all we could discover harborless; till in a moment rounding the great headland of its northern end the crescent arms of the harbor were about us — and we were there!

What a scene! Twin lofty mountain masses flanked the entrance and from the back of these the land dipped downward like a hammock swung between them, its lowest point behind the center of the crescent. A clean and smooth, dark-pebbled beach went all around the bay, the tide line marked with driftwood, gleaming, bleached bones of trees, fantastic roots, and worn and shredded trunks. Above the beach a band of brilliant green and then the deep, black spaces of the forest. So huge was the scale of all of this that for some time we looked in vain for any habitation, at last incredulously seeing what we had taken to be boulders assume the form of cabins.

The dories grounded and we leapt ashore, and followed up the beach onto the level ground seeing and wondering, with beating hearts, and crying all the time to ourselves: "It isn't possible, it isn't real!"

OPPOSITE: ENDPAPERS FROM WILDERNESS, 1920
ROCKWELL KENT

There was a green grass lawn beneath our feet extending on one side under an orchard of neatly pruned alders to the mountain's base, and on the other into the forest or along the shore. In the midst of the clearing stood the old man's cabin. He led us into it. One little room, neat and comfortable; two windows south and west with the warm sun streaming through them; a stove, a table by the window with dishes piled neatly on it; some shelves of food and one of books and papers; a bunk with gaily striped blankets; boots, guns, tools, tobacco boxes; a ladder to the storeroom in the loft. And the old man himself: a Swede, short, round, and sturdy, head bald as though with a priestly tonsure, high cheekbones and broad face, full lips, a sensitive small chin — and his little eyes sparkled with good humor.

"Look, this is all mine," he was saying; "you can live here with me — with me and Nanny" — for by this time not only had the milk goat Nanny entered but a whole family of foolish-faced Angoras, father, mother, and child, nosing among us or overturning what they could in search of food. He took us to the fox corral a few yards from the house. There were the blues in its far corner eyeing us askance. We saw the old goat cabin built of logs and were told of a newer one, an unused one down the shore and deeper in the woods.

"But come," he said with pride, "I show you my location notice. I have done it all in the proper way and I will get my title from Washington soon. I have staked fifty acres. It is all described in the notice I have posted; and I would like to see anybody get that away from me."

By now we had reached the great spruce tree to whose trunk he had affixed a sort of roofed tablet or shrine to house the precious document. But, ah look! the tablet was bare! only that from a small nail in it hung a torn shred of paper.

"Billy, Nanny!" roared the old man in irritation and mock rage; and he shook his fist at the foolish-looking culprits who regarded us this time, wisely, from a distance. "And now come to the lake!"

We went down an avenue through the tall spruce trees. The sun flecked our path and fired here and there a flame-colored mushroom that blazed in the forest gloom. Right and left we saw deep vistas, and straight ahead a broad and sunlit space, a valley between hills; there lay the lake. It was a real lake, broad and clean, of many acres in extent, and the whole mountainside lay mirrored in it with the purple zenith sky at our feet. Not a breath disturbed the surface, not a ripple broke along the pebbly beach; it was dead silent here but for maybe the far-off sound of surf, and without motion but that high aloft two eagles soared with steady wing searching the mountaintops. Ah, supreme moment! These are the times in life — when nothing happens — but in quietness the soul expands.

Time pressed and we turned back. "Show us that other cabin, we must go."

The old man took us by a shortcut to the cabin he had spoken of. It stood in a darkly shadowed clearing, a log cabin of ample size with a small doorway that you stooped to enter. Inside was dark but for a little opening to the west. There were the stalls for goats, coops for some Belgian hares he had once kept, a tin whirligig for squirrels hanging in the gable peak, and underfoot a shaky floor covered with filth.

But I knew what that cabin might become. I saw it once and said, "This is the place we'll live." And then, returning to our boat, we shook hands on this great, quick finding of the thing we'd sought and, since we could not stay then as he begged us to, promised a speedy return with all our household goods. "Olson's my name," he said. "I need you here. We'll make a go of it."

The south wind had risen and the whitecaps flew. We crossed the bay pulling lustily for very joy. Reaching the other shore, we saw, too late, crossing the bay in search of us the small white sail of the party that had brought us partway from the town. So we turned and followed them until at last we met, to their relief and the great satisfaction of our tired arms.

[WILDERNESS]

C L A R I T Y

Sunday, October Thirteenth (I still keep to my chronology until we find out from Seward where we stand): A wonderfully beautiful day with a raging northwest wind. I must sometime honor the northwest wind in a great picture as the embodiment of clean, strong, exuberant life, the joy of every young thing, bearing energy on its wings and the will to triumph. How I remember at Monhegan on such a day, when it seemed that every living thing must emerge from its house or its hole or its nest to breathe the clean air and exult in it; when men could stand on the hilltops and look far over the green sea and the distant land and delight in the infinite detail of the view, discerning distant ships at sea and remote blue islands, and, over the land, sparkling cities and such enchanting forests and pastures that the spirit leaped the intervening miles and with a new delight claimed the whole earth to the farthest mountains — and beyond; on such a day there crept from his hole an artist, and, shading his squinting eyes with his hand, saluted the day with a groan. "How can one paint?" he said. "Such sharpness! Here is no mystery, no beauty." And he crept back, this fog lover, to wait for earth's sick spell to return.

This morning the magpie sang — or recited poetry; he made strange glad noises in his throat — and that in a cage! We worked, the rest of us, like mad. At five-thirty, Olson, resting at last, said: "Well, you've done a great day's work." And after that I painted a sketch, cut and trimmed three small spruce trees; and then, it being dark, prepared supper.

[WILDERNESS]

ILLUSTRATIONS FROM WILDERNESS, 1920; TOP: THE NORTH WIND;
BOTTOM: FOX ISLAND CABIN

ROCKWELL KENT

Endlessly, day after day, the journal goes on recording a dreary monotony of rain and cloud. Who has ever dwelt so entirely alone that the most living things in all the universe about are wind and rain and snow? Where the elements dominate and control your life, where at getting up and bedtime, and many an hour of night and day between, you question helplessly, as a poor slave his master, the will of the mighty forces of the sky? Dawn breaks, you jump from bed, stand barefoot on the threshold of the door, look through the straight-trunked spruces at the brightening world, and read at sight God's will for one more whole, long day of life. "Ah God! it rains again." And, sitting on the bed, you wearily draw on your heavy boots, and rainy-spirited begin the special labors of a rainy day. Or maybe, at the sight of clouds again, you laugh at the dull-minded weatherman or curse at him good-naturedly. Still you must do those rainy-weather chores and all the other daily chores in hot wet-weather garments. That is destiny.

Most of the time, to do ourselves real justice, we met the worst of weather with a battle cry, worked hard, and then made up for outdoor dreariness and wet by heaping on the comforts of in-doors — dry, cozy warmth, good things to eat, and lots to do.

We have reached late fall — for northern latitudes. The sky is brooding ominously, heavy, dull, and raw. Winter seems to be closing in upon us. We're driven to work as if in fear. Hurry, hurry! Saw the great drums of spruce, roll them over the ground, and stack them high. Calk tight with hemp the cabin's windward eaves so that no breath of wind can enter there and freeze the food inside upon the shelf. Set up the far-famed airtight stove where it will keep you warm — warm feet in bed and a warm back while painting. Patch up the poor, storm-battered paper roof — two or three holes we find and we are sure it leaks from twenty. About the cabin pile the hemlock boughs, dense-leafed and warm, making a green slope almost to the eaves. Now it looks cozy! Outside and in, the last is done to make us ready for the winter's worst, and just in time! It is the evening of October twenty-second and the feathery snow has just begun to fall. Olson comes stamping in. "Well, well," he cries, "how's this! How does our winter suit you?" It suits us perfectly. The house is warm, Rockwell's in bed, and I am reading *Treasure Island* to him.

"What are you going to make of him?" asked Olson that night, speaking of Rockwell. I was at that moment pouring beans into the pot. . . . I slowed the stream and dropped them one by one:

> "Rich man, poor man, beggarman, thief,
> Doctor, lawyer, merchant, chief.

How in the world can anyone lay plans for a youngster's life?"

Rockwell lay in his bed dreaming, maybe, of an existence lovelier far than anything the poor, discouraged imagination of a man could reach. A child could make a paradise of earth. Life is so simple! Unerringly he follows his desires, making the greatest choices first, then onward into a narrowing pathway until the true goal is reached. How can one preach of beauty or teach another wisdom. These things are of an infinite nature, and in every one of us in just proportion. There is no priesthood of the truth.

We live in many worlds, Rockwell and I: the world of the books we read, an always chang-ing one, *Robinson Crusoe, Treasure Island,* the visionary world of William Blake, the Saga Age, *Water Babies,* and the glorious Celtic past; Rockwell's own world of fancy, kingdom of beasts, the world he dreams about and draws; and my created land of striding heroes and poor fatebound men, real as I have painted them or to me nothing is; and then all round about our common daily, island world, itself more wonderful than we have half a notion of. It is to be believed that we are here alone, this boy and I, far north out on an island wilderness, seagirt on a terrific coast! It's as we pictured it and wanted it a year and more ago — yes, dreams come true.

[WILDERNESS]

OPPOSITE, TOP: BOWSPRIT, 1930, WOOD ENGRAVING ON MAPLE, 5-7/16 x 6-31/32"

BOTTOM: CHILD AND STAR, 1927, WOOD ENGRAVING ON BOXWOOD, 3-1/4 x 2"

Fox Island, November 6, 1918

Dear Carl:

Olson returned from Seward today — after an eight days' stormbound stay — with news above all of peace. Thank God!

And he brought a fine letter from you that moves me to sit down straightaway and write to you although the chance to mail it to you is still weeks off. It is the greatest solace in the world to the loneliness of separation from one's friends to know as you tell me that I am far from forgotten here and that you have followed me here in the maps. When your letter was written, you had not yet received the card with the chart of our bay upon it that I had sent you. You doubtless have it now.

Carl, I am deep, deep in my work. Sometimes my pictures fill me with pride and again, in inevitable reaction, they look like the cheapest paint on canvas. The more I accomplish the more distant are the peaks that I am led to descry that stand there still before me to be scaled. Art is forever long, as long as one's youth, as long as the impressionable years of a life — and no longer. Here where nature in its majesty sends you each day upon your knees there is little danger of satisfaction settling upon a man. Carl, I am so continually filled with a sense of the infinite depths or heights of beauty that art has never touched that I feel indignant at the concern the manner of painting gives the "modern" artist. For such as Pach, and those besides whose disciple he is, to cry that the language of the past has expressed itself to the uttermost, that it is dead, and that we must evolve a new form of speech for this age and for the future seems to me the last confession of their own spiritual blindness. Love — and you'll forever wring from paint new glories without a thought but your worship of the living thing. When I lay blue and orange and white in their fullest purity side by side and, going to my doorway, look over the blue water at the sun upon the snowy mountains, there is then shown to me, out of sheer disgust at the inadequacy of paint to match the living splendor, the spirit of a truer realism — to make splendor of those dull paints by every distortion of value and hue that I can contrive; and there at once is born a new and personal style, and one, in that representation is its motive, is as old in principle as the oldest art and is one with every true art since.

[KENT PAPERS, ASGAARD]

MYSTICISM

I finished Coomaraswamy's *Indian Essays* today, an illuminating and inspiring book. [He] defines mysticism as a belief in the unity of life. The creed of an artist concerns us only when we mean by it the tendency of his spirit. (How hard it is to speak of these intangible things and not use words loosely and without exact meaning.) I think whatever of the mystic is in a man is essentially inseparable from him; it is his by the grace of God. After all, the qualities by which all of us become known are those of which we are ourselves least conscious. The best of me is what is quite impulsive; and, looking at myself for a moment with a critic's eye, the forms that occur in my art, the gestures — the spirit of the whole is in fact nothing but an exact pictorial record of my unconscious living idealism.

[WILDERNESS]

ABOVE: ILLUSTRATION FROM <u>MOBY DICK</u>, 1930

ROCKWELL KENT

Much of the fall it rained, with now and then a bit of snow that the succeeding sun or rain disposed of. Christmas, the ground was almost bare and a warm rain fell steadily. Christmas, the cabin was ablaze with candlelight from what seemed myriads of candles on our nine-foot tree. And if ever the love and peace on earth that Christmas means was realized, it was on that day, there in a rude log cabin in the Alaskan wilderness, and in the hearts of an old man, of a little boy, and of his father. Then, after Christmas, winter came. The snow fell and, in the breathless air, lay deep upon the ground and on the spruces and on every branch and twig of every bush; it put tall snow hats on the stumps. It frosted the forest on the faraway mountainsides and whitened the bare peaks. And then the sun came out and, honoring God's handiwork, withheld its warmth. All nature held its breath as though in awe.

Some days the north wind blew and it was bitter cold; so that from the warmer water of the bay the vapor rose like steam, and the wind lifted it in clouds that hid the mountains' foothills, leaving the dazzling peaks as though suspended in the clear blue sky. And every day and almost all the day I painted, painted in frantic haste to catch a portion of the passing glory; painted in worship of the infinite beauty. Express *myself*? What sacrilege! Who talks when God is speaking!

The steel-sharp, bitter nights, the vast and heartless depths of space that they revealed, enhanced the warmth and comfort of our cabin. There we would sit, we two, the only living beings, so it seemed, in all the universe. Reading at night, when — to the sorrow of us both — I had finished *Robinson Crusoe,* I began — to our soon great delight — to read *Le Mort d'Arthur.*

"Father," asked the boy one night, "how do kings earn their living?"

Not knowing myself exactly how they did, I told him that I guessed they didn't earn it; that the people just gave it to them.

He thought a minute: "Huh!" he said, "it sounds to me like some kind of a practical joke." Come to think of it, it does.

Whether prompted by the heroism of the knights of old or merely by his own wild spirits, Rockwell proposed, now that the snow lay deep, that both of us every morning take a snow bath. And, since a father mustn't show himself a sissy, I agreed. From then on, at daybreak I would first jump up, turn on the drafts of the smoldering airtight heating stove, and jump back into bed again; then, when the cabin was toasty warm, we'd both get up, strip and perform some frantic exercises, and, sweating hot, run out into the snow and roll around in it. After a good rubdown in the warm cabin, we'd feel like a million — no, what am I talking about! what good were dollars on Fox Island — like the good, big plate of oatmeal that was ready for us. Colds? Sickness of any kind on Fox Island? *No!* Only continuous, exuberant health, hands that grew ever harder, muscles that were strong as workmen's muscles have to be; and souls that could expand and fill immensity.

[IT'S ME O LORD]

ABOVE: CHRISTMAS CARD DESIGN, 1928

ROCKWELL KENT

DRAWING ON FOX ISLAND

Thursday, January Twenty-third: . . . For the past three weeks I have made on an average no less than one good drawing a day, really drawings I'm delighted with. I've struck a fine stride and more-over a good system for my work here to continue upon. During the day, I paint out-of-doors from na-ture by way of fixing the forms and above all the color of the out-of-doors in my mind. Then, after dark, I go into a trance for a while with Rockwell subdued into absolute silence. I lie down or sit with closed eyes until I "see" a composition; then I make a quick note of it or maybe give an hour's time to perfecting the arrangement on a small scale. Then, when that's done, I'm carefree. Rockwell and I play cards for half an hour, I get supper, he goes to bed. When he's naked, I get him to pose for me in some needed fantastic position, and make a note of the anatomy in the gesture of my contemplated drawing. Little Rockwell's tender form is my model perhaps for some huge, hairy ruffian. It's great joke how I use him. Generally I have to feel for the bone or tendon that I want to place correctly.

Last night I drew, laughing to myself. A lion was my subject. I have often envied Blake and some of the old masters their ignorance of certain forms that let them be at times so delightfully, im-pressively naïve. I've thought it matters not a bit how little you know about the living form provided you proceed to draw the thing according to some definite, consistent idea. Don't conceal your igno-rance with a slur, be definite and precise even there. Well, by golly, this lion gave me my chance to be unsophisticated; such a silly, smirking beast I drew! At last it became somewhat rational and a little dignified, but it still looks like a judge in a great wig. But a lion that lets a naked youth sleep in his paws as this one does may be expected to be a little unbeastly. When I began to write these pages to-night, the stars were out. Now it snows or hails on the roof!

Wednesday, January Twenty-ninth: Alaska can be cold! Monday broke all records for the winter. Tuesday made that seem balmy. It was so bitterly cold here last night in our "tight little cabin" that we had to laugh. Until ten o'clock when I went to bed the large stove was continuously red hot and running at full blast. And yet by then the water pails were frozen two inches thick — but ten feet from the stove and open water at suppertime, my fountain pen was frozen on the table, Rock-well required a hot-water bottle in bed, the fox food was solid ice, my paste was frozen, and that's all. My potatoes and milk I had stood near the stove. At twelve o'clock the clock stopped — starting again from the warmth of breakfast cooking. I put the water pail at night behind the stove close to it, and yet it was solid in the morning. We burn an unbelievable amount of wood, at least a cord a week in one stove. So I figure we earn a dollar a day cutting wood. We felled another tree today and cut most of it up. Still we manage to gain steadily with our woodpile, always in anticipation of worse weather. Last night at sundown the bay appeared indescribably dramatic. Dense clouds of vapor were rising from the water obscuring all but a few peaks of the mountains and darkening the bay. But above the sun shone dazzlingly on the peaks and through the thinner vapor, coloring this like flames. It was as if a terrible fire raged over the bay. This morning for hours it was dark from clouds of vapor. They swept in over our land and coated the trees of the shore with white frost.

Yesterday I had to go to the lake and chop out a bag of fish for the foxes. I returned covered with ice and the fish were frozen solid before I reached the cabin. I cut them up today with the axe and cooked a week's supply of food for the foxes.

[WILDERNESS]

ROCKWELL KENT

CARL ZIGROSSER

TO CARL ZIGROSSER

Fox Island, January 28, 1919

Dear Carl:

 Here's a fine time to write. It's only ten-thirty at night and my drawing is finished — a man asleep in his dory. I think I'm much more cheerful than I discerned myself to be the other night. When things are fine, my work flourishing, the weather sharp and clear, and my woodpile two days ahead of the stove, then I want you, Carl, worse than I ever before wanted a friend. You have been such an inspiration to me with your wholehearted enthusiasm over this adventure of mine that my very first thought in any hour of elation is of you. Gee, but I hope we can sometime try some spirited adventure together. I think that I'm a pretty good hand most anywhere now and at almost any work. I find that I need no favors or advice from anyone whatever new land I've come to, and I swear that in spite of my "bad reputation" for quarrels and general all-around ill nature I'm not bad at all to get along with. The truth is that if I don't like the other one a lot I can't stand him at all. What a lot of arrogant intolerance of other people I do express to you! Really your pride is a delight to me. How few people don't slick in a bit of Christian love over all their judgments!

 "Who loves his enemy hates his friend" is a fine line of Blake's. No wonder I find Zarathustra congenial!

 A line in the translator's introduction to that book made me stop to think (!) The translator says that Zarathustra is such a being as Nietzsche would have liked himself to be — in other words his ideal man.

 It seems to me that the ideal of a man is the real man. You are that which in your soul you choose to be: the most beautiful and cherished version of your soul is

TOP: BOOKPLATE FOR CARL ZIGROSSER

BOTTOM: THE SLEEPER, ILLUSTRATION FROM <u>WILDERNESS</u>, 1920

   ROCKWELL KENT

yourself. *To think that one is what one appears to be under the stress of life is to admit circumstances as a determining element in the judgment of character — which it is not. What are the true unusual conditions of life for any man but just those ideal circumstances with which he would surround that soul's image of his. What that character does in any other situation, even the most common and average one, is as far from the point as to submit the man to a prolonged torture — and this disarms his bad disposition. Faults of character are* breaks *of character and often the most fine-grained and sensitive natures break under the least friction so that every act may be contrary to the true nature of the man. I do think that a man is not a sum of discordant tendencies — but rather a being perfect for one special environment. And here Olson agrees with me.*

When I get so far in a discussion, I begin to think that it's probably after all nonsense. Is it a disease of the mind that a man should see us use in argument or discussion and think it not worthwhile teaching anybody anything or proving anything? I certainly have a growing distaste for propaganda. That's my one criticism of Zarathustra. Why, after all, concern himself with the mob?

In picturing his hero as a teacher has not Nietzsche been tricked away from a true ideal to such an ideal character as must be for history to record it? Of necessity the great selfish figures of all time have gone to oblivion. It's a law of life that only the benefactors of mankind shall live in memory. The true ideal is to be the thing yourself and to concern yourself not one bit in proving your worth. Be it for your own sake, not for mankind's sake, or that "beyond man" may come. Be that which you like to be. And if the true onward path of mankind seems to go another way than yours, that is not your concern.

And so — father confessor to my little provincial sins of thinking, grant me with a smile your absolution. And I'll go to bed.

Good night, you fine fellow Carl, and God bless all your household. Amen.
Rockwell
[KENT PAPERS, ASGAARD]

TITLE PAGE DRAWING FROM <u>WILDERNESS</u>, WARD RITCHIE PRESS, 1970

ROCKWELL KENT

Tuesday, February Fourth: We sawed a lot of wood today bringing our pile clear up into the gable peak. It becomes a mania seeing the pile grow. In quiet weather we cut to forestall the storm; in the storm we still cut to be well ahead for days that may be worse. It is beautifully mild now. On February first, Rockwell brought in some budding twigs. The alders all seem to be in bud and some charming red-stemmed shrubs as well. It is midnight and past. My drawing is finished, the stove is piled for the night, cereal and beans in place upon it, so — good night.

Wednesday, February Fifth: A beautiful snowstorm all the day and tonight, still and mild. Rockwell has been out in it all day dressed in my overalls and mittens. He plays seal and swims in the deep snow. We built a snow house together. It is now about seven feet in diameter inside and as cozy as can be. I'm sure Rockwell will want to sleep there when it's finished. A curtain of icicles hangs before our window.

I have carefully figured the cost of our living here from the food bills, all of which I have kept. I have bought $114.82 worth of provisions. I still have on hand $19.10 worth. For a hundred and fifty days it has cost us sixty-four cents a day for two, or thirty-two cents each — a little over ten cents a meal. This for the current high prices everywhere and additionally high in Alaska seems very reasonable living. The figures include the very expensive Christmas luxuries. What Olson has given us we returned in other foods. It has not been much at that.

Friday, February Seventh: Yesterday, THE SUN! For how many days he might have been shining at us I don't know, for it has been cloudy. However, at noon it was all over the ground about us and shining in at my window. What a joyous sight after months of shadow! Tonight the sun at setting again almost reached us. And yesterday, as if spring had already come, we began the day with snow baths at sunrise. Ha! That's the real morning bath! And today again. We step out-of-doors and plunge full length into the deep snow, scour our bodies with it, and rush back into the sheltering house and the red-hot stove. To Rockwell belongs all credit, or blame, for this madness. He will do it — and I'm ashamed not to follow. These two days have been cold and windy, North days — but how beautiful! All of the day Rockwell plays out-of-doors swimming in the deep snow, now a seal, again a walrus. Gee, he's the great fellow for Northern weather. Cooked the filthy fox mess yesterday, washed clothes today, sawed wood on both. Now it's twelve-thirty at night and I'm tired.

Saturday, February Eighth: All about me stand the drawings of my series, the Mad Hermit. They look mighty fine to me. Myself with whiskers and hair! First, today, when the storm abated a bit, we sank a bag of fish in the lake and then started on snowshoes for the ridge to the eastward. The snow lay in the woods there heavy and deep. No breath of wind had touched it. The small trees, loaded, bent double making shapes like frozen fountains. Some little trees, with their branches starting far from the ground, formed with their drooping limbs domed chambers about their stems. Coming down it was great sport. We could slide down even in our sticky snowshoes. Rockwell, who was soaked through, undressed and spent the afternoon naked, playing wild animal about the cabin. Then at six-thirty we both had hot baths, and snow baths following. I begin to relish the snow bath. Rockwell was the picture of health and beauty afterward with his rose-red cheeks and blue eyes.

[WILDERNESS]

OPPOSITE: "THE MAD HERMIT," FROM TOP, LEFT TO RIGHT:
THE HERMIT; ECSTASY; PELAGIC REVERIE; PRISON BARS;
RUNNING WATER; IMMANENCE

ABOVE: THE VISION

Sunday, March Sixteenth: And now I sit here with our packed household goods about me, empty walls and a dismantled home. Still we hardly realize that this beautiful adventure of ours has come to an end. The enchantment of it has been complete; it has possessed us to the very last. How long such happiness could hold, such quiet life continue to fill up the full measure of human desires, only a long experience could teach. The still, deep cup of the wilderness is potent with wisdom. Only to have tasted it is to have moved a lifetime forward to a finer youth. How long such a life could continue to charm, one of course cannot know; but it is clear to us now as we leave it that we have only begun to know the wonders of the life and of the land. We are both resolved in our hearts to return here and explore freedom to its limits — truly a lifetime's plan. We have learned what we want and are therefore wise. As graduates in wisdom, we return from the university of the wilderness.

Tuesday, March Eighteenth: Fox Island is behind us. Last August, Olson picked us up as strangers and towed us to his island; yesterday, after nearly seven months there with him, we climbed again into our dories and crossed the bay — and now we extend the helping hand to the old man and tow him and his faltering engine back to Seward. The day dawned cold and windy. We proceeded, however, at once to the completion of our packing and the loading of the boat.

A little after noon, the wind moderating slightly, we persuaded Olson to come with us. My engine, working beautifully, carried both boats along till the other little motor could be prevailed upon to start. In the bay the wind was fresh and the chop high. Halfway across, the wind has risen and the water flew. Olson's engine worked so poorly that most of the time I had the full strain of his dory on the line. I feared the old man's courage would give out as the sea increased, and I grinned at him reassuringly from time to time. Finally, however, as the white-crested waves seemed to rush ever more fiercely upon us, his face grew solemn. He waved to us to turn and run back to the island. But the towline was fast in my boat and I neither chose to turn nor loosen it. Showing our backs to him, we ran for the shelter of Caine's Head — and made it. From there onward we skirted the cliffs and found it smooth enough. The wind again died out and we entered Seward over a glassy sea.

And now at last it is over. Fox Island will soon become in our memories like a dream or vision, a remote experience too wonderful, for the full liberty we knew there and the deep peace, to be remembered or believed in as a real experience in life. It was for us life as it should be, serene and wholesome; love — but no hate, faith without disillusionment, the absolute for the toiling hands of man and for his soaring spirit. Olson of the deep experience, strong, brave, generous, and gentle like a child; and his island — like Paradise. Ah God — and now the world again!

[WILDERNESS]

TOP: GODSPEED, 1931, WOOD ENGRAVING ON MAPLE, 5-5/16 x 6-7/8″

BOTTOM: NIGHT ON THE SEA WITH FOUR BRIGHT STARS,
1926, WOOD ENGRAVING ON BOXWOOD, 2-3/16 x 1-1/2″

ROCKWELL KENT

TOP: TWILIGHT OF MAN, 1926, WOOD ENGRAVING ON MAPLE, 5-1/2 x 8″

BOTTOM: WOMAN WITH BASKET, 1921, WOOD ENGRAVING ON MAPLE, 1-5/8 x 1″

ROCKWELL KENT

TOP: FOREST POOL, 1927, WOOD ENGRAVING ON MAPLE, 5-1/2 x 8-1/32″

BOTTOM: GREENLAND AIR MAIL STAMP, 1932, WOOD ENGRAVING ON MAPLE, 1-9/16 x 1-1/4″

ROCKWELL KENT

THE LOOKOUT, 1930, WOOD ENGRAVING ON MAPLE, 7-31/32 x 5-15/32"

ROCKWELL KENT

TOP: IMPERISHABLE, 1927, ENGRAVING ON ZINC, 6-5/8 x 10"

BOTTOM: WOMAN AND DEER UNDER A TREE, 1921, WOOD ENGRAVING ON MAPLE, 1-3/4 x 1-1/4"

R O C K W E L L   K E N T

DIVER, 1931, WOOD ENGRAVING ON MAPLE, 7·13/16 x 5·11/32″

ROCKWELL KENT

TOP: DRIFTER, 1933, WOOD ENGRAVING ON MAPLE, 5-3/8 x 6-7/8″

BOTTOM: R. K. MARK, 1918, WOOD ENGRAVING ON BOXWOOD, 3/4 x 11/16″

ROCKWELL KENT

MOUNTAIN CLIMBER, 1933, WOOD ENGRAVING ON MAPLE, 7-7/8 x 5-7/8″

ROCKWELL KENT

TOP: THE LOVERS, 1928, WOOD ENGRAVING ON MAPLE, 6-1/2 x 10-1/16″

BOTTOM: GIRL ON CLIFF, 1930, WOOD ENGRAVING ON MAPLE, 6-1/2 x 4-13/16″

ROCKWELL KENT

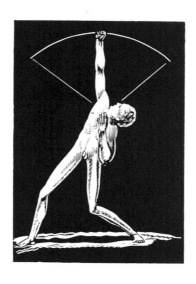

TOP: STARLIGHT, 1930, WOOD ENGRAVING ON MAPLE, 5-5/16 x 6-27/32″

BOTTOM: MAN SHOOTING AN ARROW, 1920, WOOD ENGRAVING ON BOXWOOD, 4 x 2-3/4″

ROCKWELL KENT

SEA AND SKY, 1931, WOOD ENGRAVING ON MAPLE, 10 x 6-7/16″

ROCKWELL KENT

SOUTH AMERICA
SAIL!

Down the long stretch of Broad and Famine Reach stand the white peaks and ranges of the wilderness, with all the threat and promise of their mysteries: and still beyond and high above them all the unattainable white peaks of Sarmiento. Ah, what a day! So sharp and blue, and golden where the far sky touches the circle of the world! The lower atmosphere is glistening with the spray of windblown wave crests. A double rainbow spans the west, an omen of strong wind and of good fortune; and, where it rests among the mountains of the south, there in some peaceful, solitary virgin valley lies the forever sought and undiscovered gold of happiness.

With sails all set and drawing full the little *Kathleen,* wind abeam, lies over on her side and with the main boom trailing in the water and the deck awash goes like a wild thing fled to freedom. "Don't ease her!" cries the mate. Her bows shiver the seas, the cold spray wets us. A school of porpoises is racing, leaping, plunging round us. Good luck! The gods are with us!

The wind has risen and the seas run high. Great crested waves bear down and threaten us — and laugh, and lift us tenderly, and cradle us. We *ride* the seas. Our ship is tight and strong; she sails, and holds her course unswervingly. "A beauty!" cries the mate; and with my soul on eagle wings of happiness I go below.

There in the cabin was the final word of cleanliness and order. There were convenient shelves with tins of food set out in orderly array, with pots and dishes in their place secured against the tossing of the boat, with space for linen and for books and cameras and paints; there were the racks for instruments and charts, for the compass and the clock and the lamp, and for pens and brushes, for saws and hammers and pliers and files, for the marlinspike and the calking iron, for the lead line, for the flags and pilot lights and rockets, for my canvases and paper. Our beds were cleverly contrived: on canvas, laced across, we had spread our store of clothes and made a mattress of them. The beds were laid this day all clean and sweet for night. The stove was polished and the floor was scrubbed. It was perfection in that little cabin — all but a cup or so of water that had leaked up from the bilge and slopped around untidily in a corner of the floor. I took a cup to bail it out, chatting meanwhile through the open companionway with the mate.

"With the wind holding like this," he said as a fresh squall struck and heeled us over, "we should get to Willis Bay by five o'clock this afternoon." It was now about eleven, and in an hour and a half we had covered perhaps twelve miles. Our course was for Cape Valentine on Dawson Island. In two days, we figured it, we'd reach the head of Admiralty Sound; in two days more be out and headed westward to round the point of Brecknock Peninsula.

And all the time I bailed.

Quite innocent of trouble, it occurred to me that one might have done it better with a kettle than a cup. I take a kettle, plant one foot upon the boat's sloping side to brace myself, and set to work in earnest.

The mate is singing as the spray flies over him. His is a happiness too great to bear alone. He is in love and she is many thousand miles away. A kettle of cold water on his legs startles him out of it.

A quarter of an hour has passed. I'm bailing desperately, emptying the water over the mate, his tender heart and everything. I'm standing in it to my knees, and steadily it rises. There's not one chance of beating back to the near windward shore; we change our course to run to leeward fifteen miles away. There's a gale and a high sea, and our boat is sodden with the weight of water in her. In turns we bail, work to exhaustion, both of us; and steadily, from God knows where, she fills.

OPPOSITE: LAND LEGS, ILLUSTRATION FROM <u>VOYAGING</u>, 1924

ROCKWELL KENT

And then the truth strikes home — we're sinking. And the land's too far away to reach.

We come about to lower sail. The gaff jams, and the mate scrambles aloft to trample on it. In a fury of beating and slatting and the clattering of blocks and whipping of the halyards down it comes — and we lie hove-to under the staysail.

The skiff that we carry on the deck is eight feet long, four wide, flat-bottomed; it's of no conceivable use in a sea. Nevertheless we launch it and make it fast astern, and while it bucks like an enraged animal to dislodge me, I succeed with canvas and tacks in decking it over. I stow oars and life belts and a few necessities on board, stick my opened clasp knife in the bow to cut us free at the last moment from the wreck, and the lifeboat is ready.

Seen from the skiff, the forlorn condition of the *Kathleen* was apparent. She lay there listing heavily with half the deck submerged; and every sea broke over her. Suddenly I was overwhelmed by the hopelessness of the conviction of catastrophe. There was neither thought of God nor fear of death but only a poignant vision of my life as finished and left pitifully incomplete, a lightning flash of home with the little children and their mother weeping there, a sickening shame at death so futile and so miserable as this, an instant of vertigo, a weakening of the knees, a griping of the bowels as though I hung over an immense and sheer abyss, a wild impulse to madness — to throw my arms aloft and scream. Then swiftly, at the very breaking point of all control, profounder shame swept that whole agony aside and left the mind unburdened of all memory. So that with humor I could listen to the mate's wild strong young voice sing "Smile awhile" to the swashing rhythm of his bailing; and I could note the little quaver in it, and, understanding song and quaver, laugh to think that even he got just a little touched by fear.

We stood in the cabin almost to our waists in water, and bailed in turns. The place was devastated. With the rolling of the boat, the water swashed about and swept our treasures from the shelves. Shoes, socks, linen, paper, bread, cocoa, curry powder, nuts, and cigarettes covered the tide and swirled about the vortex of the pail. My bunk was flooded so that the blankets floated out.

I took the logbook of the *Kathleen,* sat down on the edge of the bunk, and on the clean first page wrote this, "Our epitaph," I thought:

"First day out, three hours from sailing. Boat half full of water, hove-to. Bailing in turns. Lifeboat equipped to cross to Porvenir. Strong west wind blowing. Mate singing, great fellow. No chance to save anything; lifeboat is too small."

Then, tying up a few treasures in a waterproof package, I was ready.

That the *Kathleen* would sink was inevitable. For an hour we had fought against the water; we had done our best and were incapable of greater effort, and we had never for a moment checked the water's rise. The end was not a matter of guess but of exact calculation. I *knew* that in ten minutes more the ship would sink. Intelligence excluded hope.

My mate was gifted with many noble and endearing qualities: he was courageous, good-natured, and doggedly perseverant. But of intelligence — the power to reason, to deduce effect from cause — he had absolutely none. And it was pathetic not only to observe him in the face of the tragically apparent futility of all that we could do stubbornly plying the heavy pail to the everlasting rhythm of his song but to reflect that in his blindness to the imminence of death he missed the glory and the pain of life's high moment. He was too dull to know that we were doomed!

So we bailed and sang. Five minutes went, and ten. We passed the limit of the time that reason had allowed the boat to live; yet still she floated, rolling sluggishly. And as the seas piled over her there seemed each time no chance that she'd emerge again. Time brought new energy. We fought the water stubbornly.

Not daring to hope, we bailed — for it was all that there was left in life to do.

The *Kathleen* didn't sink.

Days later, when we beached her, we understood the cause of her misfortune and salvation. That day her floating was a miracle. Slowly it dawned upon us as we worked that we had stopped the water's rise; and when at last we knew beyond all doubt that we could hold our own, it was, strangely, without emotion that we received our lives again.

It was by now perhaps two in the afternoon. The water in the cabin was still up to our knees, and it required continuous bailing to hold it. Ruined supplies of every kind floated about, and our fair ship, four hours ago so trim and beautiful, was now the picture of desolation. The wind and sea abated as the day wore on; we took so little water now that by our bailing every minute showed it lower; and presently, with not a foot's depth left, we hoisted a reefed mainsail, came about, and started on a long tack for the windward shore some miles away.

The afternoon increased in beauty and in peacefulness; and as the certainty of our security became established, profound contentment arose like the morning sun within us. Life is so infinitely sweet and rich that nothing matters — only that we live.

Evening comes on, the shadows of the land creep out across the sea and cover us. It's cold. On the last breath of the dying wind we reach our anchorage.

How still it is! Darkness has almost hidden the abandoned whaling village on the shore. Dimly the forms of stores and houses detach themselves from the dark ground. In one house burns a lamp. A man is driving cattle down the silent street. Treeless sand hills enclose the little plain on which the settlement is built; beyond them stands the barrier of snow-topped mountains. . . . For long minutes we have not spoken.

We go below. There's a damp fire burning and it's faintly warm. We are dead tired. Wrapping ourselves in soaking blankets, we lie down in wet beds to sleep.

[VOYAGING]

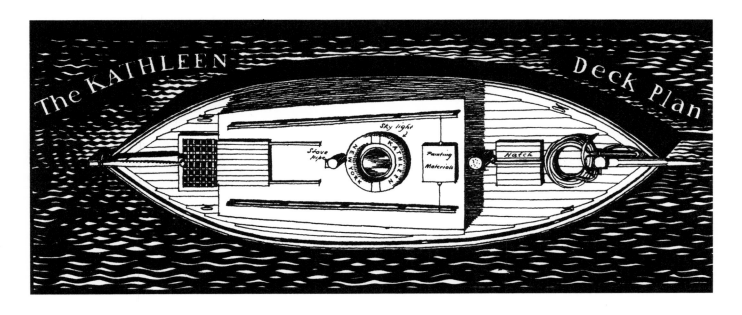

THE *KATHLEEN*, DECK PLAN, ILLUSTRATION FROM *VOYAGING*, 1924

ROCKWELL KENT

What forces drive men on to the deliberate quest of miseries and danger? Are they remote yet deeply rooted habits of a race which once delighted in adventure for the gain it held, that still assert themselves against the very soul's desire for peace and the mind's clear understanding of the paths that lead there? Is it a far-visioned life-force maintaining itself against the disintegrating allurements of ease, a militant expression of the subconscious will that's cognizant of individual weakness, an assertion in contraries of the complex of inferiority? Is bravery the cloak of cowardice?

Loving the crowd too much and shunning solitude, we seek it. Fearing our own selves' insufficiency, we must forever make a trial of it alone. Because of all things we desire slothfully to lie abed, we are possessed with energy to be about before the dawn. Never, it seems to have been willed, may men enjoy that happiness their souls desire.

ONLY THE VOYAGER perceives the poignant loveliness of life, for he alone has tasted of its contrasts. He has experienced the immense and wild expansion of the spirit outward bound, and the contracted heartburn of the homecoming. He has explored the two infinities — the external universe — and himself.

Only the voyager discovers — and by discovery he generates. For

of man's universe, which is but that portion of the infinite which he perceives, he is, by his perception of it, the creator. Thus in his own image has man created God.

The wilderness is kindled into life by man's beholding of it; he is its consciousness, his coming is its dawn. Surely the passion of his first discovery carries the warmth and the caress of a first sunrise on the chaos of creation.

WE SAILED. We cleared the Hook, the land dropped down, the hard horizon of the sea encircled us. My life became a memory and the future broke against our prow and shimmered, and was foam and trailed behind us in the steamer's wake. There was no measure of the time but days and nights, and the passage of these was forgotten in the contentment of their monotony, or concealed in the illusion of swiftly changing seasons as from the springtime of the north the steamer bore us southward through six weeks and seven thousand miles, through the midsummer of the equator to the July winter of the Strait of Magellan.

With the disappearance of land, the ship at sea becomes a planetary body moving in the orbit of its prescribed course through the fluid universe of the ocean. It has cast off from the whole accumulated "realities" of life, and these endure but in the memories of the men aboard. Activity is constrained, and the mind turns to contemplation or to thought: the true record of a voyage on the sea must be a record of those illusive imaginings of the almost unconscious mind responding to the hypnotic monotony of the ship's vibrations, of the liquid rustling of the water steaming past her sides, of the endlessly recurrent rhythm of the bow wave, and the even, seething pattern of the wake. The memory of it is of prolonged and changeless contentment.

"It is now the third of November," reads the page, "almost full moon, and a rising tide. The glass stands at 29. The west wind rakes our anchorage with undiminished force, whistling and howling. The tide rip gurgles venomously against our hollow sides, the seas strike us and hurl spray fiercely over us. Our cable creaks. The boat is rolling heavily and trembling when the squalls strike. I am driven from my reverie to bed.

"It is not easy to go to sleep on such a night as I have just recorded. Now, from another day, I look back upon it. I lay there in my bed listening to the innumerable sounds, and feeling by my close contact with the boat's thin sides her trembling response to the wild forces of the sea and wind. Sleep seemed impossible — yet, suddenly, I slept; and with that sleep all memory of the causes of my waking anxiety vanished. Still, as I must believe from the fragments of dreams that have been spared me out of that oblivion, I was by sleep transported to a world of the imagination as tragically full of peril, more harassing and, to the mind, in every way as real as the frightening actuality. I carried into sleep no memory of the daylight world, yet out of sleep I bore the recollection of experiences so terrible and of desire so hopeless of fulfillment that the mood of night clung like a pall about my consciousness. Of man's two existences, by day and night, night dominates.

"One of the ancient Christian faith would piously attribute his dreamt anxieties to visitations of Satan. But, as a pagan on the quest of happiness, I perceive them to be the warnings of a man's own spirit that he may not forsake friendship and love and hope to live at peace."

At last a day dawned overcast and calm and ominous of change. And then, toward noon, out of the pregnant stillness came — could we believe it! — a gentle east wind. With wild precipitation we weighed anchor and on the swift current of the river swept out through the narrow channel to the sound. We have a moment's memory of the friends we leave. "Farewell!" our hearts cry, "we are sailing westward!" . . .

"NOVEMBER SEVENTH. It is late at night as I begin to write. For two hours we have sat here in the darkness of the cabin. The firelight shines through the grate, casting a faint warm glow about the room. The wind blows in terrifying squalls upon us, howling, careening us — and then for a few minutes it is quite still. The boat rocks gently, the little waves gurgle pleasantly against the sides, the clock ticks loudly; there is no sound in the world besides. Then again, far off, the forests of the mountainside begin to roar — nearer comes the sound and louder. Suddenly the gurgling water and the ticking clock, the little sounds that were so loud, are lost as the wild uproar of the wind engulfs us.

"We sit in silence every night throughout the twilight. Often I play upon the flute, shutting my eyes to make the darkness darker; and my companion's head is bowed and resting on his hands. In these still hours the wisdom comes to us of knowing our profoundest needs.

"Then with fatigue the glamour of adventure wanes; and loneliness comes over us and the sense that we are destitute of all that has sustained our lives. We that have come so far and left so much then know, out of the poignant singleness of our desires, what in the confusion and abundance of life's offerings is best. But no one tells — so intimately close and dear is that desire. And when at last, suddenly in the darkness here, I ask my companion what one thing he desires most out of the whole world, tonight — he starts at the shattered silence, and, slowly emerging from far away to here, covers his thoughts and answers, 'A fair wind to carry us through Gabriel Channel.' "

However, there's an end to everything. "Mate," I said one dreary night as we turned in, "I need a new chapter for my book. Tomorrow we sail no matter what happens." And we did.

[VOYAGING]

ABOVE: ILLUSTRATION FROM MOBY DICK, 1930

RAIN TORRENT

It was my custom at every port we made to go ashore with paints and canvas and make such a record of the place as the time at my disposal and the weather allowed. The wind and the sudden storms of rain often drove me to a makeshift shelter, where I would either wait out the storm or leave my gear to be reclaimed at another time. The day following our arrival at Three Hummock, I walked to the northeastern end of the island carrying my paints and a large canvas. Across the sound towered the immense cathedral mountains of the north shore. It was a dull, moist day and against the dark precipices of the mountain face gleamed the silver of cascades that flowed from the melting snow and glaciers of the heights. I set up my canvas on the shore, bracing it against the wind with driftwood. But hardly had I begun to work when the rain came in torrents. I fled with my canvas to the shelter of a ledge of rock. Quickly I converted the picture into a roof, and, crawling under it, lay down huddled on the stones, while over me the rain beat on the canvas like the rolling of a kettledrum. It was damp and cold; so, seeking refuge from discomfort, I fell asleep.

How long I slept I do not know. At last a silence awakened me. I crept out of my dark shelter into sunlight. The storm had passed and it was breathless calm. The wet rocks glistened and the shrubbery was hung with diamonds. But the mountains! Part sunlit and part veiled in trailing vapor shadows, illumined by the rainbow mist of swollen torrents, they stood for that one transient interlude peacefully and mildly beautiful.

[VOYAGING]

ABOVE: BERTÉ'S WIGWAM, ILLUSTRATION FROM VOYAGING, 1924

ROCKWELL KENT

We lay barely fifty yards from the shore. Here, just above the tide's reach, stood the long shed of the mill. Opposite this was a small building which, we came to know, was intended as the office and the house of the manager; and farther back, suggesting the third side of an open quadrangle that faced the bay, stood a long row building in which the men were quartered. Peering out at us from the sheltered cover of the mill shed stood a man. And though we greeted him with every wave of courtesy he made no answering sign, just watched us stolidly. It's no great pleasure to be stared at, stolidly; and we muttered our opinion of the ungracious fellow.

What was our delight, however, on rowing ashore, to have him meet us at the water's edge with the most winning smile of welcome, wading into the surf to seize our skiff and help us draw it up the beach!

"Bienvenida," said he, shaking our hands; and he bade us enter the house to get warm.

There, in the kitchen of the bunkhouse, with another man who presently appeared, we tasted of a hospitality that was to last for weeks and began a friendship that is not forgotten.

These two young Chilean lumberjacks, Don Antonio and "Curly" (it was all we ever learned to call him), revealed to us that gentlemen, in that romantic sense of "those who are possessed of good manners, kindness of heart, and strict integrity and honor," do flower in life beyond the reach of education and the traditions of culture. Little did these men know of the wide world; they were ignorant, illiterate, and superstitious. But even their Christian superstition had the grace of tolerance.

One dark night, Don Antonio related to me, when the wind was blowing everything about the place, the devil came and set the machinery of the mill going and sawed some lumber. They found the new-sawn boards lying there in the morning.

"Did he do good work?" I asked.

"Lovely work," said Don Antonio. He was not a bigot.

Perhaps nothing moved me so much as their respect for my vocation and their unprompted recognition of its privacy. Only a painter can appreciate this high and grateful tribute that I pay them: they left me alone.

It cannot be said that we settled down at Bahía Blanca. We lived on board and lived in readiness for instant departure should the wind change to favor us; yet the establishment on shore became our headquarters by day, while between the Chilenos, who were the sole occupants of the place, and ourselves there sprang up a pretty interchange of courtesies that never lacked a pleasant flavor of formality.

The one luxury of the mate's equipment on the *Kathleen* was a cheap, portable phonograph with a broken mainspring, and three cracked disks. The records were beyond repair; but I spliced and riveted the springs of the machine and, having but two sewing needles and no pins on board, made needles out of nails, and tempered them — and so the thing was made to emit an enjoyable, fragmentary, ghastly kind of music. We always carried the machine ashore, that and my silver flute.

I'd play the flute awhile of an evening while everyone sat silent in polite attention. I would play the slow movements of Beethoven sonatas, "My Wandering Boy," and suchlike classical selections as my stiff fingers could accomplish. And at the conclusion they'd release their suppressed coughs and say *"Lindo, muy lindo!"* — which means "very lovely." And then on the phonograph, we'd have the undamaged last half of "Oh What a Pal Was Mary" — and to that they would say *"Lindo."* So we were very happy. We'd eat heartily of roast mutton, have more music and a very little conversation, and with mutually repeated expressions of adieu be escorted to the shore. . . .

And so, between festivities and work, the days slid by. And the west wind either blew like fury or blew moderately, or there was no wind at all and the mountains stood upon their heads reflected in the breathless calm of the green-jade water of the bay. Sometimes our watchful eyes discovered that the clouds had changed their course. In wild excitement we would bid our friends goodbye, heave up anchor, and sail out. But whatever currents might prevail among the clouds, down in that canyon of the sound there was no wind but west. We'd beat and drift and make a mile or two, and then, discouraged at such a waste of time, turn tail and sheepishly come home.

At the head of Bahía Blanca is a wide glacial moraine that extends inland to the blue-green cliffs of the glacier. The broad glacial stream pours down from a remote inland region that appears as the very desolation of antarctic winter. Flanking the glacier on the east is an immense flat mountain dome of rock, covered with ice and spotless snow. Between this ice-capped dome and the nearer mountain of the northeast shore of Bahía Blanca is a broad valley bearing southeasterly. No barrier of mountains appears beyond the relatively low horizon of this valley, so that it seems to be a highway leading south.

It was from the top of a little hill that stood at the edge of the moraine that I first saw this view; and then, and the many other times that I sat upon that sheltered hillside facing it, I was possessed by its beauty and moved to ponder on the insistent yet illusive significance that it contained for me.

Is it mere chance that the forms and humors of nature appear as symbols of the moods, experiences, and desires of the human spirit? The unbroken pathways of the wilderness are reminders of the hard and solitary way that ardent souls must travel. The glittering, virgin whiteness of high mountain fields of snow, untrodden, maybe unattainable, their mist-veiled beauty neither earth nor cloud, remote, serene, and passionless, picture the spirit's aspiration. Can it have been the fervid imagination of man that has endowed these mountains with an aura of symbolism? Rather is it the reality of mountains and plains, the sea and the unfathomable heavens, unchangingly forever dominating man, cradling him in that remote hour of his awakening into consciousness, forever smiling, brooding, thundering upon him, that have imposed their nature upon man and made him what he is.

And still, even where men dwell in the environment of their own creation, the wilderness casts its light and shadow into their dreams. Trees murmur in the city's night; men hear the thunder and the wash of seas. The moon's light shines to them on silver peaks; the wild, eternal glory of the universe appears. Unrest possesses them, and they awake to the adventurous courage of their race's past, and go.

It is not choice that draws men from comfort and security into the hazards of adventure or the miseries of solitude, but rather an impulse profounder than consciousness and more forceful than reason. It may be likened to a reassertion of the will to the achievement of high purpose. And in that the denials and perils that are sought resemble the soul-paths of virtue is concealed the truth that nature is the parent of our moral thought.

There as I sat one afternoon upon that sheltered hillside and viewed the varied beauty of the scene veiled in mistlike rain, the plain traversed by intersecting glacial streams of milky water and islanded with groves of trees and bits of meadowland, the lower mountains clothed in forests of the deepest green, the high slopes red with budding shrubbery, the dazzling summits, and the valley that forever seemed a highway to a promised land — then, as I looked far up that valley's green-clad, gently rising plain to where it dipped from view and left the whole beyond a mystery, a strange thing came to pass. The gray mist of the rain became transfused with golden light and in the broad gap where my eyes were fixed gleamed a pale rainbow. It was only for a moment; then the mists dispersed and sunlight flooded everything. That was November the twenty-fourth.

Under that date my diary reads: "It is at last dark after the long twilight, and the lights of the men's house and on the *Kathleen* are extinguished. I sit in the bare, wood-walled room of one of the mill outbuildings at a window overlooking the water. Rain beats upon the panes. Squalls sweep the bay and the surf roars on the shore. The breeze that penetrates around the window sash flutters my candle. The wind blows straight in upon us from the northwest; it never changes. We have given up all hope of sailing west and southward, for we could never beat out through this sound and Gabriel

OPPOSITE: TWO ILLUSTRATIONS FROM VOYAGING, 1924
TOP, MOUNT OLIVIA; BOTTOM, WIND-TORN TREES

ROCKWELL KENT

Channel. It is a conclusion that we have found hard to face.

"However, we will continue southward — on foot; and on the day after tomorrow we will start up the valley from the head of Bahía Blanca."

There is always a fascination in assembling the equipment and provisions for an expedition, whether it be for a picnic luncheon in the country or for a cruise of many months. This time the certain difficulties of the enterprise that we were undertaking and the uncertainty of the time that it would occupy us imposed the attractively conflicting problem of loads both light and comprehensive. Moreover, the problem of supplies was complicated by our penury. We were heading, to be sure, for the town of Ushuaia, where undoubtedly meals could be obtained and supplies purchased. But for this we had no money. And while there was the possibility of someone's befriending us with a few days' board, we had no thought of obtaining credit. Yet somehow Cape Horn was to be reached, and to that time if not beyond it we must live.

But even more of an encumbrance than our food supplies were the heavy materials of my unfortunate profession; and allied to these were the cameras. The Kodak would have been enough, but I had not entirely succeeded in repairing the damaged shutter and it was good for only very short exposures. So the bulky Graflex had to go. And there was the flute. I don't know definitely why I carried it about, for sometimes for days I would not play upon it; but then would come an hour when above all other useful things the flute alone was a necessity.

[VOYAGING]

U S H U A I A

At the head of a beautiful little bay that opens upon Beagle Channel, isolated by an almost impassable wilderness of mountains from all land communication with the world, stands the town of Ushuaia with its population of some hundreds or a thousand souls, the farthest southern "city" of the world. Overshadowing the town, by its organic importance in the life of the community if not by the vastness of its stone and concrete walls, stands the penitentiary; and from the barred windows of that prison a thousand men look out, during the months or years or lifetimes of their confinement, over the gray, cold, windswept waters of the south, or past a desolation of tin roofs and fire-devastated hills, at mountain barriers more terrible than prison walls. Yet the austerity of the visible world, far from imposing its gloom upon the inmates of the prison and the town, makes the security of their confinement and their small comforts appear as blessings wrung from the vast and pitiless desolation of the encompassing universe. Ushuaia, *because* of its isolation, is a cheerful, friendly place, where the townfolks' simple lives are just as full of gaiety as those of some great capital, and, one may venture, just as barren of real happiness; and where the carefree convicts walk the streets about their work in scarcely guarded freedom.

Into this town we two had tramped, ragged, dirty, and tired, with all the goods we owned upon our backs and nothing in our pockets. And had the people, after staring and smiling at our grotesque appearance, decided to lock us up for mad it would have been less to wonder at than that on perceiving our madness they somehow caught its spirit from us. And when to all who questioned us as to our purpose we replied "Cape Horn," they answered "Crazy! but good for you!"

Most fortuitous of all was our immediate and open-hearted welcome into the house of Martin Lawrence, who, as the first citizen of the town, at once in point of time and wealth and the deserved high character he bore, by his friendship established our respectability in the public eye and opened the wall to all that friendship and credit that was forthcoming to advance our purpose.

Yet still Cape Horn remained not only a purpose to which by our soul's desire and our outward boastfulness we stood committed, but a problem so difficult of solution that it occupied our minds to the exclusion of every other thought. That Ultima Thule of mariners is not, most readers must be told, the southernmost point of the continent of South America, nor of Tierra del Fuego, nor even of some great island nearly adjacent to it. It is the southmost point of a small rock island of a forlorn and isolated group, the Wollastons, and lies, scaled in a straight line, about seventy-five miles southeasterly from Ushuaia. We did not propose, having adventured thus far, to content ourselves with standing on the limit of the shore to gaze off seaward — and yet for that we were completely and exclusively equipped. Yet we could pace that long waterfront and look at the varied craft that lay at anchor in the harbor and discuss which one could serve our purpose best.

There was a tall-masted schooner of American build, a fine-lined vessel of that queenly type that is supreme in its class over everything that sails the seas: she was too big for us to dream of chartering. There was a smaller schooner, a clumsy, serviceable craft: she was provisioning for a sailing voyage. And there was Lawrence's big sloop, the *Garibaldi,* but she was constantly employed in traffic on the coast. One other boat was there, a smaller sloop of about ten tons: she was of the very size we wanted, and she was idle. Upon somehow acquiring her we set our hearts. And that we might in our poverty as well have coveted the yacht of an emperor never, in our fatuous and unreflecting eagerness, occurred to us.

The owner of that much desired craft was one Fortunato Beban, a Croat, a prosperous and enterprising merchant of the place — as prosperity and enterprise were measured there. In company with Martin Lawrence I sought him out. He was a tall, spare man of sixty-five, of forceful and distinguished appearance. His face was tanned and weather-beaten and from the shadow of his yachting cap his pale blue eyes gleamed with the shrewdness of a New Englander. Beban heard my story and considered. Yes, he would rent the boat; the terms he'd have to think about. And although the interview had been friendly enough my heart sank.

We *had* to wait; and with the excuse that Beban's procrastinations afforded I resigned myself to the enjoyment again of such delicious refinements of civilization as clean sheets and comfortable chairs and dainty food, and above all the society of the Lawrence household.

How pleasantly they live in Ushuaia! At evening we would stroll, my host and I, along the hilly streets up to the outskirts of the town and, in the silence that the hour imposed, look over the broad bay and channel to the hills of Navarin and the white mountains of Hoste Island. Then at twilight, while the massed clouds hung still flaming over the darkening steel-blue mountain peaks, we'd enter some quiet, comfortable drinking place and sit conversing for an hour. And Lawrence opened up the past and told me something of his boyhood there in Ooshooia where, in years before the town was built, the flag of England waved above the little mission. He spoke without illusion for, born of missionary parents, the second white child of Tierra del Fuego, he knew the harsh privations of the early missionary's life and understood the sordid humbug of it. Yet his words recalled the fact that the savages had once in thousands peopled those shores that now, thanks chiefly to the pestilence of Christian mercy, were and would forever be a solitude.*

Those days of idleness, of waiting for that mind of Beban, ponderous with craft, to form its pronunciamento, brought me some memorable acquaintances. The house of Don Julio, the barber, whom I early sought, was one of the most attractive and pretentious in the town. It stood upon a little hill and overlooked the bay. I mounted the imposing stairway at the front and rang the bell. A little man of maybe fifty, pallid, sensitive, with large mournful eyes, opened the door — Don Julio. He greeted me with the sweetest courtesy, and, conversing in French, explained that he had been at work in his garden when the bell had rung. His house, in which he lived alone, was beautifully neat and revealed in the little conveniences for housekeeping of the owner's contrivance, in the hideous collection of pictures and souvenirs disposed so lovingly about, an active personal attachment to the place that made its ugliness delightful.

But his own bedroom was one of the world's great wonders. An ornate double bedstead, a miracle in lacquered brass, stood in the central space; an ancient counterpane of yellow satin, wrought in silk and gold with twining morning-glory vines, covered the bed. Over the lace-edged pillow slips were pinned embroidered satin shams, and shadowing these hung velvet curtains from a gilded canopy. Upon the flower-papered walls hung, pitching forward, gilt-framed colored pictures of the love and hate scenes from Italian opera. On stands and scrollwork bracket shelves wonders of porcelain and painted shell rivaled the splendor of the festooned tidies that they stood upon. A crimson-flowered carpet was on the floor, and crimson, gold-edged portieres darkened the still too garish daylight of the lace-curtained window.

---

*A census of the Fuegian Indians compiled in 1883 by the Reverend Thomas Bridges, fifteen years after his establishment in Ushuaia as the first resident missionary, is as follows: Yahgans, 273 men, 314 women, 358 children; Onas, not more than 500; Alakalufs, not more than 1,500; total Fugiana, about 3,000. Ten years earlier, he estimates, the number must have been double. It was a part of the missionary program to segregate the little Yahgan girls in what were called "orphan homes." The orphan home at Ushuaia was a small cabin. The children were packed eight in one room; the window was kept shut; there was no fire. Every day the inmates were taken for a walk, under guard. Mr. Bridges's report in 1883 for a period of three and a half years shows that 38 children were taken care of during that time. Of these, 18 are listed as having died of tuberculosis, 15 are not accounted for, 5 are recorded as living. The missionary remarks in his report that he experiences some difficulty in persuading the mothers to part with their children, as they fear that they will never see them again. Forty years have passed. Mr. Martin Lawrence, of Remilino, estimates the surviving Yahgan population at 60 souls. Mr. William Bridges allows the Onas 56 men and boys, 57 women and girls, 50 little children; 16 half-breeds.

OPPOSITE, TOP: ADMIRALTY SOUND, TIERRA DEL FUEGO, 1922, O/C, 33-1/2 x 43-5/16", THE HERMITAGE

BOTTOM: COVER FOR WILDENSTEIN RETROSPECTIVE EXHIBITION OF THE
PAINTINGS AND DRAWINGS OF ROCKWELL KENT, 1925

And the people went there and admired the high mountains, the wide wastes of the sea and the mighty downward rushing streams, and the ocean, and the course of the stars and forgot themselves.

St. Augustine.

"It's wonderful!" I whispered. And going to the window drew the lace aside and looked out at the world. It was blue daylight, hard and clear; over a few tin roofs stood the concrete walls of the prison; beyond this rose high into the sky the knife-edged mountain ranges.

Don Julio's bedchamber! I peeped into a tiny room or passageway just off the kitchen. There was a narrow iron cot neatly made up, one wooden chair with a shirt and trousers hung over it, nothing more. And here he slept.

Don Julio tied an apron around my neck, put the Barcarolle from *Tales of Hoffmann* on the phonograph, and cut my hair — beautifully. Then he poured me a glass of Benedictine and himself a drop of it for courtesy, proposed "Cape Horn — and back!" and we drank.

"Wait a moment, if you please," he said at parting — and ran into the garden.

He brought me a little bunch of forget-me-nots; and, with these quite foolishly in my hand, I strode out and down the street of the real world.

A town is but the home of men and women, and its spirit can only be read in the lives of those that dwell there. Ushuaia is the resting place of a restless wanderer, Don Julio. His house is the treasury of his memories of the greater world he came from, of love and art, of pride and hope and failure. That state bedchamber is to him the symbol of the pomp he dreamed of and that might have been. Don Julio dusts its grandeur reverently, closes the door — and goes to weep upon his narrow, solitary bed.

Ushuaia is Fortunato Beban, hard and shrewd, making a little fortune for his heirs to spend. It is Martin Lawrence, cultured, intelligent, and cautious — a stabilizer; Ushuaia is old Mr. Feeque, who came there forty years ago to found the town.

This old man, a lean and feeble invalid, with the gentle face of one for whom the passion and activities of life are past, sits forever, deep in a tall-backed upholstered armchair, in a great room encumbered with a huge walnut double bed and a conglomeration of furniture, unwashed dishes, chamber pots, Catholic symbols, and lithograph portraits of the crucified Christ. Gently and very slowly the old man speaks, in cultured English; and his voice becomes at times so faint that one must sit at strained attention. And there is in his manner and appearance a beautiful and touching dignity, and in his speech the sadness of great wisdom.

I bore credentials which I offered him. "I do not need to see these," he said — and I was ashamed.

He loves his country, Tierra del Fuego, and has faith in its development; and he looks back upon past times of helpfulness to younger enterprisers in that land as on a life well spent in the service of a cause.

We drank coffee and cognac together. "Beban — " he shook his head. "Lundberg at Harberton," he counseled me, "is your man for the Horn: and if that fails get Indians and a canoe. It can be done that way if you must do it." . . .

Beban, meanwhile, "considered"; and I waited. My mate lay on his back with a foot so swollen he could hardly stand on it; yet all the time his only worry was our problem of a boat. Lundberg, at Harberton, was forty miles away on Beagle Channel. We were growing desperate.

An old-timer, who had searched the shores of all the islands to the south for gold, said one day, "I'll take you in a *dory* to the Horn."

"Good!" I cried with sudden hope.

He laughed. "Not on your life!" he said.

Despairing of getting a reply from Beban, I had set a day to cross in a small boat of Feeque's to Navarin in search of Indians — it seemed the only thing to do — when, in the stillness of the early morning, I heard the chugging of a motor in the bay. A little sloop came in and tied up at the mole. And it was Lundberg!

[VOYAGING]

ROCKWELL KENT

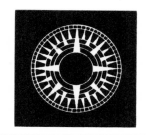

GREENLAND
A.D. 1000 VS. A.D. 1929

That *reason,* meanwhile, occupied itself with the immediate problems of the voyage and fed upon the facts of land and sea and wind as they not only displayed themselves each hour but as their nature, history, and habits were recorded in the pilot guide and chart.

Generally speaking, the hazards of that crossing were actually neither more nor less to us, with our equipment, than they had been to Leif Ericson almost a thousand years before. Our boat was possibly more seaworthy; Leif's was larger. We had only sails; Leif's ship had sails and power; and whether the auxiliary be of motor or of men they must rate alike as factors in safe navigation. We had the compass; Leif the polar star and sun — and all the wisdom of experience and tradition to read them by. They served him well enough. And if against two untried sailors and a sea cook we weigh the thirty-five sea-hardened Norsemen of Leif's ship, we may well choose, if we must cross Davis Strait, to sail with Leif.

Every spring releases from the arctic waters west of Greenland a vast quantity of floe, pack ice, and bergs to be swept southward along the shores of Labrador and Newfoundland. Through June and into July it haunts that coast, crowding the land or carried seaward as the wind blows west or east. It forms throughout its season an impenetrable barrier between Labrador and the open sea.

Down the east coast of Greenland flows a polar current. Rounding Cape Farewell, it flows west and north almost to Godthaab, hugging the shore, jamming that shore with ice from the last of March through August, not only closing the southern ports to navigation but presenting a danger as real as if the reefs and headlands of that coast were floating at the whim of wind and current.

It was our problem to avoid both the Labrador ice and the "storis" — as the Greenland ice is named. And to that end, taking advantage of the free water along the Labrador coast which the recent southwest winds had given us, our course lay north for eighty miles to Round Hill Island; thence north by east for Godthaab. And if the sun would shine by day, and stars and moon through the short hour of the night, if the wind held fair, if ice would only browse in its appointed pastures, then quicker — in view of eternity — than we could say Robinson Crusoe would we be in Godthaab. And so we were. But how!

For we knew, thanks to our charts, exactly — to the minutest contour of the shore and sounding of the waters — where we were going, and exactly — in degrees, minutes, and seconds of latitude and longitude — on which of the 16,600,160,000 intersections of the screen of our earth consciousness lay the very iron ringbolt to which we should, by God's sweet mercy and the Dane's indulgence, tie.

And because in knowing *that* we knew what Leif knew not, we were to him as gods to men.

[N BY E]

ROCKWELL KENT

The motion woke me. Where was I? I remembered. Daylight came but faintly through the fo'c'sle ports, shadowed as they were by the dinghy. My clock showed ten-thirty. How I had slept!

We were rolling violently; a sudden roll, a lurch to starboard. I heard steps on deck, voices, the sound of hawser paying out. Oh, well, we're at anchor; and no one has called. I braced my knees against the sideboard of the bunk; I had need to.

Suddenly we were careened so far that I was almost catapulted onto the floor. I got out, dressed hastily, and opened the door into the cabin. It was broad daylight there. The skipper was in bed.

"She's drifting with both anchors," called the mate from deck.

"Give 'em more rope," answered the skipper.

I reached the ladder. At that moment something rolled us over, far, far down, and held us there; and the green sea came pouring in as if to fill the ship.

"Damn it!" I cried, "and I'd made everything so neat!"

On deck a hurricane; I'd never felt such wind before. The sea was beaten flat, with every wave crest shorn and whipped to smoke; cold spray and the stinging rain drove over us.

I helped the mate. "We'll need the third anchor," I said, and started aft.

The skipper appeared. "Good, get it out," he said. . . . I went below for the last time.

The spare anchor was knocked down and stowed under the coal sacks and provisions in the after hold; it was not easy to come at. Removing the companion ladder, I set to work. Hard work it was, cramped in that narrow space on hands and knees. As I dragged the hundred-pound sacks out onto the cabin floor — always, strangely, careful not to damage anything — I'd look up and see the gray sky through the opening above my head. Then one time, glancing up, I saw the brow of the mountain; and always after that more mountain showed and less sky. And at last the mountainside itself seemed to have moved against the ship and to be towering over it.

I had laid a lighted cigarette carefully upon the chart table; this, as I worked, was always in my mind — that it should not be left to burn the wood. And so, from time to time, I'd move it just a bit. We were so careful of our boat, to mar it in no way!

But all the while I had been shifting goods and moving sacks of coal; so that at last I came to the anchor. It was a large anchor and very heavy. I dragged it out into the cabin.

"Come," I called to the mate, "and help me get this thing on deck." And as I looked up I saw the mate in his yellow oilskins, bright against the near dark mountainside.

"Not much use now," said the mate; but he came down.

It was hard work to lift that anchor up, and we seemed not to be very strong. "I lose my strength from excitement," said the mate. I thought that I did too — but I didn't say so.

We lifted the cumbersome affair head high and tumbled it out into the cockpit. As I started to follow, a great sea lifted us and rolled us over; I hung on, half out of the cabin. And I stared straight at an oncoming wall of rock so near astern it seemed about to crush us. The sea rose high against it, and broke and became churned water that seethed around us. It cradled us and lowered us gently; and the dark land drew quietly away.

Then came another sea that hurled us and the land together. Now for the crash! I thought — and I gripped hard and braced myself against it, and watched the moment — thrilled by its impending horror.

There was no crash — that time. Ever so gently, just as we seemed to draw away again, our sternpost touched the ledge; so lightly touched it that it made no sound, only a little tremor. And the tremor ran through the iron keel and the oak, and through the ribs and planking, and through every bolt and nail, through every fiber of the boat and us. Maybe we had not known that the end had come; now, as if God whispered it, we knew.

So for a third time we were floated back.

OPPOSITE: CHAPTER OPENING ILLUSTRATIONS FROM N BY E, 1930

R O C K W E L L   K E N T

Then, as if the furies of the sea and wind were freed at last to end their coquetry, they lifted us — high, high above the ledge — and dropped us there. And the impact of that shock was only less than those that followed for that half an hour until *Direction* sank.

JULY FIFTEENTH, 10:30 TO 11:00 A.M.: That half an hour! We lay, caught in the angle of a giant step of rock, keel on the tread and starboard side against the riser; held there by wind and sea; held there to lift and pound; to lift so buoyantly on every wave; to drop — crashing our thirteen iron-shod tons on granite. Lift and pound! There the perfection of our ship revealed itself; only, that having struck just once, she ever lived, a ship, to lift and strike again.

A giant sledgehammer striking a granite mountain; a hollow hammer; and within it a man. Picture yourself the man. I stayed below, and was.

See me as Adam; set full blown into that pandemonium of force, his world — of wind, storm, snow, rain, hail, lightning and thunder, earthquake and flood, hunger and cold, and the huge terrifying presence of the unknown — using his little wit toward self-containedness against the too-much of immensity; and quietly — for Adam lived — doing the little first-at-hands one on another in their natural course, thinking but little and reflecting less. Adam and Man; and me in that compacted miniature of man's universe, the cabin of the yacht *Direction* on the rocks of Greenland.

We live less by imagination than despite it.

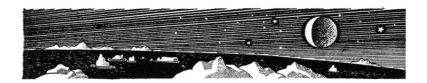

MATCHES: They're in the fo'c'sle cupboard. I get out a lot. Next: keep 'em dry. A big tin on the shelf. Lentils! I pour them out on the floor — no, not all; we don't need all that room for matches. Pack in matches, put on the cover. Good. Now something to put the tin into. Sam's little bag lying there; the very thing! Good neckties and white collars! Out with them!

Put in the tin of matches; add odds and ends of food; close it; that's done. Kerosene: five-gallon tin too big to get ashore. The one-gallon. Buried under stores. Over the coal sacks into the after storage space. God, what a mess! Dig in the stores; dig — and find it. Good! Alcohol for priming: find it — a small bottle. And the primus stove? Crushed on the floor.

There's another in my packsack with pup tent, nest of pots, etc. Under the starboard fo'c'sle bunk. Smothered under spare sails, spare rope, spare clothes, painting supplies. Out with everything. Ha! the sack! Flour, rice, butter, beans, dried soups, coffee, bacon, chocolate, cigarettes: fill up the sack with them. Done.

Chronometers, the beauties! I take them from their boxes and wrap them carefully in layer on layer of clothes. I partly fill a duffel bag with blankets; put in watches; add the sextant, my silver flute, my movie camera, more blankets. And this and all the rest, plus now and then a garment or a blanket, I pass on deck to the mate. Enough! I think with pride.

"Come out of there," calls the mate for the fourth time, peering down into the havoc of that hold. Havoc! It's no-man's-land; a mass of wreckage: doors, drawers, shelves, sheathing, stove lids, pots and pans and crockery, springs, mattresses, tools, beans and butter and books — torn, splintered, crashed, and mashed, lifted and churned and hurled again with every shivering impact of the ship.

Over my writing table in the fo'c'sle, nailed to a timber, was my sweetheart's picture. I had not forgotten it. I will take that picture, I had thought, tuck it for safety next to my skin; and carry it, last thing, ashore with me. Then on my return I'll say, "Look, darling, what I have brought

ABOVE: ILLUSTRATION FROM LEAVES OF GRASS, 1936

ROCKWELL KENT

home!" And I'll take the picture from over my heart and show it to her. And with not so much modesty as to hide my valor I'll tell how in that hour of confusion and terror I had thought of her. And what a fine fellow I shall be!

So I now clambered, somehow, back to the fo'c'sle; found her image looking out serenely over the carnage; took her down and tucked her next to me; put an envelope containing my money, my passport, and my permit to land in Greenland next to me too; and — wading, climbing, dodging, holding on for dear life — made my way out and to the deck.

THE MATE, working like ten stevedores, was getting things to shore. It was not far: a jump from deck to rocks, jump on a rising sea and scramble out of it and up before that step of rock was flooded. Hurling a sack, he'd follow it; clutch it and drag it to the safety of a higher ledge.

The sack containing the chronometers rolled back into the water. It was retrieved intact. Some things, washed from the rocks, were lost. The tide was littered with our gear and goods.

The thrashing of the main boom added confusion to the deck. Only the too stout standing rigging saved the mast.

The skipper was on shore desperately struggling to secure a masthead line to a great boulder. Finished on board, I leaped to help him. The yawing masthead tore the line away from us each time we'd nearly made it fast. But once as the mast leant far down toward us we got two turns of line around the rock; we braced ourselves and held. The three-inch cable snapped like grocer's twine!

Direction's end was near. Quickly undoing the sack, I got out the movie camera. Listen! Even above the noise of sea and wind and rain I hear for a short minute its small whirring like the beating of a heart. And by that sound, what happened there, in Karajak Fjord in Greenland, at eleven in the morning of July 15, 1929, achieved soundless immortality.

[N BY E]

NEW YORK BREWER & WARREN 1930

TITLE PAGE SPREAD FROM N BY E (TRADE EDITION), BREWER & WARREN, 1930

ROCKWELL KENT

HOME WITH SALAMINA

The house that we have come to, with the family, is small: one room. There is a sleeping platform in an alcove, and over it a trapdoor to a low and narrow loft. There's a low cellar underneath; there had to be, on that side hill. It proved as cold in wintertime as all outdoors. I hadn't planned that house for family life, and when I'd signed on Salamina and her brood in Umanak, I'd thought to add a room, and told her so.

But one night, soon after we had all returned, as I was sitting there drawing, and Salamina sewing, and the children — there were only two, she'd left one child behind — the two children asleep in bed, Salamina, lowering her work, looked up and said, "Why do you build another room? One room is quite enough." And I, thrilled at escaping all that work — I had a shed and a storehouse still to build — said, "Good! we'll go on as we are." So far, one thing alone had troubled her: my sleeping on the floor. She was in all respects, I was to learn, a stickler for propriety; she cared what people said. The master's sleeping on the floor reflected, she contended, on her credit. She wept at my insistence. I told her that in America men always gave their seats to women — and offered them their beds.

So lived we four, for weeks; until Frederick, the elder child, aged maybe eight, was taken to the sanitarium in Umanak: incipient T.B. That left us three. Two, I might almost say: that little mouselike, silent, five-year-old Helena, one rarely heard a whisper from her lips, never a cry. She answered yes by arching up her brows, and no by wrinkling her small nose. That is the Greenland way. She'd sit an hour on the platform edge without a movement or a sound. A sweet, round, healthy little child, her playground was outdoors. She kept what hours she pleased, did as she pleased — except when, rarely, given an order. Then she obeyed, at once, implicitly. She was never punished; Greenlanders don't punish children. Is it in consequence of this that Greenland children are so good?

To Salamina I relinquished all the cares of housekeeping, except — this brought contention — instruction in the art of cooking. She knew a little that she'd picked up here and there; that little made the trouble. She was glad to be shown things that she knew nothing about — such as how to make baked beans or cook spaghetti with tomato sauce — but she didn't like my criticism of her bread nor being told her sauce had lumps. When she would listen, she was quick to learn, but having learned she didn't like man's meddling in affairs that were, she held, exclusively a woman's. And over bread-making we had unbelievable scenes. I'd show her how: I'd mix the yeast, the sourdough, and ripen it. She'd never worked with sourdough before. I'd mix and knead the bread. I'd fix it for the night, tuck it up warm against all drafts. I'd work it into loaves and stand the loaves to rise. She'd watch me scornfully. And the minute I'd be out of sight she'd pop the half-risen bread into a half-ready oven, and ruin all. Again I'd make the bread — to have it again ruined by her defiant disobedience. Once, having set the loaves to rise and strictly ordered her to lay no hand on them, I flew into such a fury at her putting them ten minutes later into the oven that I pulled them out again and hurled the lot outdoors. That tamed her for the moment; she left the house in tears. I made and baked new bread. It turned out — God be praised! — perfection. That settled things. And now Salamina, using old-time sourdough — she swears by it — makes the only first-class A-1 white bread that I've tasted in North Greenland. If you're going to do a thing, you'd better do it well.

ABOVE: ILLUSTRATION FROM <u>N BY E</u>, 1930

OPPOSITE: AND <u>THIS</u> — IS ANNA,
ILLUSTRATION FROM <u>SALAMINA</u>, 1935

ROCKWELL KENT

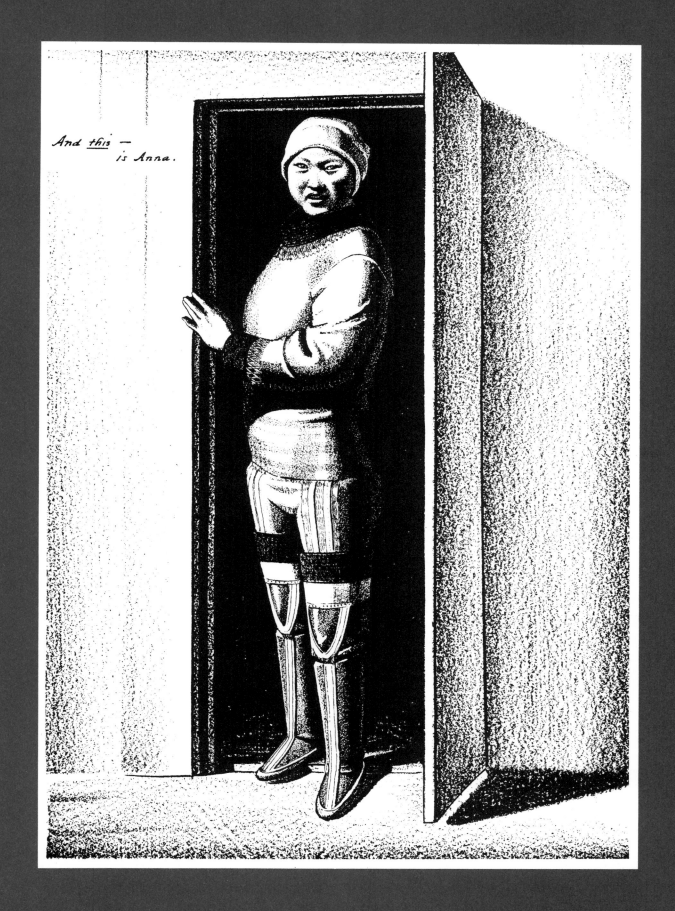

And *this* —
is Anna.

That might, in fact, be Salamina's motto. She did things well and took great pride in it. If my kamiks were not well cut and made, my anoraks — the hooded cotton shirts that all men wear in Greenland — not exactly right in cut and fit, and *clean,* if the house was not always in order and the floor and benches scrubbed, she held it to be a reflection upon *her.* "What will people think of *me?*" she'd say. She was of incorruptible integrity in her craftsmanship. She was a kifak, to be sure, an employee; but not to be employed except to do things well.

And she was more than that, took more than mere employment on herself. She made herself the mistress of the house. In the absence of another woman there, that was, to her, her right, responsibility, and privilege. Her immediate and ruthless disposal of Anna was but the first act of cleaning our *her* house. No interlopers should be there; she'd have no carrying over of old debts or old encumbrances. Or did she sense that I *liked* Anna?

That too was her concern. The house, the home, and me: the lot, as one, the woman's chattel — hers. Liberty in the choice of friends and guests, in choice of whom I'd greet on promenade, or promenade with, liberty in general which I had so taken for granted as not even to have thought of it, was suddenly made something to aspire to, to scheme toward, assert. It was, to put it mildly, disconcerting for one who liked in general the conducting of himself to find himself a chattel of the house, pursued, dogged, watched, and spied upon, whenever he was pleased to stroll abroad. That we should attend each other when invited out to kaffemiks, or on evening calls upon our mutual friends, was natural enough; and I was as punctilious in the observance of established social conduct as she, my social sponsor, was herself. Then, too, we strolled together — sometimes; *always* was what got me. The inevitability of her dear company on *every* stroll, of her constraining company. For let me but address myself — address? smile, *look* — at any human creature but a male or a babe in arms or a woman over sixty, and at a look from Her they'd flee. She had strong character; all knew that, felt its force. They visited their fear of her on me; my friends avoided me. Escape! There was one loophole to a week of freedom: a plan I'd made with Anna and Johann.

[SALAMINA]

ILLUSTRATION FROM N BY E, 1930

ROCKWELL KENT

SALAMINA

[Saturday, August 29, 1931] Salamina chose last night to have a little party — inviting Stjernebo, Anina and Helena, in my name. They came all dressed up, greatly to my astonishment, for I'd hardly understood even that they were coming. But Salamina had made the house clean and tidy, put up the curtains, spread the new oilcloth tablecloth, polished the elegant, brass seal-oil student lamp and filled it. The floor was, of course, scrubbed; the pots scoured till they shone — oh, everything was done to make the whole place right. Then came along the guests — Anina in a new secondhand outfit that became her well for, praise God, she concealed her silly bowlegs in kamiks [native boots]. Helena was entrancing in her Greenland things, with red predominating. Her round cheeks shone like apples, her tiny nose had — as it always has — little pearls of sweat upon it; the dark down above her upper lip like a shadow made her curved red lips stand out even more provokingly; her innocent round black eyes glistened in their setting of dark lashes. And her black hair hung in two heavy braids to her waist. Especially was it nice when the lamp, for the first time, was lighted. There, at last, was the house adorned and illuminated, with dressed-up guests drinking coffee about the garnished table. And Salamina, mistress of it all, presiding! . . .

It was the night before that brought the event. I had gone to bed and Salamina was out. Coming home, she undressed in the dark. I called her to me. She came under the covers and nestled close. She resisted my advances, yielding when I desisted. Then at last, against the mildest show of protest, I had my way. And Salamina revealed herself to be affectionately warm, taking an elemental satisfaction in being possessed by a man, but revealing not one quiver, note, or sign of passion.

And now today Salamina is all ardor. It would all be ridiculous if it did not all appear so childlike on the part of S., and so charming.

[GREENLAND JOURNAL]

ABOVE: ILLUSTRATION FROM "SKAAL SALAMINA!,"
ESQUIRE MAGAZINE, AUGUST 1934

ROCKWELL KENT

And though she has had to
wait till winter time, she
has found it.

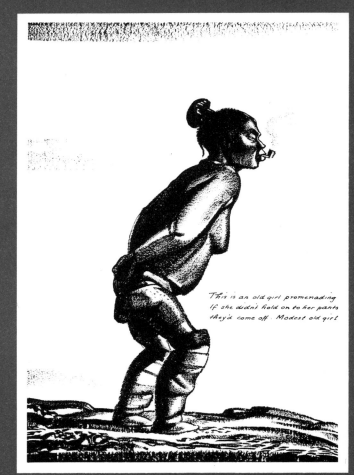

This is an old girl promenading.
If she didn't hold on to her pants
they'd come off. Modest old girl.

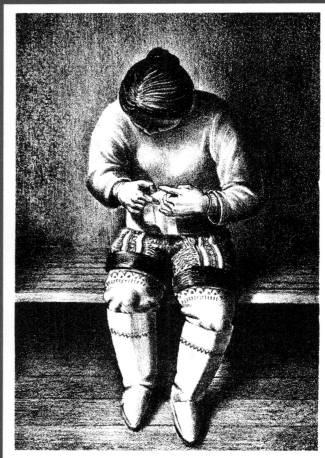

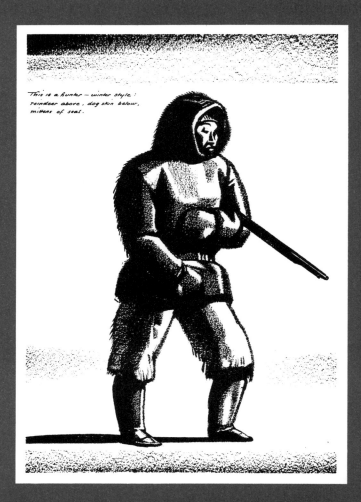

This is a hunter — winter style:
reindeer above, dog skin below,
mittens of seal.

IGDLORSSUIT

[October 23, 1931] As I look over the settlement from my window, Igdlorssuit is like a stage upon which the epic drama of the lives of these people deploys unendingly. There, seen in sunlight and in shadow, rain and snow, wind and calm, day and night, as if responsive to the elements and hours that bestow their mood upon each day and hour of the drama, the people come out of their houses and in all the perfection of entire artlessness perform their parts. Nor does the drama ever halt or wane in interest, nor for a moment, even, leave the stage unoccupied. And if the interest is sustained at no high pitch, that is only in keeping with the eternal duration of the play; it may not change its even pitch or pace lest change lead to an end. It is an *epic* drama in that it is at once local and universal. Its elements are the essentials of all human life presented here as though this were Bayreuth or Oberammergau, colored and costumed in the conventions of this unique and special culture as though that culture through its character of unrestraint were best fitted for self-revelation and as though the place, the climate warm and bitter cold, and all that natural environment out of which the culture has matured, would best cause man to act the part of man.

The front part of the stage is the land: the settlement of Igdlorssuit and the broad smooth crescent of the strand that reaches right and left to the lookout head and the mountain that like two wings shut off the backstage world from view. From behind these wings enters from time to time the unexpected; a boat from Umanak or north or anywhere — always a great event that stops all lesser actions on the stage and at the cry *"Umiatsiaq!"* or *"Pujortulêraq!"* (a boat! a motorboat!), picked up and swelled by every throat, brings people running out of every house, stops work, calls in the scattered fuel gatherers, the strollers, lover pairs, brings in every living thing — men, women, old and young, children and babes in arms, and dogs — down to the shore; and groups them there by that first principle of art, one thought. Or maybe the cry is *"Umiâr!"* or *"Umiârtorpoq!"* — and then bears in impressively the great, high-sided skin boat of the Eskimos, stately and slow, with even, rhythmic dipping of its paddle oars as tireless women oarsmen raise their bodies to each stroke. Slowly it comes, a laden freighter. Whole families are there with all that they possess of children, household goods, tents, feather beds, pots, kettles; nets, implements, and dogs; kayaks are lashed to the gunwale or towed astern. And at the steering oar, high up on a mound of goods, sprawls the skipper, owner, leader, family head. But most often there appears a kayaker, empty-handed maybe after hours away; a bird or two perhaps. And only now and then a seal.

But are these workaday happenings all? What else goes on? It is Sunday night. All day intermittently the snow has been gently falling — floating downward, it seemed, to lay itself most gently over all the world. Calm it has been and still. And now that it is night the stillness and the calm are absolute. And it has cleared and from a sky veiled with soft clouds the full moon shines, illuminating the white world with somber brightness. Whiter than snow appear the moonlit mountains; and the shadows are luminous with the reflected light of the white universe. By ones and twos the young people have come out to stroll along the shore. And gradually the little groups, meeting along the pathway on the strand, have joined. Then some begin to sing, then all. And now a great band, young men and boys and mostly girls, walk in broad ranks together, arm in arm. And their voices heard in harmony are as beautiful as the night itself, and, like the moonlight, clear and sweet.

OPPOSITE: TOP, LEFT AND RIGHT; BOTTOM, RIGHT: ILLUSTRATIONS FROM
SALAMINA, 1935; BOTTOM, LEFT: YOUNG SEAMSTRESS,
1962, OFFSET VERSION OF LITHOGRAPH ON STONE

ABOVE: VIEW FROM IGDLORSSUIT, FROM GREENLAND JOURNAL, 1962

Early this morning the clouds lifted like a curtain rolling up. It was all gray at first. And then as the lower mountains showed themselves, the color-reflected dawn crept over them, and they were bright with it. Then all at once a shaft of the true sunlight shot somehow through the ceiling of clouds and fell upon a far-off, snow-white mountain peak. And by the splendor of that, all that had seemed bright before was now as though in shadow. All day the cloud curtain hung suspended just below the height of the higher mountain peaks. Night was its cue to lift. And sometimes all between was visible and clear, and sometimes the falling snow shut out the world. The sea was motionless but for the tide. This bore the innumerable little icebergs past in unending procession. They are like Lohengrin's swan boat, I thought.

As a flower is sometimes described as so beautiful that it looks like wax, so have I described the region of sea and mountains surrounding Igdlorssuit in terms of canvas, compo board, and paint. Yet the reduction of the infinite to terms of human comprehension is all that art and science ever can achieve or try. That, in recognition of the limitations of human faculties, is the function of art and science.

[GREENLAND JOURNAL]

NORTHERN NIGHT, 1930, WOOD ENGRAVING ON MAPLE, 5-9/16 x 8-1/8″

ROCKWELL KENT

It is my belief that advances in the study of evolution will eventually demand that, for the proper explanation of the many coexistent differences and likenesses between isolated races of mankind, environment must be distinguished as a trinity, and we may as follows name its parts, and qualify them: the Local — climate, resources, and manner of life — by which man's physical attributes are affected; the Incidental — the exigencies of daily life under the limitations of the various cultures and their resources — by which character is formed; and the Cosmic — the aesthetic aspects of physical law — by which man's sensory organism is determined. Take this hypothesis, or leave it; facts are our concern. To the recorded evidence of Salamina's sensibilities, and Martin's, let me add that the Greenland people's taste in the combining of colors, their feeling for harmony in music (they use our scale today), their sense of flavor in foods (disregarding prejudice as to its form and nature), their sense of what smells good and what feels nice are like our own. Their quiet voices, their gentle, noiseless ways, their abstinence from quarreling: these are degrees of sensibility that we may envy them. Environment so peaceful *should* breed quietness; environment so beautiful *must* tune man's nature toward itself. Outdoors — I've told of that — is more to them in Greenland than to us. They nearly are — we've coined the term ourselves — a nature folk.

Character is another matter. It is largely the antithesis of sensibility; it disciplines it, keeps its carefree self-indulgence within bounds: a killjoy role. I have hoped, in this story of Greenland, to avoid overstressing the hardships of the life of the Greenland hunter. His land — the frozen North; his element — the sea; its risks — storm, ice, the hazards of the hunt: these are enough to send a shiver through the spine. To play them up would be to melodramatize the North, and to falsify completely the truth that they are undramatic everyday to Greenlanders. The hunter takes his risks, endures his hardships, easily. That's character.

To have to get up out of a warm bed — he likes warm beds and has one — and, breakfastless, in the darkness and the bitter cold of a January morning, lift his kayak upon his head, carry it across a mile or two of rough ice to the open water, launch it there, and paddle out to where at the first streak of the day's twilight seals may come; to stay there hours on end, be cold, get frozen cheeks and wrists; no factory whistle, time clock, boss: to *will* that of yourself and do it, day succeeding day, makes character. They're men, strong men, inured to hardship and hard times, to working on their own, to shifting for themselves. They've needed no Lycurgus for their laws; necessity imposes them. They are heroic men, and I'll venture that there are more Danish Royal Diplomas for exceptional bravery framed on the walls of the turf houses of the peaceful fifteen thousand Greenlanders than we can show of Congressional Medals among millions.

But now that we have set the Greenlanders upon a pinnacle, let us climb up there ourselves and, finding it perhaps crowded, push a few of them off. The Greenlanders are good men: they endure hardships uncomplainingly, stand exposure, hard work, hunger, cold, mosquitoes. And so can we. In the high temperature of the foundry of the Ford works at Detroit, they employ mostly Negroes: it has been found that they endure the heat better than white men. That may be race, or Southern cotton fields. A Negro stood with Peary at the Pole. It used to be said that Eskimos could not long survive a temperate climate. That is sheer nonsense; plenty live in Denmark. It is popularly thought that Eskimos don't *feel* the cold as we do: that too is probably a myth. At any rate, their fat cheeks aren't an asset; they freeze while our lean jowls stay warm. And almost pure white Greenlanders work side by side with those almost pure Eskimo. They're no bit better, but they're just as good. A white man

ABOVE: DRAWING FOR DUST JACKET FOR "A GREENLAND LETTER"
(LATER PUBLISHED AS S<small>ALAMINA</small>), PRINCETON UNIVERSITY LIBRARY

if he *will* can stand most anything. And like it. Doubt it? My son, of whom I have spoken, aged fourteen (I am now writing of 1935), accompanied the post to Umanak in February. They attempted one route and, encountering thin ice, were compelled to take another, the land passage at the head of Kangerdlugssuak. Conditions were bad: on the sea ice, they broke through the covering of snow into water; on the land, they found deep snow and heavy drifts. The passage overland that takes normally from two to three hours occupied them most of two days. It took them four days to reach Umanak; and two nights were spent in the open. The days and nights were the coldest of the winter, the temperature falling to between 35 and 40 degrees below zero. Two of the Greenlanders — there were, all told, four in the party — wore reindeer garments. The boy wouldn't take his with him: "Too hot," he said. All four slept sitting up in the boy's three-by-six-foot sledge tent. The boy got his nose frostbitten, the Greenlanders all froze their cheeks and noses, and one went lame from strain ("water on the knee"). The boy arrived home in perfect shape and fine spirits. "It was fun."

These Greenlanders whom I have praised so much are not, remember, moral or romantic; and the affecting friendship and gratitude of a few friends may not be taken as characteristic of the people. For what one does for them the masses are not grateful. To begin with, they don't understand why Europeans should be rich while they are poor; why *anyone* should have a lot of property when others haven't. (I tried explaining it, but got mixed up.) In times of scarcity, when one is fortunate he shares his meat around the settlement. All share in it by ancient communistic right; and no one thanks the giver. When I hand around a hundred dollars' worth of stuff at Christmas, few say thank you; and most of those don't mean it. They know it flatters us: they're skillful flatterers.

It is hard to tell just what they think of us; they are secretive with the European. They respect ability as it is shown in work; they don't call adding figures work. And they don't appreciate that the fatiguing nature of "brainwork" entitles men to an enormous wage and the privilege of lying in bed. (I didn't try explaining that.) They've mostly never seen a white man lift his hand. They don't respect us and, I think, don't like us.

When you buy from a Greenlander, he won't mention the price. "These simple, trusting, childlike people!" says the tourist. Simple as Satan; trusting as a banker; childlike as Henry Ford. Try bidding low: they'll catch you up on that. They want the limit that your ignorance will yield. The Danes, we learn, encourage them in that. And let the visitor be Santa Claus himself — most visitors play Santa — on high advice they'll soak him in a trade. "The Director has told us," say the Greenlanders, "that we should charge outsiders thirty kroner for a dog, but not the Danes." Ten kroner is the price. Sweet business principles! They'll flatter to an end, they'll cheat on price; they lie.

In the fall of '34, Peter, of my Three Musketeers, was lost at sea. They found his kayak later, torn to shreds. Only a walrus, it is thought, could have done it. At Christmastime, Amalia, Peter's sister, comes with a present: it is an anorak, a secondhand one neatly pressed. "It was Peter's," says Amalia almost tearfully. "We've kept it for you." It was a pleated anorak such as the dainty Olabi makes for himself. She had bought it off him for a pittance only the day before. They think *we're* children.

They steal. Through the generosity of an American woman, I came in '34 with fifty pounds of coffee, to be given to the people of Igdlorssuit. At the general kaffemik in the dance house at which the coffee was distributed, I left my cup, for just a moment, standing on the table. It was stolen. A young woman whom I had brought in my boat from Söndre Upernivik to visit relatives at Igdlorssuit, and fed and treated well en route, next night was reaching through my cellar window stealing canned goods. My friend Boye, the young hunter, while a guest at dinner at my house, loaded his pockets with my cigars. I saw the bulging pockets, guessed the fact. "Come out with me," I said to Boye. We stood outside together in the dark. "Let's have them, the cigars," I said. There was a moment's pause. Then Boye brought them out and gave them to me. "Thank you," I said. "No, wait," said Boye, "there are more." He gave me more. "Still more," he said. "And cigarettes." I put the lot into my

ROCKWELL KENT

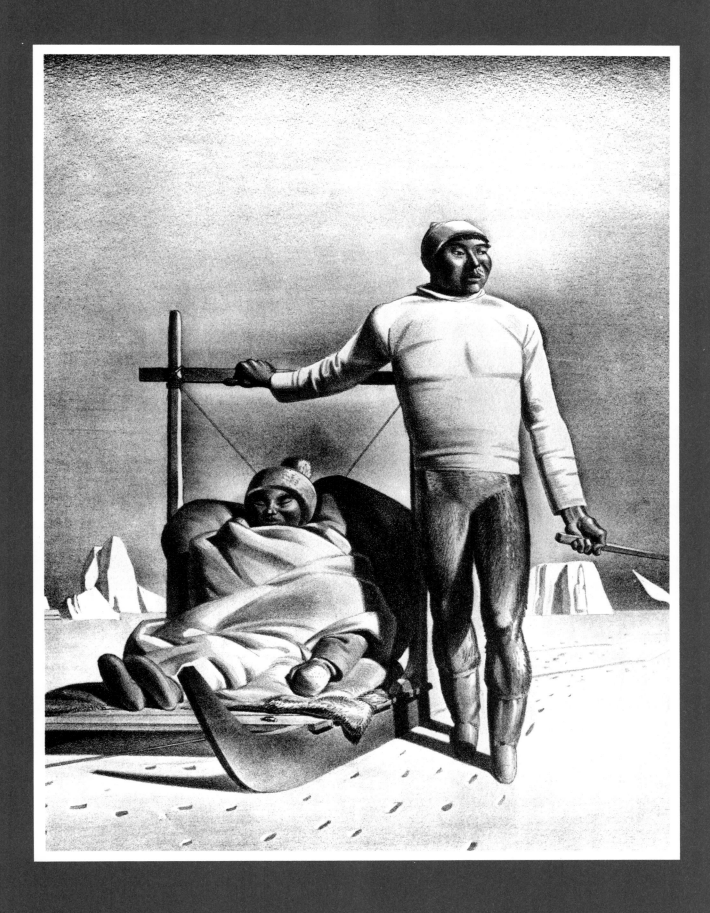

pockets; that was ended. "Now, Boye," I said, "would you like some cigars? Here are cigars, take them, they're for you. I give them to you." Boye was hit. "No, no," he said, "I can't. I am bad. Yes, I am bad. It was Sahra who told me to take them." (I didn't doubt it in the least.) "No, I can't take them." I forced them on him. As Boye left for home that night, he drew me to one side outdoors. He said, "Here, take these. I can't keep them. I am bad." "No, you are good," I said. "Good night." Two or three times, coal was stolen from my bin; it stood outdoors. Someone entered my meat shed once and took a small piece of white-whale meat. One tent pole (it would make a good pike handle) was taken from a pile of such things. That, in more than two years' time, is all.

Greenlanders' guile is artless, unprofessional; a class to prey upon is new to them. But we have come, we whites; and to a lot of them we're only prey. Potbellied clerks, or measuring worms that crawl about their hills, or putterers with paint: how can we qualify as much to them? Why should they in their hearts feel more respect for us than self-respecting workmen feel for nitwit bankers' sons? They have their pride.

[SALAMINA]

BELATED RUMOR

[October 23, 1931] Two nights ago the rumor got about that I was to meet Cornelia in the loft of the church at nine o'clock. There was, it seems, wild excitement, and people rushed to tell the catechist. The catechist was outraged at the proposed desecration of the church. He'd lock the door at once. Thereupon Salamina, immediately satisfied, came running home. What she expected to find there, of me, I can't guess, for it was about nine when she came in. Doubtless to await my chagrined and crestfallen homecoming. But, while the catechist and innumerable men, women, and children gathered about in every nook and hiding place that the not too dark night afforded, to watch the rendezvous, there sat I quietly at home reading. Nor did I stir to keep my rumored tryst. The whole story of the planned tryst was completely false. The hour for it was eight o'clock — not nine; we'd met and passed a happy while together and, with Cornelia pocketing a package of cigarettes, parted mutually gratified. But the church is now locked at night — which is certainly more bother for the catechist than for me.

[GREENLAND JOURNAL]

OPPOSITE, TOP: TASSIUSAK, 1932–33, O/C ON WOOD, 25-3/4 x 46-3/8", THE HERMITAGE

BOTTOM: GREENLANDERS, C. 1932, O/C, 20 x 24", COLLECTION OF IRVING AND SHELLY CANTON

ABOVE: PENCIL STUDY FOR THE ARTIST IN GREENLAND, C. 1935,
COLLECTION OF SALLY KENT GORTON

CULTURE OR CIVILIZATION?

The work that I am reading on the culture of the western Eskimo (Bureau of American Ethnology report), with its minute description and picturing of innumerable products of their handiwork, leads me to reflect upon that aspect of culture among the people of Igdlorssuit. First as to what they possess. The average house has: 1 kayak, 1 harpoon, 1 lance, and miscellaneous accessories, 1 gun, 1 dogsled, a whip, 6 to 12 dogs; clothes for the man — 2 pair trousers, 3 anoraks, a timiak, 2 pair kamiks, 1 half jacket (for kayak), 1 pair sealskin mittens, a cap, underwear — possibly socks; for the woman — 2 or 3 anoraks, 2 pair pants, 2 pair kamiks, a worsted cap, wristlets, underwear, mittens. They have a couple of dogskins, a small amount of cotton-covered feather bedding. A kettle, a pot, a chamber pot (of course!), a cup, a spoon, a woman's knife, a pocketknife, a chest, a table, a stove, two or three very cheap brooches, a tin cracker box, a tin can or two, and a soapstone lamp. Of all these things, only the kayak with its accessories, the sledge, the whip, the woman's pants, one pair of the man's, the chest and table, the kamiks, the timiak, and the half jacket are indigenous products. The anoraks, of European cotton, are sewn by the women. The rest of all that little stuff is European. The western Eskimo had, at the time of the report that I'm reading, innumerable utensils and tools and weapons — all, without exception, of native manufacture. Most of them are made of hard materials such as stone, bone, or ivory that must have required countless hours of patient work to shape — for not only are they shaped to their end but often extended into the field of art both in form and in the elaborate decoration of their surfaces (and all with primitive tools!). Moreover every article of apparel was made by hand out of the skins that the hunter procured, or woven out of grass. And the articles of adornment, that were many, were exclusively of native make. Now if one should lay the lives of the western Eskimo and the Greenlander of today side by side, one would find them almost identical in respect to hunting and housekeeping, and then where the primitive Eskimo continues with innumerable activities in the arts and crafts, the Greenlander does nothing. And there, in having taken away from the Greenlander the incentive, the need, to fill his time with profitable and absorbing work, is where the European has most sinned. If there has been, in Greenland, a disintegration of culture and in racial character, its cause is not Christianity but commerce. One must fully realize what thousands of hours in the lifetimes of primitive folk must have been devoted to the fashioning of articles of use and adornment to appreciate the void that is left in their lives when, as though suddenly, the whole incentive for such work is removed. And one must measure the effect upon them of this annihilation of industry, not only in terms of the demoralizing effect of idleness but in terms of a positive loss to them of their whole creative activity. That was no ordinary activity; not one to be compared to the majority of those that our civilization offers. I will content myself with merely asserting that the devising and making of individual useful articles because they are needed, and the fashioning of them into such lines of beauty as the fancy may dictate, is an activity of an infinitely higher order than being a clerk, salesman, bank president, day laborer, servant, mill hand, chauffeur, tradesman, or being occupied with any of the regular rank-and-file vocations of our civilization. Measured merely by its effect upon the individual, it is only to be compared to our arts and sciences, and it has the advantage over them spiritually of being unprofessionalized. The early missionaries to Greenland made it their first business to abolish, often by violence, those ancient festivals of dance and song that were so important in the social life of the pagan Greenlanders. And it has been felt by later observers of Greenland life that in that abolition lay the cause of most of the lassitude of the present-day Greenlanders. But lives are not sustained by anticipation, nor by occasional happinesses. It *is* unfortunate that there can occur now no event in the life of a Greenlander more exciting than drinking coffee at a neighbor's house or the uninspired singing of uninspired Protestant hymns in a cold and cheerless church on sunlit Sunday mornings. But the real

ROCKWELL KENT

tragedy is that in the innumerable hours when men are not hunting, hours that mount to days and weeks and months throughout each year, they have absolutely nothing to do. And it's all very fine for us who have behind us the tradition of property accumulation to say, "Build up your homes, work, save to buy things for your houses!" They have before them the example of Stjernebo [the Danish trader] and his museum of useless stuff, and of two or more women and a boy endlessly polishing brass and silver, scrubbing, washing, dusting chairs that no one has sat upon, pictures that no one has looked at, horrid knickknacks and the tidies they rest on to protect a tabletop that's never used or seen. Having apparently an ineradicable common sense, they're just not interested.

The Greenlander has been started along the road that should lead to what we call civilization. With the first step, he entered the field of commerce and left behind him forever his entire previous activity in the arts and crafts. Our civilization will at last offer him an education, employment in business or industry, money and the things that money can buy — including, of course, machine-made things to take the place of everything his people used to make. And it will never give him, probably, the slightest chance to work at anything comparable to that making of beautiful things out of stone and ivory that his forebears practiced. Now we may leave the definition and discussion of civilization to college professors: none of us care much whether we're called civilized or not. The quality of our humanity is another and infinitely more important thing; it is the one common factor of every equation of happiness. And if it shall appear that the environment and conditions of a culture different from our own are more favorable to the maturing of fine natures, let us, without bothering to call it relatively savage or barbarian, frankly call it good. We are, it is to be feared, hopelessly prejudiced and academic in our consideration of alien cultures. Education, Christianity, cleanliness, industry, property, efficiency, etc., are to us the components of civilization, and civilization is absolute. A number of great men have come up from the gutter, and *because* of the gutter. If it could be shown that everyone who amounted to anything had risen from such environment, would we abolish schools? Certainly not. "Of course I don't believe in religion," says the average man. "But I think my children ought to go to church." There's little, however, that we *can* do about it, for we're all swept along by the current of Western civilization. But in regard to other peoples we can, at least, try to keep our hands off. And I suspect that if the Danes *really* loved the still primitive east Greenlanders they'd move out bag and baggage and leave what still is well enough alone.

[GREENLAND JOURNAL]

GREENLAND HILLS AND MOUNTAINS, 1931, LITHOGRAPH ON STONE, 10-1/2 x 15-3/4"

ROCKWELL KENT

PAINTING IN THE ARCTIC

Let us assume that you are dressed as I am; you're wearing ordinary woolen underwear and woolen socks (you see, the Greenlanders have long ago abandoned the more primitive and doubtless warmer caribou underwear of their forefathers); you're shod in sealskin, knee-high kamiks with their inner dog-fur socks; you have on windproof sealskin trousers, a heavy Faeroe Island sweater; and over it — no, don't put on that reindeer parka; you'd smother in it — just a fairly wind-resistant, cotton anorak with a hood to keep the wind from the back of your neck; a heavy woolen toboggan cap, and good warm mittens. You see, it isn't cold; here in the shadow it's only 20 degrees below freezing; and when we get out into the sun it will be warm. Good: now you're dressed; come help me pull the sledge down from its rack. You know I put it there to keep it from the dogs: they'd chew its rawhide lacings. I see you're interested in the sledge: yes, it's quite different from the Alaskan type, being adapted to travel on the usually smooth plain of the frozen fjords. My sledge happens to be about nine feet long and three feet wide, five and a half feet of its length being covered by broad slats to make a platform. But see how I've adapted the two stanchions and their crossbar at the rear: they form my easel. I fix my big canvas to it before I start, placing it, as you'll notice, so that while I paint I'll be sitting on this warm reindeer skin that covers the platform. Now for my bag of paints and brushes: just hang them on the stanchion; and lay the palette in its box anywhere that will be out of our way when we're aboard. Now for the dogs.

Generally we have no trouble catching them; they stay around the house. I think they like to go on trips. Here's one: I'll slip this bit of rawhide harness over his head so that it fits across his chest, over his shoulders, and around his forelegs; the long, single trace is, as you see, attached to it. When we've put them all in harness, we'll gather up the separate traces and, bunching them, tie them to the — what shall we call it? — this ten-foot, heavy rawhide loop that is attached to the end of the platform. All ready now? Jump on. And away we go, lickety-split downhill to the shore, with me hanging on to the stanchions from behind and digging in my heels to try and slow us up a bit. Down to the shore and over the edge of the three-foot shelf of ice the tide has left, crash bang down onto the level snow-covered plain. I jump aboard. "Eu, eu!" I cry and tap my whipstock on my boot. We're off! And whether we drive a mile or two along the shore of our island, or cross the ten-mile-wide fjord or sound and, pushing on, explore the narrow mountain-walled fjords that lead to glaciers and the inland ice, is up to us. The dogs, well fed, well trained, and, let us hope, well driven, are game for anything. And on the wind-packed snow they only break their trot to gallop. But we have come to paint; and arriving at a spot where, let us say, a turquoise and pale emerald iceberg stands silhouetted against the rich-hued, deep-toned land, I halt the dogs, move my sledge-easel with its mounted canvas into position, squeeze out my colors, and am ready to begin.

I am sorry, my dear friend and guest, at not having been able to take you on one of my painting trips of several days' duration. When, with food along for dog and man, I'd camp in one place or another as suited my work and my convenience, cooking and sleeping and spending leisure hours in the little sledge tent I had contrived. In less than half a minute after arriving at a campsite the tent would be up, the primus roaring, and I'd be at home. But the three-by-six-foot house is only big enough for one.

[IT'S ME O LORD]

ROCKWELL KENT

DRAWN SHADES

Love, as *we* understand it, as we, fabricators throughout the centuries of the now top-heavy structure of romantic love, have made ourselves believe it to be, is all but unknown in Greenland. It is as though the interdependence of the sexes both for the satisfaction of their sexual appetites and for the performance of the routine of living had left no need for the romantic stimulant. They fornicate: they like to. They mate: they have to. And mutual possessiveness with its attendant jealousy, which is virulent in Greenland, only appears as a safeguard of the economic partnership and of its biological result, the family. In studying a transitional civilization like that of Greenland one must be careful to distinguish between indigenous traits and those which show imported influence. Between the highly Europeanized family of a Greenland pastor and the family of an outpost hunter there is the blending of the two in all degrees. It is, however, with the immediate transitional moment that we are concerned; our subject is the hybrid people, hybrid culture, of today. Two hundred years of missionary work and trade prosecuted with energy, and backed by the prestige of economic, social, and cultural superiority: they worship the Holy Trinity and accept the precepts of Christ; they read and write; they deal in money and exchange; they have their legislators and their written laws. Two hundred years: and they're not moral yet. I think that few of them have ever felt for anything they've done the torturings of conscience. They function, and don't agonize. If one steals, it is but one's appropriation to his own use of another's property — his meat, his chunk of coal, his wife — that then and there is wanted. It is done secretly through fear. They fear — both punishment and ridicule. And the ridiculous calisthenics of love are practiced secretly. The *fact* is not ridiculous: they tell about it — afterward. It is possible that if the promiscuity of the unmarried were more fruitful, there would long ago have been developed a taboo against it. It is far from fruitful. And to forestall some ponderous explanation of so strange a fact let me here hazard that girls' breeches are its cause. Let speculation start with that.

Jealousy, the fear of losing to another what is ours, is so closely woven into the fabric of romantic love that only those of us who don't much care, or who are preternaturally wise and self-controlled, are free of it. In Greenland life, its sordid nature stands exposed, and none are free. Its object is the establishment, of which the man and woman are to each other the personification. With allowance for temperament, it is proportioned to what is risked. And whether in the establishment, native or foreign, the woman be the mistress, wife, or servant, it is a direct expression not of her status, not of love, but of the privileges, authority, and *prestige* with which she is invested.

Salamina, until the coming of my wife, enjoyed unbounded privilege, assumed unlimited authority, and basked in a prestige that she supported well. And if I view her attachment to me, and her fantastic jealousy, as consequence, I must yet find it too instinctive and uncalculated to be classed as mercenary. She was touched by kindness, generosity, and thoughtfulness, by such human virtues as might show themselves in me *for her;* their evidences were the material and worldly advantages which I bestowed. We may not, even among our romantic selves, distinguish harshly between bought and given love. One *wins* love: how?

Enjoying as she did, until May 4, that almost unlimited authority at home which is the pre-

ABOVE: DEDICATION PAGE FROM <u>GREENLAND JOURNAL</u>, 1962

ROCKWELL KENT

rogative of Greenland women, one might have looked for some show of resentment at the prospect of being superseded by a lawful and desired housewife. She showed none. And she was too emotionally uncontrolled to have concealed the slightest shade of jealousy. I believe that her own pride in those virtues of household management which had made her so indispensable to me led her to be confident without a passing fear that she would be as indispensable to both of us. That in good-fellowship we'd be alike, she had no doubt; she judged my unknown wife by me. She'd be *our* friend. But there was more than that. The indefatigable vigilance, that *damned* vigilance and energy with which she'd dogged my steps, I had not valued; Frances would. "Here," was her attitude, resigning me, "here, take him now. He has given me a lot of trouble but I've done my best. We'll see now what we two can do." And, sure enough, up she'd come running with what tales she could: "Kinte is talking to Amalia on the beach" — and such.

Salamina, an attractive widow in her late twenties, was not one to sit her life out on the sidelines. And although her principles, her taste, perhaps her common sense, forbade a second marriage, neither her conscience nor her sense denied her love.

Among the careers that the Danish administration has opened to Greenlanders, one of the most honorable is that of carpenter, one of the most honorable, useful, and, possibly, ennobling careers in the world. A man's work makes him, in the end; and carpentry was starting well with young Jens Lange. *Life* started well with him: gave him good looks, good brain, gave him a lot of charm. Gave him, I'll say, good taste. He picked out Salamina.

And certainly in part of Salamina's holiday — we gave her three weeks off at home and Umanak — she was beguiled by Jens. How must she have been thrilled when we sailed off to fetch a carpenter! There was but one. So Salamina stood there on the shore to welcome us — and Jens. From that time on — almost until we sailed for home — Marghreta's house, where she now lived, was Jen's too. It was the only native house with window shades. They drew them: let them be.

[SALAMINA]

GREENLAND COAST, 1931, LITHOGRAPH ON STONE, 10-1/2 x 15-1/4"

OVERLEAF, TOP: COMMUNING WITH NATURE, 1934, LITHOGRAPH ON STONE, 8-1/2 x 13-1/2";
BOTTOM: JUSTINA, C. 1935, PENCIL DRAWING, 12 x 9", COLLECTION OF SALLY KENT GORTON

FACING OVERLEAF: GREENLAND COURTSHIP, 1934, LITHOGRAPH ON STONE, 14 x 10"

ROCKWELL KENT

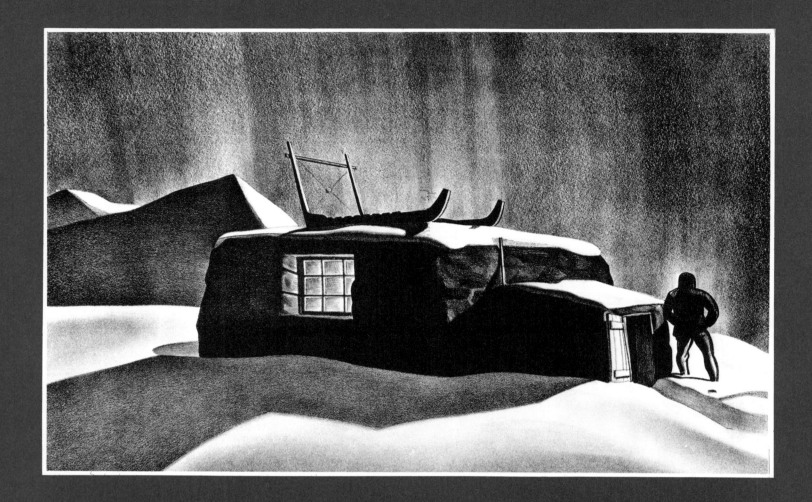

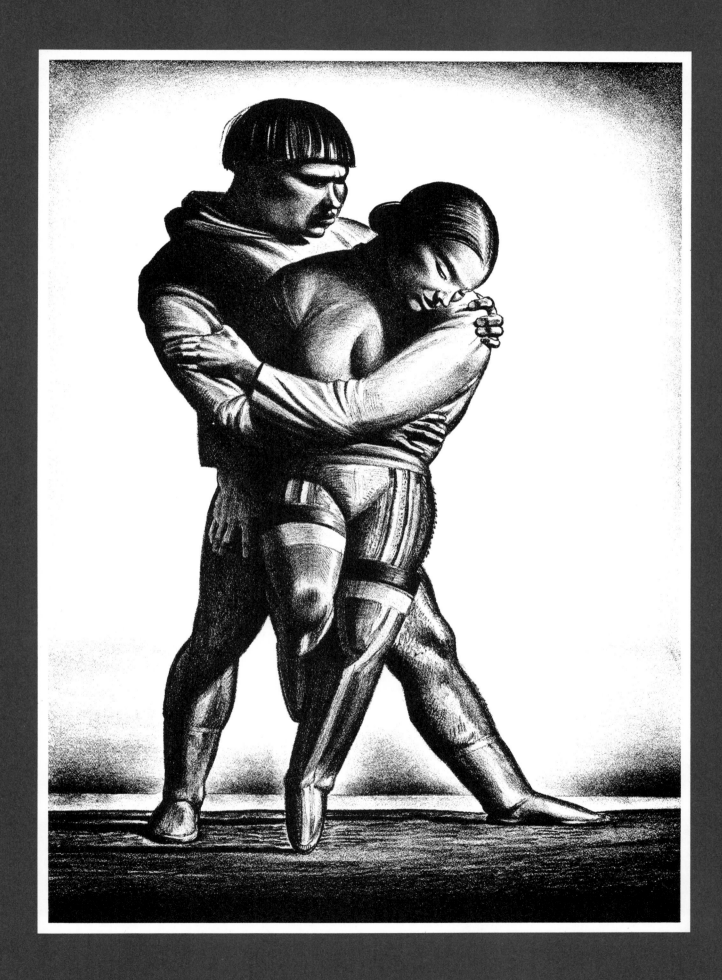

ASGAARD

HIS NEW HOUSE

Woodstock, N.Y., September 6, 1927

Mr. Ray Trumbull
Keene Valley, N.Y.

Dear Mr. Trumbull:

Mr. O. Byron Brewster has strongly recommended my asking you for an estimate on the house I propose building at Ausable Forks. I am sending you a tentative eighth-scale plan that I have prepared and beg you to please send me a rough estimate of what such a house would cost to build.

The property lies about a mile and a half south of Ausable Forks at no great elevation from the river; it is accessible by good roads. The land is flat and free from stones, and promises no difficulties in excavating.

The house is to be of simple farmhouse construction, typical in every way of the farmhouses of that section; the only unusual feature of the plan I submit is that the ceiling of the living room, and consequently of the floor of the hall and three bedrooms above it, is two feet higher than the rest of the second story.

The trim, both inside and out, will be without moldings. The windows will all be of the stock double-hung type. The house will be plastered throughout except the ceiling of the living room, etc., where timbers are indicated on the plan; and the studio is to be finished with Celotex. The studio window should be of stock metal factory window, the nearest stock size to that indicated in the drawing. The outside of the house is to be finished with clapboards and the roof of shingles.

Only the portion under the kitchen will be excavated and finished as a cellar. The foundation walls to a depth of four feet would carry the rest of the house. The cellar and foundation walls should be of cement. The chimneys and fireplaces are to be of common brick and the floor of the porch is to be of brick.

The three bathrooms should each be furnished with a toilet, washbasin, and tub, of a good grade. The floors of the ground floor should be of hard pine and the second floor of clear matched spruce.

I call your attention to an error in the drawing, viz: the two windows in the west wall of the studio have not been shown on the elevation.

I will be in Ausable Forks in about a week. If you could let me have a rough estimate on this plan before then, I would appreciate it. I can then give it my consideration in advance of meeting you.

> *Very truly yours,*
> *Rockwell Kent*

[KENT PAPERS, ASGAARD]

DAILY ROUTINE AT ASGAARD

The routine of our lives when we were left in peace was simple. To begin with, it was conditioned by the farm which, despite its being mainly conducted by an employed farmer and hired labor, remained an integral part of our lives and an influence on our habits and, I must suppose, our thoughts. The farm was in no sense an appendage to our estate; rather, were we — our house, my studio, our tennis court and pond — an excrescence upon it that its owners (we) and their farmer tolerated, *provided* we in no way trespassed on its cultivable land or "fed or annoyed" its animals. (If only those same pampered animals, the cows and heifers, had had some comparable social consciousness about our lawn and shrubbery!) Our house stood but a stone's throw from the barn. Toward the east it looked out over the entire expanse of the farm's cultivated land, in the foreground of which and bordering what little lawn we had was the vegetable garden. Across our meadows shone the morning sun; and it became our practice even in midsummer to be up to greet it, as in the pre-dawn darkness of the winter we would match the barn lights with our own. More and more, as years go on, it has dawned upon me that the best that I have come to know or believe in is contained in Mother Goose. "Early to bed and early to rise," for example. That for fully nine-tenths of my whole life I have gone to bed early and got up at dawn or before must have had something to do with my rarely having had to *stay* in bed. And while we're far from being wealthy — though that's, of course, all relative — Mother Goose would call me wise in that I believe in her.

Early to bed. In summer it was often scarcely dark (for in our region so-called daylight time is in force) when we'd turn in. We had to, for full eight hours' sleep before the dawn. And in winter, breakfasting as we did by lamp and firelight, our appointed bedtime was scarcely much later. Our days were long in things accomplished and too short and swift for all that every day we had to do and for the happiness our occupations brought us. Frances, who was my secretary as well as our business executive, accountant, housekeeper, cook-at-times, mender of socks, sewer-on of buttons, knitter of everything, interior decorator, and landscape gardener, began her secretarial duties as we lingered over our morning coffee. And ended them when at night, knitting and reading to me as I worked, she'd fall asleep. "What do you find to do?" her city friends would ask her. Do? How in ten lifetimes find the time to do it!

Pastimes were not a part of life for us. Life was too short to pass an hour by. More from a sense of duty to ourselves would we occasionally play a set or two of tennis. We liked it — but there wasn't time. And the short daily rides on horseback that for years, winter and summer, were a part of my own day's routine, were gradually so encroached upon by work that needed, or that I wanted, to get done, that at last I scarcely rode at all. Yet this, even in the interests of my work, I must regret; and only increasing necessity and a growing sense of the impending end of life could force me to it.

[THIS IS MY OWN]

OPPOSITE: JEWELRY DESIGNS, C. 1940, COLLECTION OF SALLY KENT GORTON

ROCKWELL KENT

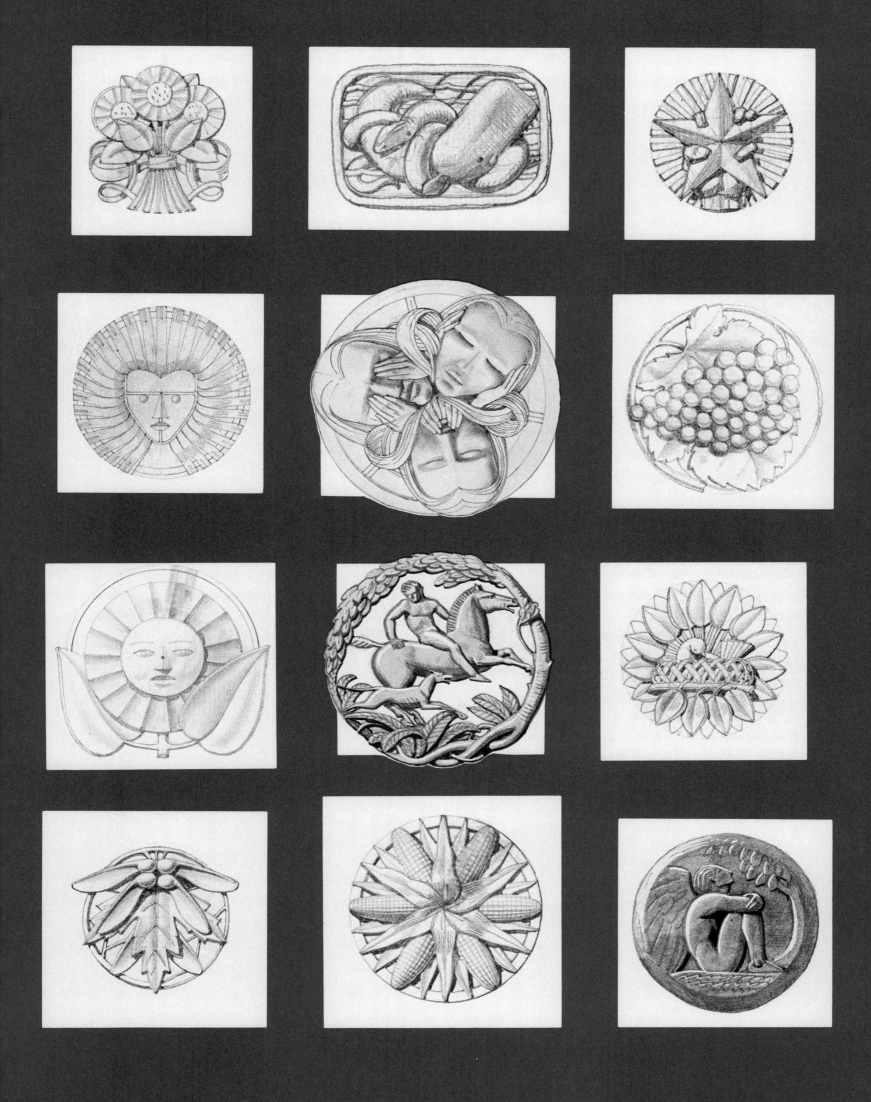

Of our life, tidings and tales have, in a lesser way, been told, for many good and riotous and happy times have here "been had by all." And since what really was done and drunk and eaten is, as with all good tricks of conjuring, of little moment as compared to what guests *thought* went on, I quote our friend and twenty-five-mile-distant neighbor, Louis Untermeyer — a chieftain in his own right, but not, like Snorri, an ambitious one; like Snorri, famous as a poet; and, again like the great Icelander, a historian of his times and chronicler of how his friends the gods (his friendship makes them gods) perform.

"A party at Rockwell's," writes Louis (having just described — cringing, craven, timid back-seat driver that he is — a gentle motor trip with me) — "A party at Rockwell's is even more breathless. His daughters have been married *al fresco,* on the side of a hill, between Rockwell's living room and an oversize swimming pool. The weddings have been something between a community affair, a marriage feast out of Breughel, and a robust ritual in which only the fittest can hope to survive. The ceremony begins long before Supreme Court Justice Brewster puts on his officiating robe. Many toasts are solemnly proposed in what is the most comically intimate bar ever built by an artist who is not afraid to satirize himself. After the legal stamp has been put upon the proceedings, the varied guests — among whom are eminent publishers, hired men, Broadway actresses, members of the Vermont Symphony Orchestra, local contractors,

assorted artists, and nearby roadhouse keepers — entertain each other with acrobatics on the lawn, high diving, ground and lofty tumbling, quartet playing, and kayak stunting. I remember seeing Tony (of 'Tony's') practice his yoga, standing on his head and singing the entire prologue to *Pagliacci* without missing a note or disturbing a grass-blade.

"Dinner follows, in the Kentian tradition, gay and Gargantuan. There are tables of more *smörgåsbord* than were ever set in Sweden. There are whole roast piglings, haunches of 'mountain lamb' (the native euphuism for venison), a variation of Shepherd's Pie invented by Frances Kent, vast communal bowls of salad, great cakes and lordly cheeses — baronial to the last mouthful. All this is interlarded with fresh toasts during which the ceremonial *aquavit* (a caraway-flavored gin) is washed down with goblets of beer."

This must be true: I've read it in a book. See L.U.'s *From Another World.*

Each morning-after from "another world," our guests, in time, wake up. (Good record for some thirteen years!) And it was in tribute to a few more favored ones — believing that they would not want through too prolonged a sleep to miss too much of day, and knowing them to be too thoroughly unfit by temperament for "treasons, stratagems, and spoils" to not love music even in the morning — it was our custom occasionally, not always, to put a magnificent orchestral record of "The Ride of the Valkyries" on the phonograph and, ever so gently, so as by no little sound to disturb the sleeper, place it just within the chamber door. And set it off. Can a more delightful awakening be imagined?

What, at these periodic weekend riots of enjoyment, do we do? Just what we please. In summer in the Adirondacks it is hot: the cold pond is the place for us. One end of it is ten feet deep, and there's a platform and a springboard there. On getting up, all (*all?* Well, some; the brave ones) take their naked morning plunge. At noon we gather there and sprawl and bask; get hot, dive in, get cool

ABOVE: KENT WITH HIS SILVER FLUTE AT ASGAARD, C. 1945

again, climb out again, and bask some more. The farm bell at our gable peak clangs *lunch!* We're ravenous: we eat. We feel convivial: we talk. We argue. "Look at the mess they're making of things in Russia," shouts a young hopeful of Canadian finance.

"Look at the triumphant accomplishment of their five-year plan!" shout I.

"Read Lyons's book," retorts the banker.

"Read Rhys Williams," scream I. "*Skaal,* Frances!" cry we all; and stand, and drink to her in aquavit. And we all love each other again.

Tennis, or what you please, at four or when you please. Good tennis, medium tennis, bad tennis; silly tennis, with the gallery laughing and drinking Tom Collinses. But, gee, it's hot! Let's swim again.

Many a torrid summer night, when the air was heavy with impending rain that somehow wouldn't fall, we'd bathe again. One night the rain did fall. And lightning flared and thunder crashed and rolled. And *how* it poured! Then all of us — it must have been past midnight, and the darkness was intense — all of us, and there were many there, went out into it and down to the pond, all hidden from each other by the darkness. But that now and again, often terrifyingly close to us, the lightning would flare and for a split second show the naked forms of the bathers livid against the black water. God! how the thunder crashed!

Talk? Yes, and plenty of it. And room enough, with the living room and the bar, and the porch and all outdoors between, for all opinions, interests, moods to find expression, if not listeners. Room even for our music, with the whole night world to flee into. Music! The Kents — oh, stranger, be forewarned! — are musical. Rockwell (Junior or Third) sings bass; Kathleen plays the violin and the piano; Clara sings; Clara's husband, C.A.P., like a certain stentorian ex-brakeman down-east preacher of my memory, can't sing, but he can make "a joyful noise unto the Lord"; Barbara sings — ever so sweetly — and plays the recorder; Barbara's husband, Alan, conducts the Vermont Symphony Orchestra and plays the viola; Gordon plays — let's see: What does he play? — the trumpet (Lord have mercy on us!), clarinet, and flute (not all at once) *and* sings; and Frances sings — so that it melts your heart to hear her. And I? I play my silver flute. At the piano, when we're at our best and at full strength, sits Louis: and his skill, like Alan's, is unequaled but by the goodness and the patience that incline him hours, maybe, at a time to play with us. So there we stand all crowded at his back and play and sing. Let voices tire and crack: they do. They keep on singing. Let the lips of the winds get cramped and petrified: they do — and keep on blowing. Quietly, Louis's Esther and Kathleen's Peter tiptoe from the room, the last to go. Let music reign: it does.

Then Sunday evening comes. Often when the weather is fair — in spring, in the summer, in the fall, even in the dead of winter when the snow is deep and the temperature is at zero or below — we go for supper to one of two commanding hilltops not many miles away, and over an open fire cook a simple meal; eat, drink, sprawl on the grass, or huddle warmly by the flames, talk, sing, or just do nothing.

[THIS IS MY OWN]

TO CARL RUGGLES

Asgaard, July 2, 1928

Dear Carl:

If you won't come and see us — and you should, of course, to see five beautiful children, one beautiful wife, sixteen elegant cows, one super bull, five horses, one Shetland pony about the size of a rabbit, a hundred flat acres of crops, romantic woodland, staggering mountains, and a sheltered swimming pool to lave your limbs in — if you won't come immediately to see all that and a house more beautiful and convenient than any you have ever entered, and a new barn surpassing any and all barns ever built before — if you won't come and bring my powder horn with you, please send it to me for I'm fond of it.

Finished the Rachmaninoff painting. A good one, I think; but nothing to do with Rachmaninoff.

Love to all.

Affectionately,
Rockwell
[KENT PAPERS, ASGAARD]

THANKS FOR THE CHAMBER POTS

Asgaard, May 14, 1934

*Dear Cuties:**

I enclose the telegram that was your christening, and I acknowledge, with all the emotions of a coffee addict, the receipt of those two chamber pots that make it possible to square the one-cup conscience with drinking a gallon of coffee at a time. Those cups would do for bathtubs in Greenland, and if you two darlings are seriously considering coming to Greenland with me corner a few more of them and bring them along. What fun it would be for all three of us to sit around in separate little bathtubs like those and all get clean together; and then, of course, jump into bed. . . .

Yours, Rockwell
[CARBON COPY, KENT PAPERS, ASGAARD]

---

*"Cuties" were two sisters. One of them, Charlotte, was a favorite model of Rockwell's. — ED.

BEOWULF

NEW YORK · RANDOM HOUSE · 1932

Tubac, Arizona, August 27, 1935

Dear Elmer:

. . . Let me good-naturedly beg you to somehow correct in print a rather damaging misstatement that you have committed. It is in a fine illustrated article of yours (included in a beautifully printed book on bookmaking) on the making of Beowulf.* In that article you describe in some detail my making of the Beowulf lithographs on paper, transferring those papers with great care from Ausable Forks to New York; and how "in the studio (or shop) of George Miller" they were transferred to stone. Now: a lithograph done on paper and transferred to stone has neither the quality of a fine lithograph nor, to collectors, the same value. Actually, it is merely a reproduction of a drawing in wax crayon. It may be that subsequent work upon the stone, by the artist himself, will give the design the quality of a true lithograph. I have made a few paper lithographs; invariably all the subsequent work on the stone has been done by me. That the stonework on the Beowulf lithographs was done by me is not even suggested in your article: "in the studio (or workshop, or however it reads) of Geo. Miller" would be understood by the reader as eliminating me. So much for that.

The hand holding the sword which decorates the title page of Beowulf was first drawn. The transfer on the stone turned out very poorly. I practically redrew the entire design. That redrawing was done in the studio of George Miller. It was done, of course, entirely by me. (For George Miller is a thoroughly capable lithographic printer; and neither he nor anyone in his employ claims to be an artist.)

The title-page design of a hand holding a sword is the least pretentious and, in fact, the least important of the many lithographs in Beowulf. It is merely a decoration. Of the many illustrations to Beowulf, not one was drawn first on paper, not one was a lithographic transfer. All of them were drawn directly on the stone, by me. And the statement that they were lithographic transfers is false and damaging; damaging to me, damaging to the publishers of the book and the dealers in the prints, and damaging to the collectors who have purchased the book and the handmade prints of the illustrations which were sold separately.

That your damaging statements were made unintentionally and in ignorance of the truth I am convinced. Yet having been made by you, the printer of the book, and in collaboration with me, its designer, lends the error the weight of authority. You will, I am sure, want to correct yourself in print. I want you to; and I suggest that you give this letter of mine as for publication, as the most authoritative of all means of correction. You may, of course, refer this letter to George Miller for endorsement of the facts.

I write this in no unfriendly spirit, Elmer, but with real feeling that you have inadvertently misrepresented me in a matter that relates clearly to my professional pride. If Beowulf — the Random House edition — was worth writing about, misstatements about it are worthy of prompt and full correction.

Faithfully yours,

Rockwell

[THE ADLER COLLECTION, PRINCETON UNIVERSITY LIBRARY]

---

*Kent here refers to Elmer Adler's article in *The Dolphin*, No. 2, Limited Editions Club, New York, 1935. The bone of contention was Adler's bald statement on page 149: "The stonework was done at the studio of George Miller." There is no doubt that Kent worked on the actual stones until he was satisfied with them, then turned them over to Miller for pulling the final proofs. According to Dan Burne Jones, *The Prints of Rockwell Kent*, proofs from the original stones were pulled by Miller and the stones reground. A proof from each stone was transferred to zinc and 950 copies were printed in reverse by offset for an edition of *Beowulf*. — ED.

OPPOSITE: TITLE PAGE FROM BEOWULF, RANDOM HOUSE, 1932

ROCKWELL KENT

To my sweet Valentine, Cathie:

I fondly hoped, my darling wife,
That you'd be mine throughout my life.
How could I guess, my hope, my joy,
That you would leave me for — a Boy!

FATHER TO DAUGHTER

December 15, 1935

Kathleen darling:

First: please send me the name of your boss. I want to send him the copy of
Candide *which I promised him.*

Second: During your Christmas shopping keep your eyes open for gold fish —
plain and fancy — and get prices. Also on small aquariums. Frances wants a pet and
fancies gold fish. She's getting so sexy in her tastes!

Third: Are you going to Grandmothers at Christmas? If so, bring along a
beau. Frances is asking your mother to come here at New Years.

Fourth: Are you well and happy?

Fifth: Answer all these things immediately.

Sixth: Do you want my love and kisses?

Seventh (making a whole week): Here they are

x o x o x o x o x o x o x o x o x o

I adore you,

Father

[COLLECTION OF KATHLEEN KENT FINNEY]

ABOVE: A VALENTINE TO ANGUS CAMERON'S DAUGHTER, CATHIE, C. 1954,
PENCIL DRAWING, COURTESY OF CATHERINE FRUITERMAN

OPPOSITE: PENCIL STUDY OF KENT'S DAUGHTER KATHLEEN, C. 1923,
COLLECTION OF SALLY KENT GORTON

SALLY

Combustion: to be sure of understanding a process of nature with which we are about to become concerned, I have opened my Columbia Encyclopedia to the subject. "Combustion, commonly burning," I read, "the rapid oxidation of a substance, in which process heat and light are evolved." And, continuing presently with a description of the phenomenon known as spontaneous combustion, the article concludes by citing haystacks and piles of oily rags as among its likelier victims. It forgot to mention human beings.

The *slow* oxidation to which spontaneous combustion is attributed had been in process with Frances and me for some years without either of us, I believe, being aware of its potential danger to our marriage. Repeated friction had engendered heat; and which of us should first burst into flame depended partly upon chance but mostly on our relative combustibility. To my own mind, our recent formal agreement — yes, it had come to that! — to six months' separation out of every year, dooming me, as I gloomily viewed it, to half-time happiness for all that still remained of this, my only life, was a compromise only by me to be endured as salvage from an otherwise wrecked future. From the practical viewpoint — and this, in our life together, was closely interwoven with the emotional — her absences were disruptive to a serious degree. Deeply involved, as I had become, in innumerable activities of citizenship in that critical era of our nation's life, my correspondence was not only so large as to require a secretary's help but mainly of so impassioned a nature as needed just such sympathetic interest and heartfelt cooperation as, I had come to believe, only Frances, functioning as secretary, could offer. And now — we return to our narrative — in the fall of 1939, having finished in short order the writing of one book, I was about to begin the long order of writing another. For a good six or eight months, as I figured it, I'd sit at Asgaard, nose to my paper, pen in hand — I've never learned to type — turning out pages of minutely written, altered, interlarded, scratched-out, nearly indecipherable manuscript that who but Frances could interpret! For six long months, or eight, I'd be no use to anyone. But help I needed: who'd put up with me? Me and the book, my correspondence, and the winter solitude of Asgaard: who'd take a job like that?

"And beside all this," I continued to the friend who had offered to help me find a secretary, "if we're to live at peace up there she should be lovely to look at, lovely to listen to, lovely to have about day in, day out. . . . But don't misunderstand me," I added hastily, laughing at my own ridiculous extravagance, "it's just a secretary that I want. I have a wife." All right: she'd see what she could do.

ROCKWELL KENT

The letter that I received a few weeks later from a Miss Johnstone was written in an easy, good, clear, well-formed hand — and that, to my old-fashioned eyes, was good — and stated that she had heard about the job and its conditions, and that she'd take it. I liked the letter. And on my next visit to New York I called on her at Brentano's foreign-book department where she was employed — called, and invited her to lunch. I don't know how much time Brentano employees are given for lunch. I didn't care. From that hour, or hour and a half, or two — however long that luncheon lasted — but for the customary period of grace, her days at *selling* books were over. For in my own heart there was begun a ferment or, let us say, a speeding up of the process of oxidation, of which the swift developments of the succeeding weeks were, on my part, the inevitable consequence.

It was a *real* winter, that of '39 and '40. The snow that fell in December stayed, as I recall it, until March; and by January it was already more than eighteen inches deep. Fair, clear, cold days began the new year; and although on the morning of January second when Miss Johnstone — no, let us call her by her Christian name — when Sally, bright and early, came down to her first breakfast the sun had not yet risen, no sooner had she looked toward the west where Whiteface stood above the foreground of snow-laden pines than suddenly — as though her eyes had been the sun — the summit glowed with the rosy light of sunrise. The unearthly beauty of the glowing peak against the still gray, early-morning sky so moved her that, watching her face as it reflected her emotion, I could have knelt in homage. From that time on it wasn't easy to conceal my love.

It wasn't easy when every hour that we were together — the hour or more of dictation, our meals together, our times outdoors when, shutting shop, we'd wander through the woods on snow-shoes or go skiing on the pasture hills, and our long evenings at the fireside where, conversing, I delighted in her thoughts, her voice, her crystal-clear enunciation — it wasn't easy when every word of hers and every motion, every look, endeared her more to me. In fact it soon became so far from easy that in a few days I just gave up trying. And driving her one lovely afternoon to the foot of a high hill, floundering afoot with her through the deep snow to the top, and there revealing to her enraptured eyes the whole wonderland of that North Country world, I said to her — almost in these very words — "All this will I give thee if thou wilt fall down and worship me." So next day Sally packed her things and left.

Never before had Asgaard seemed so utterly forlorn, the house so empty, the hours so interminable, the days, my life, so purposeless. Fair days, blue skies, the world dressed in its winter best: what for? Whiteface at sunrise: beautiful? Who cared! And the nights, half sleeping, half awake on the hard floor close to the telephone: would that phone never ring? Would morning never come? And morning: what had another day to offer? Hope, Sally had not given me. She'd think. She'd weigh things over in her mind: weigh her own hopes, her heart; weigh men, for all I knew. Two, three, four, five days passed; a week. And then, unable to endure my growing hopelessness, I phoned. And in her answer — no matter, I've forgotten her words — in the ardor, love, and poignant need of me her voice conveyed there spoke the promise of which our happiness throughout the years has been the fulfillment.

Frances, though bound for Arizona, had lingered in New York. I asked her to return. And here at Asgaard she met Sally — met her and took her to her heart. Out of the deep goodness of a heart that in that crisis let her only think of me, she gave us two her blessing. Of her sincerity, today's affectionate friendship is the evidence.

To Sally, the meeting with a family whose youngest daughter was of her own age must have been, in prospect, an ordeal far more fearsome than, with her dignity and self-possession, she let me know. Yet at the big coming-in party that she and I together gave for her she won their hearts. And throughout the years she has so kept them that not long ago my forthright daughter Barbara said to me: "Rockwell, the best thing you ever did in your whole life was marry Sally." Amen.

[IT'S ME O LORD]

RIGHT: ILLUSTRATION FOR <u>LEAVES OF GRASS</u>, 1936

ROCKWELL KENT

TO PAUL ROBESON

Asgaard, May 29, 1941

Dear Paul:

Beyond just stating that no human voice moves me as yours does, I want to say very little. That is perhaps enough.

But I must add that I know too much about art to not be aware that it is you, in all the quality of mind and heart that that implies, who, through your voice, move me and all of us.

For You, and the integrity and courage that keeps you standing with us, we just thank God.

> *Faithfully yours,*
> *Rockwell Kent*

Asgaard, June 25, 1945

Dear Paul:

At the fire-side Saturday night, you told us all how much you loved the party, the people there, the night, the world and the people in it, and life itself — very much as the wood thrush at sundown tells us how wonderful it finds life to be. Our spellbound silence while you sang must have communicated to you how deeply we were moved.

There was an aspect of the moment of which you may hardly have been conscious. That was your own gigantic figure swathed in the poncho and clinging to you in utter devotion and trust that lovely, golden-haired young girl. She, as the youngest of the party, will have more years in which to remember that night.

I am writing this letter now — or, I should say, we are writing it, for Sally is taking it all down for both of us — to confirm the agreement, if I may call it that, that your son is to be married here; and to tell you that, if we are not already planning the festivities, we are at any rate looking forward to them as to one of those high moments of life that we all hope will come to us but are rarely, as now, definitely able to foresee.

Meanwhile, we will hope to be able to at least drop in on you at Enfield, to meet your wife, and you again; and we are looking forward to your coming, you two, to visit us in the fall.

With warmest regards from us both, I am,

> *Faithfully yours,*
> *Rockwell*

[COLLECTION OF PAUL ROBESON, JR.]

ABOVE: ILLUSTRATION FROM <u>IT'S ME O LORD</u>, 1955

ROCKWELL KENT

ASGAARD/ *January 23, 1952*

Riette dear, who the hell am I
  To rate so rare a token?
What have I done to merit it
  In what I've writ or spoken?
In what with grease on litho stone,
  Or graver's tool on wood;
With pen or pencil, brush and paint —
  Try as I damn well would —
What, tell me, have I ever done
  To win this signal honor,
To wit: a photo of yourself
  Indicted by the donor?

Believe me, dear, when things go wrong,
  When, let us say, I'm broke;
Or when my wife embraces some
  Ingratiating bloke;
When rheumatism racks my bones
  And gall-stones bruise my bladder,
When ulcers and dyspepsia
  Reduce me to a shadder;
Then, dear, your photo I'll take down
  And for the hundredth hour
Your features — forehead, eyes, nose, hair,
  And luscious lips — devour.
And for the Hundredth time I'll read
  The sentiments you've stated,
'Till, reading them and seeing you —
  My ailments thus abated —
I'll yield to that sweet sorrow, dear,
  Of hopeless, vain regret:
What life had been had I but been
  Forever yours, Riette!

Dear Madam: Please find here enclosed
  Thanks, halting, but well meant.
  I have the honor to be yours
    Affectionately,
    Kent (Rockwell)
[COLLECTION OF MRS. ALBERT E. KAHN]

ABOVE: DECORATIVE INITIAL LETTERS FOR
THE MODERN SCHOOL, 1917 – 22

ROCKWELL KENT

Asgaard, November 15, 1954

Mr. Henry Davis
The Rapid Blueprint Company
818 Santee Street
Los Angeles, California

Dear Henry:

   Under separate cover I am sending you the drawing of the Tower of Babel.*
With your justified criticism about the impracticality, to put it mildly, of moving the
great stone blocks in my design, and your equally justified criticism of the architecture
shown in my sketch, the research department of my mind got to work, to learn as
follows:

   The Tower of Babel was erected probably prior to 6000 B.C. at or near Babylon,
a flourishing city on the Euphrates. In that region, stone as a building material was
utterly nonexistent. The remains of Babylon which have been unearthed show the city
to have been built entirely of brick. The Babylonians' knowledge of engineering limited
their brick construction to very simple forms. However long the building might be, they
had perforce to be narrow; for although the arch was known at that time, its use was
probably restricted to subterranean construction where the earth itself could serve as
abutment for the arch's thrust. Moreover, timber was all but nonexistent there on the
Euphrates; and though it was used for ceilings, the spans were relatively short.
Furthermore, there was little timber available for scaffolding. There were few
openings — i.e., doors and windows — in Babylonian architecture of the period, and it
was in general characterized by flat wall surfaces, occasionally paneled.

   How the tower was constructed is not known. But there is still in existence a
minaret in Samara that, despite its being of a much later period, is of a form of
construction that might have been known at the period and could have been built of
brick with an earth filling. It is spiral, and its ascending roadway would allow
materials to be transported to whatever height was called for. The tower that I have
drawn is a vastly enlarged version of the minaret at Samara. The bricks used were
probably mostly sun-dried, for the shortage of fuel would have prohibited the use of
kilns. I haven't attempted to show the process of brickmaking, for I don't know
anything about it. The bricks as I have shown them are already assembled in piles in
the neighborhood of the tower and being transported there on donkeys' backs.

   Well, here goes your Tower of Babel. I hope you like it. It is drawn with a
combination of lithographic crayon and pen-and-ink; and, judging by my Shakespeare
illustrations which were done in the same way, should reproduce well by linecut and
certainly by your offset process.

   It is hardly the season yet to wish you a Merry Christmas, but just right to
send you my warm Thanksgiving greetings. I do.

                    Faithfully yours,
                    Rockwell Kent
          [K E N T   P A P E R S ,   A S G A A R D]

---

*Kent had been commissioned to make this drawing for use on a Christmas greeting. — ED.

OPPOSITE: THE TOWER OF BABEL, COVER FOR A CHRISTMAS GREETING, 1954,
LITHOGRAPHIC CRAYON AND PEN AND INK, 9-1/4 x 11-1/2"

E·JOSEPHINE·HOLGATE

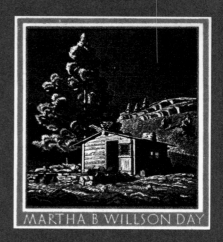

MARTHA B WILLSON DAY

LUCIE ROSEN

GEORGE HENRY COREY

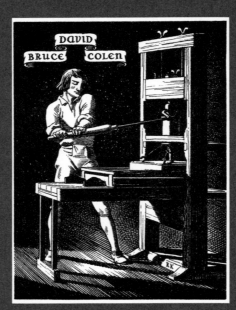

JACQUIE & DAN
BURNE JONES

A POOR PRINTING JOB

Asgaard, January 30, 1957

Dear Dan [Dan Burne Jones]:

Your own disappointment at the bookplates doesn't equal mine. I am thoroughly and completely disgusted with them. If they had been under my supervision, I could have had an infinitely better job done by the local newspaper office.

But let's start with the paper: that glossy paper is fit for nothing but the pulling of engraver's proofs, and not properly fit for that, for engraver's proofs should be pulled on the paper that is to be used for the job. Linecuts should never be printed on coated paper. It is just thoroughly nasty stuff. The ink used looks more like shiny shoe blacking. No first-class printer would use such ink nowadays. Lakeside Press, in the printing of Moby Dick, experimented a long time to get an absolutely matte ink. Such inks are now on the market. Of course they are out of register — badly so. This is particularly noticeable in the small ones — in which, for some reason or other, my design has been altered to show the lettering in black instead of in white. You will notice that the black plate is not vertical in relation to the tint plate. The "S" of the "JONES" is nearer the bottom line than the "B" of "BURNE." It looks as though no makeready had been used. The fine lines are badly clogged and thickened. Take, for example, the string for the kite on the larger prints, and the kite tail.

I don't believe that this printer of yours can do a decent job. As you know, I was reluctant to have the printing go out of my hands, for, as I think I wrote you, I like first of all to see the proofs of the plates and be able to make corrections on them if they are needed; and I invariably see trial proofs before the editions are printed. I indicated a buff for the background. I would have changed this to a gray — and a rather dark gray. The buff is much too light. The boudoir pink strikes me as horrible. This is not, as Fred Bartz believes, the fault of union printers. Elmer Adler's printers were union men. Colish's are union men. I would suspect by the appearance of the work that they were not union printers, for the union has an enforced apprentice system.

If I were you, I would condemn the job and hand it to another printer. And whatever you do please let me see proofs. I will enclose a sample of the second color that I suggest.

Affectionately,
Rockwell
[COLLECTION OF DAN BURNE JONES]

OPPOSITE: A SELECTION OF BOOKPLATES

ABOVE: FINAL, CORRECTED BOOKPLATE FOR MR. AND MRS. DAN BURNE JONES

ROCKWELL KENT

THE PUBLIC MAN
REAPPRAISAL

It is approaching spring of the year 1926, and he whom we used to call "our hero" — a term that at the moment appears singularly inappropriate — has nearly reached the age of forty-four: let's look at him. It is now twenty years since we last sized him up as, standing on the deck of the old schooner *Effort,* he was embarking on that Monhegan Island adventure which was to have so large a part in shaping the pattern of his life. What has time done to him? Outwardly not much. The onetime lofty brow is now an unadorned bald head; the former naked upper lip now wears the light mustache that he had grown in Alaska. There are, of course, the incipient wrinkles and crow's feet of middle age, but they are the result of much exposure to the wind and sun rather than of care. Life has been good to him. And work, hard work: it has been good — as his broadened shoulders and deepened chest give evidence. No, outwardly he hasn't changed, not much. Nor, as I came to know him, inwardly. For although many of his earlier faiths and principles may be said to have gathered dust, or to have gotten smeared and soiled by contact with the world, they are essentially the same as twenty years before. Unchanged, though rusty through disuse, are his social and political principles. And if that holier-than-thou puritanism which so distinguished his youth has been seriously if not irreparably damaged by experience, he has been sufficiently adroit with the processes of rationalization to leave himself un-burdened by remorse. Unchanged, too, and bright as burnished gold are the principles by which his art is guided, for, against the winds of fashion which for moments had caused him to waver, he has squared the shoulders of his mind and marched ahead. I am reminded, as I write about his art, to raise my eyes to the weather vane on the gable of my barn, here in the Adirondacks. The vane is of two parts: one, rigid, points toward the north, unchangeably; the other, pivoted, veers with the wind. Kent's art points north. And whether, as some say, this is a sign of his limitations, of his inability to "grow," or of mere steadfastness in a true belief, only time, measured it is probable by vast social changes, can give a final verdict.

But what, we may well ask, has social change to do with the evaluation of the art of one who in the past twenty years has lived so much apart from the affairs of men, and who, even when living in the very midst of things, New York, and in so momentous a period as the Twenties, would seem to hold himself aloof from all of it? What — and this is the real question — has the form and condition of society got to do with the evaluation of *any* art? And to this question my own answer is an une-quivocal *everything.*

In support of this conclusion I will cite the contrasting currently "approved" arts of two currently contrasting societies: the abstract art of the United States, and the realistic art of the Soviet Union. About our art I will say, quoting from a letter of mine in the *Times* magazine, that "the cur-rent, generally incomprehensible abstractions appear as the inevitable and perfect expression of a mor-ibund culture. Their acceptance by the patronage of our galleries and the masters of our press is less to be interpreted as a surrender to fashion than as further evidence of that renunciation of humanity implicit in our purposes and evidenced by our acts. Abstractionism is the cultural counterpart of the atomic bomb." And, of Soviet art, that its current realism, however academic much of it appears to be, is an equally inevitable expression of a *Socialist* culture. Meant to be understood, it is a people's art and aims to deepen mankind's love and understanding of his fellow beings and our world. That So-cialism will at last and everywhere prevail, I as a Socialist can have no doubt. Its arts, democratized and free, will be evaluated by their service to mankind.

Returning to the subject of our book, the life and adventures of the artist Kent, and Kent's apparent aloofness from public activities throughout the twenty years prior to the moment of our story, and admitting, as we must, that the carefree periods he enjoyed were most productive of good

OPPOSITE: LAYING PIPE SECTIONS OVER A BRIDGE, 1941, LITHOGRAPH ON STONE, 12-11/16 x 9-3/8"

ROCKWELL KENT

work, we may still question whether any citizen of a Democracy may for long, and to his own advan-tage, avoid his civic responsibilities. Admitting, as Kent in his pigheadedness might argue, that what may be good or bad for him is none of our affair, that, as he makes his bed — or, in the case of Kent, lets others make it for him — so must he lie in it, there is still the question of whether or not any cit-izen — butcher, baker, painter, or wood engraver — is entitled to renounce his civic obligations at the mere picking up of the tools of his trade — even, let us say, if the renunciation is to his own advantage. For, to get right down to hard tacks, our involvement in the European war in 1917; for the conse-quent, unprecedentedly vicious suppression of our civil liberties; for Mitchell Palmer and his acts; for the frame-up and arrest and final death of Sacco and Vanzetti; for Prohibition and the resultant drunk-enness and crime and deaths; for the revival of the Ku Klux Klan, its bestial torturings and lynchings; for labor racketeers; for strikes and their repression by violence and injunction; for the weakening of organized labor; for Teapot Dome; for the ugliness of clothes and morals; for the whole weird night-mare of the Twenties and the cold gray dawn it was to lead to; for all of this, not the winds or waves, or sun or rain, not natural elements or God, but *people,* were responsible. Are such things not for art-ists to concern themselves with? Aren't artists people? Sometimes one wonders.

[IT'S ME O LORD]

AUGUST XXIII, MCMXXVII (SACCO AND VANZETTI), 1927, WOOD ENGRAVING ON MAPLE, 4-15/16 x 3-3/16"

ROCKWELL KENT

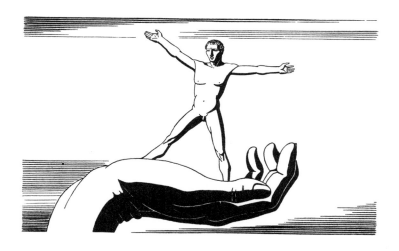

TO MARTIN DIES

October 16, 1939

Congressman Martin Dies
Dies Committee
Washington, D.C.

Dear Sir:

The press reported on Friday afternoon, October 13, that the Dies Committee investigator J. B. Matthews stated before the committee: first, that I was a Communist; and second, that the United States Department of the Interior had paid me $40,000 for a mural painting. In regard to the first charge, you will be pleased to know that if, by "Communist," Matthews meant what the majority of uninformed, biased, and ignorant people mean by Communism, or if he meant that I was a member of the Communist Party, or if he meant that my opinions and public actions have ever been influenced by the Communist Party or by Communists, or if he meant to suggest that I have ever held or advanced views that are to any degree inconsistent with our American democracy, you, I repeat, will be pleased to know that I am not a Communist and that your investigator's statement was fortunately completely false. In regard to his second statement, about a mural painting for the Department of the Interior, I must tell you:

One: That I have never been commissioned by the Department of the Interior to make a mural painting.

Two: That I was commissioned by the Treasury Department to make not one but two mural paintings.

Three: That the price paid me for both mural paintings (i.e., the total price) was $3,000.

In view of the conflict between your investigator's statement to the Committee and the truth, one has the choice, which I trust the members of your Committee will duly exercise, of holding Matthews to be either a liar or an irresponsible ass. In either case, as a taxpayer and consequently one of Matthews's employers, I wish to protest to you that he is unfit for the work upon which your Committee has employed him. As a taxpayer, I object to the squandering of public funds upon such worthless fellows.

Your Committee in its search for the truth would do much better, it appears to me, if it would turn directly to those chiefly concerned in the immediate matter of your investigation. If the Dies Committee wishes to inquire into my views, I am at all times available to give them. Meanwhile I must ask you to rule out, as it concerns me, such slanderous, backstairs gossip as your investigator Matthews purveys.

[THIS IS MY OWN]

ABOVE: ILLUSTRATION FROM LEAVES OF GRASS, 1936

ROCKWELL KENT

January 23, 1941

Dear Mr. Jerome:

    I had not known until my conversation with you on Tuesday that your articles on "Intellectuals and the War" had been reprinted as a pamphlet. The pamphlet was sent to me as you had instructed, and I now have it before me. It came during my absence on a lecture tour and it has remained in a pile of printed matter that accumulated during that period, to be gone over when I had the time. . . .

    I had read your whole series of articles with great interest. The problem of the intellectual is one that has troubled me a great deal. Counting myself as one of that shady category, I am inclined to attach less importance to us than others do. I make a distinction in my mind between Power and Directive Force. Power is exclusively inherent to the worker. In social terms it is evaluated by the basic importance of the work he does. In political terms, under democracy, it counts as 1, and in America as, roughly, one thirty-millionth — or, more accurately, one divided by the voting population. The pen is not mightier than the sword, for its value is only to be defined in terms of the swords it can control. The intellectual's role is like that of the engineer in the control of water power. It's control, not power.

    The phenomenon of backsliding intellectuals is one for which I have not yet found an explanation that satisfies me. I am inclined to think that it is an involved psychological problem and not to be generally explained as selling out. I knew the leading Socialist intellectuals before and during the last war, for I lived for a year with J. G. Phelps Stokes on Caritas Island, Stamford. I was thrilled by their original, unquestioned altruistic fervor. It was too genuine, as I recall it, to permit of an easy explanation of their change of heart. The result of that change of heart was too devastating to themselves to invite an easy explanation. It made a wreck of Stokes.

    When I accepted the vice-presidency of the IWO, I warned the delegates against my kind and me; warned them to watch me. I warned Bedacht when he spoke to me about the nomination. His reply will amuse you. He smiled and said, "Well, to tell you the truth, I have never thought that artists were intellectuals." Because I incline to believe that the backsliding of an intellectual is due to some strange and unexplained aberration of the mind, I incline, if not to be actually distrustful of myself, to warn others to be distrustful. I can't conceive of me going wrong. But then, being extremely well and healthy at the moment, I can't conceive of my getting the grippe. There is, however, an advantage in being old. Before my last trip to Greenland I inquired of the doctor about the chances of my getting T.B. living closely with the people, 50 percent of whom had it. He said, "If you haven't had it yet, you won't get it. You're too old." "Thank God," I said. "Now I can go to Greenland and kiss all the girls without fear."

    Maybe people like Dreiser and me, being so old, can move around among their thoroughly infected fellow intellectuals without the slightest risk of getting the intellectual T.B. of reaction!

Faithfully yours,
Rockwell Kent
[KENT PAPERS, ASGAARD]

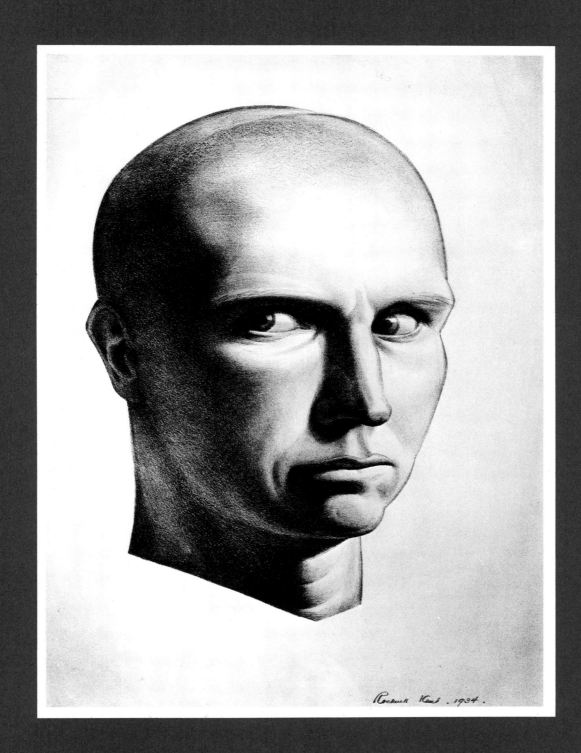

ON PICASSO

Editor, New Masses:

If we ever get to have a people's art, it will be an art that people can understand. The people have got to help the artists by telling them honestly whether or not they do understand.

Let me, as one of the people, start this honesty by saying, apropos the article on Picasso (New Masses, *March 13*) by PFC Jerome Seckler, that I don't understand Picasso. Let me, all for the sake of honesty, go a little farther; say that such pictures as are shown with that article strike me as just plain silly; that, as they appear there, they haven't a single redeeming feature.

It is nothing in Picasso's life whether we understand or not. "I paint this way," he is quoted, "because it is a result of my thought. I can't use an ordinary manner just to have the satisfaction of being understood. I don't want to go to a lower level." Reconcile this, if you can, with his statement "I am a Communist, and my painting is Communist painting."

People who think of Communism as a revolutionary movement mustn't get the notion that it is to herald in a general revolutionary free-for-all. It is a people's movement; and whether it is called revolutionary or reversionary it rests upon popular understanding and participation in every activity that it involves. There were, as I recall it, a lot of artists in old Russia who welcomed the Revolution as entitling them to the irresponsible luxury of being misunderstood. They soon found out it didn't. If the "Revolution" means anything, it means increased social responsibility for everyone and an end to such silly, ivory-tower self-expressionism as Picasso boasts.

Picasso is apparently a modest man. He hasn't sought publicity for his ideas. An interview was all but forced upon him. But he did give it. He did talk. And he read over and edited the remarks attributed to him. Well, read them. For significance and profundity I can think of nothing comparable but an answer of Churchill's printed in the Carson City (Nevada) Chronicle and quoted in The New Yorker: "London: In answer to a question put to him in the House of Commons today Winston Churchill, Prime Minister of England, said 'No.'"

>Faithfully yours,
>Rockwell Kent

[KENT PAPERS, ASGAARD]

ABOVE: MURAL FOR THE G-E BUILDING AT THE NEW YORK WORLD'S FAIR, 1939, 15 x 50'

TO A DETRACTOR*

August 12, 1948

Dear Sir:

By your letter to the Parker Pen Company — which they have courteously forwarded to me — you reveal yourself as one who is not only, in a progressive sense, politically ineffective but one of those who are assisting in that betrayal of American democracy which is in progress. The millions of good Americans who, like myself, write with the excellent Parker pen might take some satisfaction in knowing that men of your persuasion don't. It might well be used as an idea for Parker advertising.

Yours,
Rockwell Kent

[KENT PAPERS, ASGAARD]

---

*In 1948, as part of a national advertising campaign, the Parker Pen Company featured a photograph of Rockwell Kent, "one of America's best-known artists," as a regular user of Parker pens. A Houston, Texas, man tore out one of these advertisements from *Look* magazine and sent it to Parker with the following remarks: "Sirs: Kent is also one of America's best-known Reds — if, in fact, not an avowed Communist. It is strange, indeed, that a free-enterpriser like Parker Pen, & a recipient of the Benefits of the American System, should dignify its ads with such as Kent. You may be sure that I & many of my friends will avoid Parker Pens." — ED.

ABOVE: FROM A SERIES DRAWN FOR THE CHICAGO TRIBUNE, 1927

DEATH OF A CIVIL RIGHTS LEADER*

January 11, 1952

Dear Angie [Dickerson]:

. . . I didn't get a chance to tell you what a deep impression these two days in Florida have made upon me — not only the moving experiences of the first day but the extraordinary happenings of the second — and to express my appreciation of the character of the delegation that the Civil Rights Congress had assembled. All of us went to Florida with a feeling of smoldering fury over the planned atrocities that were in progress there. The funeral service and the subsequent visit to the scene of the tragedy intensified this fury. But that the entire delegation could, on the following day, so quickly readjust itself to the spirit in which the Governor received us and conduct itself with what I believe to have been eminently proper moderation is due largely to the extraordinary diplomatic gifts of our leader, Mrs. Bass, and of yourself.

I detected an inclination on the part of some of us to feel that we had been taken into camp and disarmed by an uncannily shrewd politician. If the purpose of our mission in seeing the Governor was to put ourselves on record as having bravely, and in high places, aired our indignation, or — to put it more strongly than that — if our purpose was to stage a fight, he unquestionably defeated us. But he defeated us first of all by receiving us and by the manner of his reception; and then by promptly aligning himself with us in our fury at what had occurred, our determination to find and punish the murderers and to put a final end to such outrages by making Florida a state in which that equality of man proclaimed in the Declaration of Independence should prevail. Beginning by recognizing our right and duty as American citizens to demand that Florida toe the mark of human decency, he gave us what I think we must accept as a straight account of his constitutional limitations. He assured us of his acceptance of our demand for a big public hearing; he declared his enmity to the Ku Klux Klan; he announced his purpose to increase the reward for apprehension of the killers; and he finally, and as though lightly, gave evidence of his full acceptance of the principle of social equality by his astonishing invitation to be the guests of the Governor of Florida. In short, he exceeded, in his conduct and in his promises of action, the utmost that we could have hoped to win. None of us are so naïve as to

---

*In 1951, Harry Moore, the Florida state director of the NAACP, was murdered and his wife mortally wounded when a bomb exploded under his house on Christmas night. Kent was part of a racially mixed delegation who attended the funeral and were received the day after in Governor Fuller Warren's mansion.

ABOVE: MANY MORE, C. 1939, TWO-COLOR PLATE FROM A PORTFOLIO
PUBLISHED BY THE SCHERING CORPORATION

ROCKWELL KENT

believe that the policy of the Governor was determined by anything but the considered best interests of the property owners of Florida and of himself as their Governor (and a presumably ambitious politician) — in short, by political expediency in response to world pressure. But we must not forget, as he took such pains to remind us, that he is also a human being. I had a long talk with his secretary — a professional newspaper man, a Northerner (six years on the Herald Tribune) and, I gathered, a liberal. He told me that the Governor was really moved by what he had heard that day. We must not fail to recognize that this too was a factor in his treatment of us and may presumably be counted upon as a factor in what he does from now on.

Whatever sort of a picture we individual delegates may choose to present to our various constituencies, I feel strongly that they should be urged to assume the entire good faith of the Governor; that, on this premise, he should be embraced (with a bear-hug, and let him try to wiggle out of it!) by Negro leaders, and labor leaders, and by the leaders of the civic organizations as their declared ally — not only in stopping genocide in Florida but in working to promote the end of Jim-Crow, social and political, within that State and within all the states of this, as he reminded us, "indivisible Union." If you and the Civil Rights Congress, as the organizer of this delegation, feel as I do about this, I suggest that you send a letter of recommendation to each of the delegates.

I have heard — and you have doubtless heard — all sorts of expressions of distrust and criticism of the Governor and of ourselves for "falling" for him. I will just mention one: "Where," said somebody, "was the Governor's wife?" It's none of our business where she was. Maybe she had a previous engagement. Actually, she would have had, unless she is just a woman who stays home and knits. Maybe she is just a hard-boiled Southerner whom he would have been ashamed to introduce to his guests. Or maybe she is a human being and has rights of her own; and, having rights of her own, is not to be told that she must attend a spur-of-the-moment function. Or maybe, my wife adds, she was in the hospital having a baby. . . .

I wish that you could be everywhere, all the time and — for example (and I speak for the two Kents) — at this moment here.

Faithfully yours,
Rockwell

P.S. I am sure that all of us were troubled by the complete absence, in the funeral addresses, of any thought that might rouse the Negro people's resentment, rouse them to action, against the murderers and the society for which they acted. But, on reflection, I have come to realize that the position of the Negroes in the South today is closely parallel to that of the oppressed classes under the Roman Empire; and that Christianity is to them what it became to the first Christians — a repudiation of this life and all that it might hold for people, an acceptance of its utter hopelessness, in favor of a life hereafter that, in early Christian days, led to almost wholesale suicides. As the condition of the lives of Southern Negroes parallels that of the early Christians, so does their faith appear as the truest survival in this day of early Christianity. That faith will be hard to contend with. The Negroes are spoken of as a "very religious people." A truer way to put it would be that they are a people all but destitute of hope in this life.

R.K.

RIGHT: ILLUSTRATION FROM MOBY DICK, 1930

ROCKWELL KENT

MINE EYES HAVE SEEN THE GLORY
OF THE COMING OF THE LORD;
HE IS TRAMPLING OUT THE VINTAGE
WHERE THE GRAPES OF WRATH ARE STORED;
HE HATH LOOSED THE FATEFUL LIGHTNING
OF HIS TERRIBLE SWIFT SWORD;
HIS TRUTH IS MARCHING ON.

GLORY, GLORY, HALLELUJAH!
GLORY, GLORY, HALLELUJAH!
GLORY, GLORY, HALLELUJAH!
HIS TRUTH IS MARCHING ON.

TO THE McCARTHY COMMITTEE*

July 1, 1953

I will state, to begin with, that I believe in constitutional government and that, as an American, I accept the Constitution of the United States in its entirety and without equivocation — including, of course, Article Five of the Constitution which provides for its amendment. I hold the first ten Amendments, known as the Bill of Rights, to be fundamental to that democracy of which our Constitution is the implement. Holding entire allegiance to the Constitution, I abhor any act, or series of acts, or conspiracy to act, toward the overthrow by force and violence of our Constitutional government.

I believe the investigations into the political beliefs of American citizens and the political tenets of groups of American citizens to be in clear violation of provisions of the Bill of Rights. Observing the widespread nature of these investigations and noting by whom they are sponsored and conducted, I am forced to the conclusion that there exists a conspiracy to deprive entire political minorities of American citizens of their Constitutional rights. And this deprivation of their rights being virtually the silencing of a political minority, I am forced to the further conclusion that the conspiracy exists for the purpose of overthrowing our democracy in favor of a Fascist, totalitarian government. I have no hesitation in charging that this Committee plays an active part in that conspiracy and that its Chairman, Senator McCarthy, is its leader. Moreover, and in view of the forces at the disposal of this Committee, I charge the conspiracy to be one to overthrow our form of government, if need be, by force and violence.

Not only my personal abhorrence of such activities but what I conceive to be my duty as an American citizen constrains me to not only refuse any cooperation with the committee in what it is aiming to do but to oppose it by every legal means available to me. There is yet another ground on which I refuse to cooperate with this Committee:

The Declaration of Independence lists, among the unalienable rights with which mankind's Creator has endowed him, the rights of life, liberty, and the pursuit of happiness. It states "that to secure these rights, governments are instituted among men. . . ." The Preamble of our Constitution states that our Union is formed to "establish justice, insure domestic tranquillity . . . and secure the blessing of liberty to ourselves and our posterity."

---

*Kent was not permitted to read his prepared statement into the committee record in consequence of his refusal to testify if he was or was not a Communist. — ED.

OPPOSITE: GLORY, GLORY, HALLELUJAH, 1944, LITHOGRAPH ON ZINC, 7-3/8 x 8-5/8"

ABOVE: ILLUSTRATION FROM <u>LEAVES OF GRASS</u>, 1936

ROCKWELL KENT

The work of this Committee, and of other committees of Congress, the prosecutions instituted by our Department of Justice, the notorious invasions of citizens' privacy and legal rights by the Federal Bureau of Investigation, the widespread investigations of the personnel of our schools, colleges, and industries, of the fields of entertainment and of publication, together with the deliberately engendered war hysteria that has made us unique among the nations of the world, has so thwarted the aims of our Government as stated in the Declaration of Independence and in our Constitution, that the American people, far from enjoying "domestic tranquillity," live in a state bordering upon hysteria. There is a conspiracy afoot to make us a demoralized people that fears discussion, fears association with friends, fears even to think. And the effect upon our children is demoralizing to an incalculable degree. I charge that this Committee, and all similar committees, and all those in Government or in private life, who abet, sustain, or countenance the current inquisitions and the Cold War that is related to it, are entirely responsible for the attempted demoralization of the American people. . . .

It is stated that Mr. McCarthy wants his witnesses to give their views. I hold my views in general to be my private concern and the very request for my views to be in violation, in spirit, if not in letter, of Article One of the Bill of Rights.

In conclusion let me say that I intend to avail myself of every legal and Constitutional right I may have before this Committee. The cards are stacked. I will not play the game.

Rockwell Kent

[DELETED FROM IT'S ME O LORD MANUSCRIPT; KENT PAPERS, ASGAARD]

ABOVE AND OPPOSITE, BOTTOM: ILLUSTRATIONS FROM <u>THE SAGA OF GISLI, SON OF SOUR</u>, 1936

OPPOSITE, TOP: INK DRAWING FOR THE COMMERCIAL NATIONAL BANK AND TRUST COMPANY OF NEW YORK

ROCKWELL KENT

ON MYSTICISM AND SYMBOLISM

In many of my engravings and lithographs, and in much of all my work in black and white, people have inclined to find a mystic quality that is so obviously at variance with my own proclaimed belief in realism, and my fundamental disbelief in Deity, as to deserve consideration. Mysticism, to begin with, is not subject to easy definition, for it is premised on the belief in an omnipresent unifying principle or spirit that by its own illusiveness is indefinable and inaccessible to understanding. I believe that all things can, and someday will, be understood. I believe in Man as the supreme consciousness; and in the arts as the supreme expression of his spirit.

Be that as it may, my prints and drawings were intended to imply no mystery remote from Man himself, and no spirit not implicit in his mood; and of that mood, his gesture is the visible expression.

Of mankind's obsession with attributing ulterior meaning to plain statements, what better example is there than the Anglican Bible's *précis* of the chapters of the *Song of Solomon:*

> *Thy navel is like a round goblet, which wanteth not liquor; thy belly is like an heap of wheat set about with lilies.*
> *Thy two breasts are like two young roes that are twins, etc., etc.*

This, the church fathers, avid for inner meaning, tell us is "a description of the church's graces"!

Defending my Tierra del Fuego paintings against any suspicion of ulterior meaning, I quoted in the introduction to the catalogue of my 1925 show these words of St. Augustine: "And the people went there and admired the high mountains, the wide wastes of the sea and the mighty downward rushing streams, and the ocean, and the course of the stars, and forgot themselves." "That these paintings," I concluded in my own words, "may convey to those who see them some of the elation of self-forgetfulness is all they are meant to do."

Symbolism is quite other than mysticism. As an expedient of expression, it is unrelated *per se* to any faith, serving in general merely to lend concrete form to mental concepts or to phenomena perhaps not otherwise apparent. In New York harbor stands "a mighty woman with a torch," the dated symbol of the Liberty once universally believed inherent to America. Of justice, the time-honored symbol is the woman, blind to prejudice, bearing in one hand a sword and, in the other, scales — though for the bandage we would latterly have equipped her with colored glasses and substituted for the scales a paintbrush. In my own work I have often employed symbols — notably in the many drawings in which, in literal acceptance of a term of speech, I have shown soaring figures. And when, to these figures, I have chosen to give wings, it is through no belief in the existence of celestial beings but rather as a rationalization of midair suspension — mixed, perhaps, with a little bit of wishful thinking.

[IT'S ME O LORD]

OPPOSITE: NIGHTMARE, 1941, LITHOGRAPH ON STONE, 10-7/8 x 8"

ABOVE: COLOPHON PAGE OF <u>THE BRIDGE OF SAN LUIS REY</u>, PYNSON PRINTERS, 1929, LITHOGRAPH ON ZINC

ROCKWELL KENT

ON COMMERCIAL EXPLOITATION

That competent artists should of necessity be dependent for their livelihood on work at which, it may be assumed, they are less competent, or that work into which, to risk extravagance of phrase, they have poured their heart's blood should be exploited for commercial ends, is of itself such a commentary upon our society as must cause the thoughtful to reflect. That this fair world of ours should be desecrated and mankind's love to travel be exploited has caused the people of some states — I have in mind Vermont — to not only reflect but, on reflection, act. Vermont has outlawed roadside advertising — in belated pursuance, I pretend to believe, of my own covert, one-man crusade back in the early Twenties when, on occasional dark nights, I'd drive out with my horse and buggy and stealthily chop down the more obnoxious signs. I don't like advertising. And against the charge that, in saying so, I bite the hand that has fed me, I say, and on higher authority, that the laborer is worthy of his hire; and that, believing the advertising work that I have done to have been a fairly exact equivalent of the fees I have received, there are no obligations of mutual loyalty. But this belief, as we shall learn, employers do not share.

[IT'S ME O LORD]

PROBLEMS OF THE PAINTER

The problem of the painter, you know, is not essentially unlike that of the poet whose aim it is to make the studied cadence of his soundless, written lines convey the mood and cadence of impassioned speech. To make the plane of a stretched canvas have the third dimension, depth; to transmute pigment into light; and to reduce the bewildering infinitude of nature to an ordered finitude which shall be comprehensible to the human mind: these are the artist's problems. And however apt other painters may be at their solution, from me they call for hours of reflection extending sometimes over months and years; and, on each picture, days or weeks of work.

[IT'S ME O LORD]

Asgaard, April 19, 1958

Dear Albert:

. . . *Though we are still trying to catch up with accumulated mail I will tell you a bit more about the Supreme Court hearing:*

To get seats, we arrived there at half-past eleven and were shown in before the general public by arrangement with the Marshal. There was quite a group of us, for Leonard's family was there [Leonard B. Boudin, general counsel of the National Emergency Civil Liberties Committee], a number of Clark Foreman's friends were there, a number of lawyers who were interested in the case, and Dr. Briehl, my fellow appellant. Before Court opened the public had been admitted and the seats were full. Moreover, since the first case to be heard was an insurance matter, about three dozen insurance lawyers packed the space reserved for that privileged profession.

Our case didn't start until about one-thirty, and Leonard's argument was interrupted at two o'clock for, presumably, a half-hour snack period for the judges. . . . Leonard continued for a few minutes and then reserved for rebuttal ten minutes of his allotted three-quarters of an hour. He was constantly interrupted, principally by Frankfurter, who apparently is notorious for speech-making, having, it appears, contracted the habit while Professor at Harvard. He sits slumped down in a rocking chair with only his eyes and the top of his head visible to the public, though when he talks he rears up a few inches. When he concludes his harangue he looks right and left at the other judges as though to say "Pretty fine, wasn't I?" Whittaker took rather ill-natured exception to Leonard's reference to the passport regulations as "outrageous." Leonard replied that he withdrew the adjective and left it to His Honor to characterize them as he pleased when he had read them. Warren, Brennan, and Douglas asked questions or made comments of non-committal character. . . .

The Government was represented by Solicitor General Rankin, who was fair enough in that he resorted to no rabble-rousing stuff about the "Communist menace" or security. He helped us a good deal, for he frankly had no case. He merely recited the State Department's rules and claimed that they took precedence. To questions put by the judges he appeared often at a loss for an answer.

Many of our crowd, judging by the attitude of the Court, felt that we might lose the case. I put my faith on its merits and don't see how we can lose it — though Clark and two or three others will certainly vote against us and will doubtless find spurious rationalizations of their stand. We are told that the judges reach their decision at a meeting the morning following the hearing; that the writing of the majority opinion and of the dissenting opinion is then assigned, and that we may have to wait months before judgment is announced. On issues of this nature, i.e., major issues that have been discussed in the press, the judges are assumed to have made up their minds before the case is even heard. They may not even read the briefs. We count on Black, Douglas, and Warren, with Whittaker, Brennan, and Frankfurter as possibly being with us — though, to return to Frankfurter, he was distinctly disagreeable. Douglas, as I am told is his custom, appeared to be busy writing most of the time. They say he is writing his next book. Black, in our case, didn't say a word. I think his mind is undoubtedly made up and he is merely bored by argument about it.

When Kent wrote this letter to his friend Albert Kahn, two more months were to elapse before the United States Supreme Court was to hand down its landmark decision (June 16, 1958) in the highly publicized Kent-Briehl passport case. Altogether, Kent's attempts to obtain a passport were spread over nearly eight years. — ED.

RIGHT: DECORATIVE INITIAL LETTER FROM <u>CANDIDE</u>, 1928

ROCKWELL KENT

We spent an hour with Tamara [a representative of the Soviet Union in Washington, D.C.] and her assistant, Gene. They had important business to discuss with me: the Soviet Union wanted to buy some of my pictures. They showed me a list of the ones in which they were particularly interested — two paintings and a considerable number of black and whites. "What," said Tamara, "would be your price for these pictures?" "Why," I said, "the price is written right there on your list. That is the price I put upon them. But of course," I added, "pictures sold to a gallery are sold at a discount, and certainly when you are buying such a number I should give you a generous discount." "No, you don't understand us," said Tamara, "The values you have put on the pictures are for insurance purposes only. We want to know what you would sell them for." I answered that for insurance I had cut those values by 50 percent and that my price for the pictures was as listed and that they should get a discount. This left them literally staggered. It was ridiculous to them that I should charge so little. "We are a rich country," said Tamara, "and we want to pay you well." But Sally and I stood pat: we certainly would not charge the Soviet Union more than we charged other people. And so the matter was left until we discuss it further. "One thing I have learned about America," said Gene, "is that pictures are cheap." I think that to them it is a graphic illustration of the little respect that is shown for art in this country. . . .

    We are delighted at what you write about your book. I only hope that when you get your galleys you will go over them for nothing but typographical errors and not show the galleys to anyone!

    Spring has come to us at last. It has been the most amazingly swift transition from snow to fields that are already turning green. Asgaard will be beautiful for you.

With love to you all,

Faithfully yours,

Rockwell

[COLLECTION OF MRS. ALBERT E. KAHN]

A SHORTCOMING OF ART SCHOOLS

A shortcoming of the art schools of my student days — and for all I know a shortcoming of the art schools of today — was their complete unconcern with a "graduating" student's future, except of course as that student's subsequent renown might reflect credit on the school he'd sprung from. Nor was the fact of having put in years of study to the point of finally, as it were, being graduated, of the slightest advantage in breaking into the picture market. Yet, considering the very limited nature of school instruction and experience, how could it be? Having studied drawing and painting from still life and the nude, you could, at last, paint nudes and still lifes well. And so what? one might ask. Who wants such things? The answer is, of course, just nobody. You've learned the alphabet of art: so far, so good. The world awaits your saying something with it. And in the period of learning how to do just that, you've got to live. Ah, there's the rub!

Once, as a boy, I had gone upon a train trip with a small dog toward whose transportation in the baggage car I had been carefully instructed at home — even to being provided with a quarter with which to tip the baggageman. Duly arriving at my destination, I reported to the baggage car and was handed the pup by a man of such years and dignity, and such condescending kindness to me and my pet, that it came over me that not for the world should I insult him by tendering him money. So, gratefully shaking his hand, I just said, "Thank you very, very much." "Say, Mister," said the baggageman, "I got my pockets full of them." So I gave him the quarter, and right away he was nice to me again.

He was, of course, quite right. Now, as a picture painter I had received veritable ovations of praise every time my paintings had been shown. Yet, except the first two not very good pictures which I had exhibited at the Academy, none had been sold. Praise? yes; but money? not a cent. Well might I have said to the public, "Messieurs, I've got my pockets full of praise!" Often enough throughout the years I've thought it. But the public is not a little boy, so what's the use?

[IT'S ME O LORD]

ABOVE: NUDE, ALASKA, C. 1918, PEN AND INK DRAWING

ROCKWELL KENT

ART BELONGS TO PEOPLE

Dear Dan [Dan Burne Jones]:

One result of telling you of my gift to the Soviet people has been the provoking of you to write a singularly beautiful and affecting letter. The whole matter is very simple:

All my life I have been provoked by the habit of our press of bestowing upon rich art collectors — i.e., the buyers of art like Morgan, Frick, and others — the title of "art patron," my feeling being that the most that can be said of them is that they are a kind of glorified furniture movers, their patronage of art consisting only in taking works of art away from one people and giving them to another — or, as it happens, for the lifetime of most of the "patrons," isolating them from all public gaze by hanging them on the walls of their own exclusive residences, to be looked at for a lifetime by probably no more than a selected few of the most unappreciative class in the world. And art belongs to people, and those who love it most have the first title to its custody.

The manifold virtues of the American people as a whole are not to be questioned. Nor is it to be questioned that, relative to the peoples of some other lands, their interest in the arts is not to be counted as one of them. Moreover, though there are unquestionably many virtues in our form of democracy, in the field of culture the concept of a people's art has not only not been entertained but discouraged, even scoffed at, by the arbiters of culture and the whole branch of commerce — the dealers, critics, galleries, and showmen — into whose hands the destiny of American art has fallen. The simple fact is this: that in the course of five or six exhibitions held in one short year in the Soviet Union, many times more people have seen and loved my work than in the whole course of my long life in America. That is of itself enough. My pictures are for them.

Until recent years, throughout my life in America my pictures have been available to the public, or, I should say, to those few individuals of the public who promised in my dealer's eyes to be purchasers; and pictures have from time to time been sold — and, in consequence, lost for a lifetime at least and maybe, through neglect, deterioration, and destruction by fire, to me and everyone forever. Most of my life's work is — and doubtless will remain — in America. There are possibly eight or ten pictures on display in public galleries. There are many more than that buried in the galleries' cellars. There are few private collectors — you, of course, among them — who, having a number of my pictures, can be counted upon taking care of them; but relatively few people will see them, and their eventual destiny is quite uncertain. Where are the rest? God only knows!

In the course of my life, I have frequently exhibited my pictures in public galleries or in one-man dealer's shows. Much of the expense of such exhibitions has been borne by me — such matters, for examples, as framing, packing, shipping,

OPPOSITE: NIGHT FLIGHT, 1941, CHIAROSCURO WOOD ENGRAVING
IN BLACK AND BLUISH GRAY, 8-1/2 x 6-3/8"

ABOVE: TITLE PAGE VIGNETTE FOR <u>MOBY DICK</u>, VOL. I,
THE LAKESIDE PRESS, 1930, COPPER ENGRAVING

ROCKWELL KENT

insuring, and the cost of advertising and of printing catalogues. Since the public has in general been free to attend these exhibitions, my rule, like that of American artists in general, has been that of an unpaid public entertainer. But today, due to political prejudice and the vagaries of fashion, coupled with my own unwillingness to stoop to the demands of the marketplace, all public shows are closed to me and in consequence my pictures . . . are piling up to fill to overflowing the wooden storage shed attached to my wooden studio, resting in a bed of inflammable pine needles in the midst of a pine woods, waiting only for the first unextinguished match to be dropped to be reduced to ashes.

As to the welcome you feel would be accorded my pictures by one of our museums, I have only to remind you that six or seven years ago I offered the entire collection to that beautiful, small, richly endowed museum in Rockland, Maine — a region dear to me through my years on nearby Monhegan Island. As you know, the pictures were accepted and a preliminary exhibition had been planned — until, following my appearance before the McCarthy Committee, the whole idea was abruptly canceled by the Boston bankers who were the museum's trustees. . . . I could go on at length with personal reasons for wanting my work to belong to the people who love it. I will now give you the other, and deeper, reason why I want to make this gift.

Forty-three years ago the people of Russia embarked on a momentous political experiment: Socialism — which as an ideal, or a Utopian concept, had for centuries been in the minds of thoughtful men and prophets — was at last launched on a vast scale. It was an experiment that deserved not only the interested attention of the peoples of the whole world but from the American people, themselves arisen from a revolution, the hand of friendship. We met it with overt hostility — and if that hostility is not directly to be charged to the American people, they at least, loyal to their form of government, must bear the full blame for the attitude and acts of their elected representatives. That hostility, mitigated only in the crisis of the last war, has continued ever since; and instead of gratitude for what the Soviet people did for us and all mankind, we think, officially at least, of nothing but their ultimate destruction. As an American, I have a weight of guilt upon my conscience and, to epitomize the war by Stalingrad, a debt of gratitude to pay. If, as you believe and write me, my pictures are in truth a treasure that belongs to the American people, all the more eagerly do I — an American — give it, in the name of America, to the Soviet people. But the gift would be in token not only of my gratitude for what they have done but a sign of my deep and heartfelt appreciation of their stand today for worldwide peace. It is not necessary for me to attach to my work the importance and value that you do. I think of it only as that thing of most value which I have to bestow. I can only hope that, recognizing the spirit in which it is given, they will do me the honor of accepting it.

But when all is said and done the matter boils down to this: accepting without qualification the principle of the brotherhood of man as transcending race and bounds and nationalities, I am merely giving my pictures to those brothers of mine overseas who have shown me that they love them.

I have been so long dictating this letter to Sally and become so immersed in the "grandeur" of this enterprise that I won't attempt to write about more immediate personal happenings — especially since there have been none.

Affectionately,
Rockwell

LEFT: BOOKPLATE FOR SALLY AND ROCKWELL KENT

OPPOSITE: ON EARTH, PEACE, 1944, O/C MOUNTED ON WALL, 16 x 11', MURAL FOR HOUSE COMMITTEE ON INTERSTATE AND FOREIGN COMMERCE, LONGWORTH HOUSE, WASHINGTON, D.C.

ROCKWELL KENT

A "SOLUTION" TO DISARMAMENT PROBLEMS *

We have had an idea that I will pass on to you: to invite, if you feel like it, your derision. It seems to be agreed by many experts that we can only quit our war production slowly in order to avoid a disaster to our economy. But what nonsense, once disarmament has been agreed upon, to keep on making arms! Many of the arms manufacturers make other articles of peaceful use — automobiles, for example. Good! Let's keep on spending billions (only gradually reducing our appropriations), ordering motor-cars — billions of dollars' worth if necessary — and presenting them to underdeveloped countries. The same with machine tools, machinery of all sorts, and even plants. Airplanes? Why shouldn't we equip all the underdeveloped countries with freight and passenger planes, sending them instructors and mechanics. Electronics? We could convert much of our production to the uses of space exploration. And also — why not? — bring the backward countries up to date electrically. Just think of the friends we would make! Meantime, pour some of the billions that, apparently, the pump of our economy needs to be primed with into higher wages — paid, if necessary, by the government. And if there still remain unemployed let's send 'em to school. Anyhow, unless something of this sort is done the idea of gradually reducing our production for war is ridiculous on its face, for from the moment that disarmament is agreed upon all war products are destined for the scrap heap.

Well — I guess artists have no business thinking about such things — though artists, just like other people, want to keep alive and, again like others, have to pay their taxes.

[COLLECTION OF VICTOR PERLO]

*Excerpt from a letter to Victor Perlo, March 5, 1962. — ED.

OPPOSITE: THE KNIGHT, FRONTISPIECE FROM
THE CANTERBURY TALES, 1930

ABOVE: ILLUSTRATION FROM GISLI, 1936

ROCKWELL KENT

ROCKWELL KENT

AN EXHIBITION OF HIS WORK

36 University Place

FOR THE MONTH OF MARCH

An Address by the Artist on the 28th at 8 P.M.

ON CRITICS

What, on the whole, I did say in my lectures on art was aimed at strengthening people's confidence in their own judgment. Art being essentially an embodiment of human personality was no more to be accepted or rejected upon the authority of others than are friends or lovers to be chosen on a psy-choanalyst's advice. In art there is no good or bad but what seems good or bad to each of us; and the pictures we would choose to live with, like the books upon our shelves, the records in our albums, like our homes in their entirety, should be as revelations or reflections of ourselves. Toward the clearer un-derstanding of art and its finer appreciation I quoted the timeworn cliché "I don't know anything about art, but I know what I like." After a lifetime as an artist, I told my hearers, that was all I knew. And in vindication of myself and, I might assume, of most people, I would quote Emily Dickinson: "If I read a book and it makes my whole body so cold no fire can ever warm me, I know that is poetry. If I feel physically as if the top of my head were taken off, I know that is poetry. These are the only ways I know it. Is there any other way?"

And at this point, observing the nods of approval, the smiles of satisfaction and almost of triumph, hearing the murmur of approbation or, it might happen, the applause, I'd know that the peo-ple knew that they were hearing the truth. "Don't let the critics fool you or coerce you," I'd continue, "into praising anything that you don't truly understand and like." And I would tell them the story of *The Emperor's Clothes,* paraphrasing it to make the weavers of the story foreign artists plying their trade of "Abstractionism" in the show window of a Fifty-seventh Street dealer: how the first critic, fearing to betray his blindness to the super-values of the work, acclaimed it as a masterpiece, how suc-ceeding critics and, at last, the patrons and the people, each in turn afraid of being thought insensitive or blind, contributed his mite of praise to the snowballing humbug; and of how at last at the words of a little child — a symbol of the simple honesty in all of us — the whole fantastic fabric of the lie col-lapsed; and the whole world roared with laughter.

I know from the response of the many thousands whom, in the course of years, I have addressed that in these times of humbug people hunger for the truth. They yearn for freedom from the pretense that has come to dominate their lives. Only the truth, as we are told, shall make us free.

[IT'S ME O LORD]

ABOVE: ANNOUNCEMENT FOR AN EXHIBITION AT PYNSON PRINTERS

SAINT-TROPEZ

I *started* home, but not in so great a hurry as to forbid my stopping off at the Mediterranean artists' colony of Saint-Tropez; in the course of a week's nightly attendance with artist fellow countrymen and others, at their long table on the sidewalk of a bohemian café, to perpetrate such a fraud upon the artist intelligence as, borne in mind today, illuminates the current madness in the arts. In this worthy enterprise I had as a confederate a Scot, named McCance, who was equipped with, or inspired to, just such a vocabulary of pseudoscientific terms as would impress, astonish, and convince our credulous listeners. Just what we *called* the basic theory of art which we expounded, I have forgotten; but its underlying principle was this: that all actions of the mind and body of man are compounded of two elements; that these are human energy and cosmic force. Upon the perfect and precise apportionment of these mystic impulses in any given action all true accomplishment depends. And in support of the theorem we cited — always in conversation between ourselves but calculated for the eager ears of others — so impressive a number of alleged French, Swedish, Polish, and Russian authorities, and drew such bewildering geometric diagrams all over the tablecloth as brought the crowd at last to awed attention.

"We get the *principle*," put in one neophyte, "but how is it applied? Can you paint pictures by it?"

"*Can* you!" one of us two replied in rude exasperation. "What else did Greco do? How were the paintings in the cave at Altamira made? And how about Cézanne? Haven't you read his journals? And Picasso in his latest phase! *Can* you paint pictures by it! Huh!" And the next thing we knew, we were being escorted by the whole crowd to a nearby studio whose owner had offered a brand-new canvas for a demonstration. We were on the spot.

How — with the canvas on the floor and all the artists in a circle round us — we plotted the design is too complicated for description. Using a metric scale, dividers, compasses, and all our wits, we laid down arcs and circles, drew tangents, intersected them. Using buttons as tiddlywinks, we snapped them on the taut canvas, and, designating where they landed as "isotropic radiation centers," tagged them with the different colors of the spectrum. We drew, connecting them, what we termed conjunctive "isochromatic radii." And finally, having squeezed gobs of appropriate paint onto the "isotropic centers," we flooded the canvas with turpentine and with big brushes got to work — to finally produce a picture that, resembling nothing that was ever seen in the heavens or on the earth, was unanimously acclaimed a superb and highly original work which, but for the slight Kandinskian influence that it showed, might be said to have blazed a new trail into the never-never land of abstract art. It would be false modesty to hide the fact that the influence of this work by McCance and Kent is to be seen in many recent acquisitions of New York's Modern Museum, and in the prize-winning pictures of the 1952 and '53 Carnegie Internationals.

[IT'S ME O LORD]

ABOVE: BOOKPLATE DESIGN

ROCKWELL KENT

On our return to our hotel [in Tashkent] we found the elevator still not working and, of course, our room two long flights of monumental stairs away! So, in the dauntless spirit that, without any reason whatever, I like to think of as characteristic of the Kents, I start to climb for a few steps and, breathing hard, sit down. It took a long time but, at last, I made it. And — Sally opening the door — I collapsed onto the bed. And Sally, alarmed, called for a doctor.

The doctor, coming, and on examination not alarmed, decided that the one thing needed was a rest; and that, quite fit to fly, I should, and soon, fly back to Moscow. "But what?" cried our Tashkent friends. "What about our scheduled visit to the state farm? . . . And what about your visit to Samarkand?" Our hosts insisted that we stay; and we, supported by our doctor, that we go. And there arose such a to-do about the matter that, as a welsher on agreements and a general killjoy, I was thoroughly ashamed. And although a lot was said about the impossibility of getting plane tickets, Edward, who had meanwhile telephoned Tamara in Moscow, did get them. And when a few hours later we landed at a Moscow airport, there was Tamara, in spirit arms outspread, awaiting us. And there, too, was an ambulance with uniformed attendants and, believe it or not, a stretcher to bear me into it — and at the very sight of it the "corpse" revived, picked up his bags, walked to the car, and packed them into it.

Promptly following our arrival at our Moscow home, the Hotel National, there came a group of doctors to examine me. . . . At last — if not with flying colors — with hands and arms stretched out in gratitude, we set out for the famed sanatorium of Barvikha.

And what a truly lovely place it proved to be! Set near the shore of a beautiful lake in gardened, flower-planted grounds, surrounded by a forest of pines whose very presence and aroma may have added to Barvikha's healthfulness: if we two always active Kents could ever find enjoyment in plain idleness, here was indeed the place to look for it. And idleness was here imposed — on us and virtually all our fellow patients. . . .

[Of the patients] none were there but those who above all yearned and worked for peace on earth — some guests who in their own countries had suffered and been punished for their love of peace — such as Paul Robeson, who had stayed there formerly; and the distinguished Negro leader Henry Winston, who, blind from mistreatment in his country's prisons, bore without bitterness what had been done to him, becoming, at Barvikha, a close, dear friend of us two fellow countrymen; and, to conclude a list that might become interminable, Hilda and Gerhardt Eisler, who, years before, had fled America and jail for nothing more, essentially, than wanting peace on earth too much. Among the fellow countrymen of ours we were to meet were Louise Patterson, an old friend and associate of mine in the days of the now-ever-to-be-lamented International Workers Order . . . the Pitmans (he the Moscow correspondent for the *Daily Worker*) and his successor, Art Shields and his Esther, and John Howard Lawson and his wife, and, later, our dear friend Holland Roberts. So, with meeting at Barvikha so many fellow countrymen and a growing acquaintance and friendship with English-speaking Soviet men and women of consequence, our days, though not productive of work done, were fruitful of friendship and, in consequence, of happiness.

[UNPUBLISHED MANUSCRIPT, KENT PAPERS, ASGAARD]

OPPOSITE: BEOWULF: FUNERAL PYRE, 1931, LITHOGRAPH ON STONE, 15-5/8 x 10-1/4"

ABOVE: DECORATIVE INITIAL LETTER FOR <u>THE MODERN SCHOOL</u>

ROCKWELL KENT

THE WHITE HOUSE AND VIETNAM

February 27, 1965

President Lyndon B. Johnson
The White House
Washington, D.C.

As one of the more than eighty million people now on record as opposing our war in Vietnam, and of the world's hundreds of millions who are losing all respect for American pretensions to be a land of freedom and justice — and, I may add, as one of the many millions of Americans who, believing you to be a man of peace, actively supported your candidacy — I write to urge you to put an end to our continuously murderous interference with the lives of a foreign people who have inherently the same right that we Americans once exercised to determine their own way of life.

The excuse, frequently uttered in Washington, that by withdrawal from Vietnam we would lose prestige in the eyes of the world has no validity when compared to the fact that by our actions there we have already lost much of our prestige in the eyes of the peoples of the whole world. There can be no excuse for continuing an evil policy.

I am, Sir, Respectfully yours,
Rockwell Kent

February 11, 1966

Vice-President Hubert Humphrey
The White House
Washington, D.C.

Sir:

I wonder if you realize that your hog-calling, baby-kissing act in Vietnam is adding the final touch to the disgrace you have brought upon yourself in the minds of the American people. Shame!

Faithfully yours,
Rockwell Kent

ABOVE: COLOPHON PAGE FOR BEOWULF, 1932, LITHOGRAPH ON STONE, 3-1/2" IN DIAMETER

ROCKWELL KENT

July 28, 1965

Senator Robert Kennedy
United States Senate
Washington, D.C.

Dear Senator Kennedy:

If the war in Vietnam is to be continued, it must be under a mandate of Congress — the Congress being far more representative of the American people than an Administration already proven to be false to its pre-election promises.

Our entry into the Vietnam civil war is, as all informed Americans know, in complete violation of the Geneva agreement, with which our country expressed its accord. Our persistence, for the sake of what we term our "honor," in the course we have begun suggests that the notorious Jack the Ripper, having committed one or two murders, continued murdering to save his "honor" in the judgment of his gangster friends.

There is just one way to now save our honor in the eyes of the world; and that is to get out of Vietnam and indemnify the Vietnamese people to whatever extent we can for the tragic wrong we have inflicted upon them. Only by such withdrawal can the American government regain its honor not only in the eyes of the people of the outside world but in the eyes of the millions of truly decent American people who today are tragically mortified by their country's unutterably shameful conduct.

I am, Sir, Respectfully yours,
Rockwell Kent

TO THE NEW YORK TIMES

Asgaard, January 6, 1969

Editor, The New York Times

Sir:

In your article of Sunday, December 22, 1968, entitled "The Law, the Tourist and the Fine Print," it was stated that Rockwell Kent was denied a passport "because he had openly espoused Communist beliefs."

It is with some authority that I may state that Kent was denied a passport merely on the ground that he simply refused to answer the sixty-four-dollar question, holding it to be irrelevant to the issuance of a passport. The Supreme Court sustained him in taking this stand.

I am, Sir, Yours,
Rockwell Kent

[CARBON COPIES, KENT PAPERS, ASGAARD]

B O O K   B U R N I N G

Asgaard, September 8, 1969

Mr. Grant C. Roti
Department of English
State University of New York at Albany
Albany, New York 12203

Dear Mr. Roti:

The only "book burning" of books with which I have been associated that I know of was the ordered destruction of whatever books of mine were in our overseas libraries — and that, of course, might include Pakistan. But the list of books originally given out by McCarthy and his gang included only books written and illustrated by me. They included, ironically, a little Christmas book called On Earth Peace, *and my first book,* Wilderness: A Journal of Quiet Adventure in Alaska. *When I asked to be allowed to buy them all back, I was told that they had to be destroyed.*

By a recent "Act of God" (lightning), all my own copies of books which, as illustrator or writer, I had been involved in producing were burned. I consider myself most fortunate in having, about ten years ago, given the Soviet people not only eighty paintings of mine but copies of all my prints and drawings and of all my books, as well as the manuscripts. In the U.S.S.R. they are classed as "national treasures," and when, a year ago, I asked to borrow the manuscript of Wilderness *in order to have it microfilmed, it was conveyed to me by hand by a representative of the Soviet Embassy. McCarthyism is a virulent disease, and the germs of it are still alive in America.*

If you do get authoritative information on other book burnings in which books of mine have been involved, I would be most appreciative of your informing me about them.

Faithfully yours,
Rockwell Kent
[CARBON COPY, KENT PAPERS, ASGAARD]

ABOVE: BOOKPLATE DESIGN

TO JAMIE WYETH

Asgaard, March 3, 1970

Dear Jamie (as an ancient mariner in art, I take the liberty of calling you by your first name):

What a wonderfully warm letter you have written me! It adds to my delight at learning that you had bought the house at Lobster Cove that I had built — and, somehow, to the deep respect I have for what is now three generations of Wyeth artists.

The picture of mine that you have is undoubtedly one that had belonged to my mother and that came to me again following her death about twenty years ago. Its being mounted on plywood is probably due to the canvas having been in rather bad condition when I received it. The picture was painted from the steep hillside overlooking Gull Rock. I must have sold the painting after I fell heir to it, but how it got into the hands of Hirschl and Adler I have no idea, for I have never even heard of them.

It has always amused me to think, and even speak, of my paintings as my "children." I am consequently delighted at learning that this one has found so loving and so gifted a foster parent.

About the situation of the house, you will be interested to know that when I built it so very close to the sea I was warned by old Monheganers that it would never stand up against stormy weather. But since there was grass growing in the scanty soil on that site, I was certain that the sea would never reach it. But for a year or two after I had built the house, I had nightmares over its being washed away and of myself swimming about in the wreckage.

Traveling back and forth between your Maine and Pennsylvania homes, do sometimes — maybe this summer — come by way of where we live and see the new house that we have built (not with my own hands!) on the foundations of the larger house we lost last spring. We would love to meet the loving foster parent of the early Monhegan painting of mine.

With very warm regards, I am,
Faithfully yours,
Rockwell Kent

[CARBON COPY, KENT PAPERS, ASGAARD]

ABOVE: BOOKPLATE DESIGN

OVERLEAF: ROCKWELL KENT LETTERHEAD, 1925

ROCKWELL KENT   **239**

ROCKS, MONHEGAN   1906, 37-5/8 x 27-5/8″, OIL ON CANVAS, COLLECTION OF JAMIE WYETH **241**

242 THE SEINERS   C. 1910, OIL ON CANVAS, 34 x 43″, HIRSHHORN MUSEUM AND SCULPTURE GARDEN

TOILERS OF THE SEA 1907, OIL ON CANVAS, 38 x 44", THE NEW BRITAIN MUSEUM OF AMERICAN ART **243**

1907, OIL ON CANVAS, 34-1/8 x 44-1/8″, THE CLEVELAND MUSEUM OF ART

1950, OIL ON CANVAS, 28-1/4 x 34″, SUNY COLLEGE AT PLATTSBURGH

MAINE HEADLAND, EVENING C. 1950, OIL ON CANVAS, 34 x 44″, COLLECTION OF PETER BRADY **247**

248 MONHEGAN VILLAGE, MAINE: MORNING C.1907, OIL ON CANVAS, 28 x 44", THE KIEV MUSEUM OF WESTERN AND EASTERN ART

THE WRECK OF THE WILLIAM McKINLEY 1940, OIL ON CANVAS, 27-3/4 x 43-3/4", COURTESY OF PETER BERGH ASSOCIATES **249**

C. 1947, OIL ON CANVAS (DESTROYED BY FIRE, 1969)

1907, OIL ON CANVAS, 33-7/8 x 44″, THE METROPOLITAN MUSEUM OF ART

ROAD ROLLER
1909, OIL ON CANVAS, 34 x 44-1/3", THE PHILLIPS COLLECTION, WASHINGTON, D.C. **255**

1903, OIL ON CANVAS, 28 x 30″, SMITH COLLEGE MUSEUM OF ART

1909, OIL ON CANVAS, 34-1/8 x 43-7/8″, COLUMBUS MUSEUM OF ART

NEWFOUNDLAND ICE

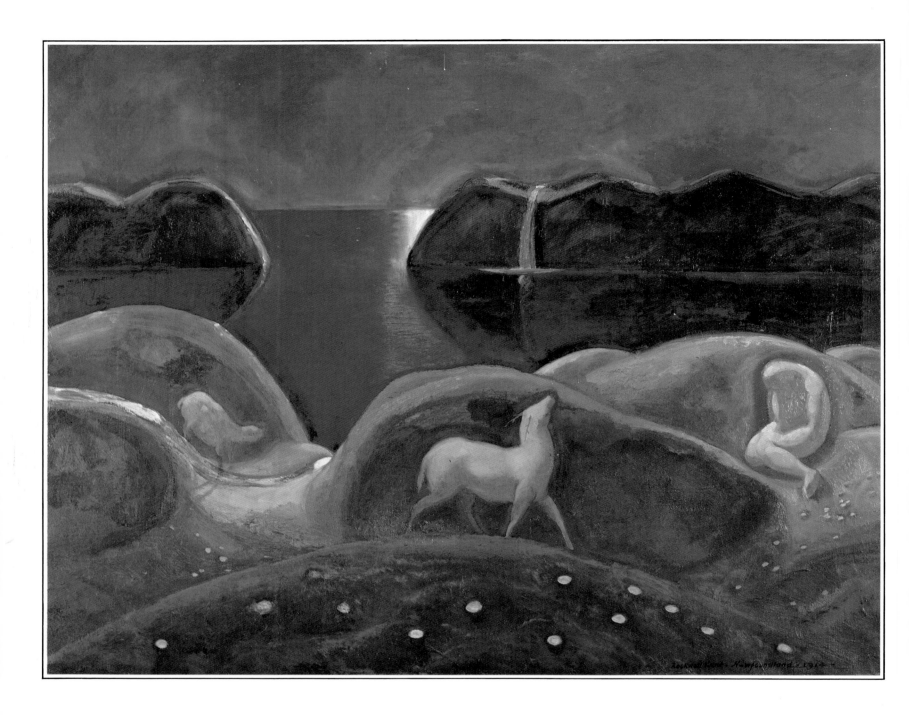

1914, OIL ON CANVAS, 33-1/8 x 44-1/8", COLUMBUS MUSEUM OF ART

PORTRAIT OF A CHILD (MY DAUGHTER CLARA) 1914, OIL ON CANVAS, 21 x 28″, THE PUSHKIN MUSEUM OF FINE ARTS

262 HOUSE OF DREAD

1915, OIL ON CANVAS, 28 x 38″, SUNY COLLEGE AT PLATTSBURGH

BEAR GLACIER   1919, OIL ON CANVAS, 33-1/2 x 43-1/2", COLLECTION OF JOSEPH M. ERDELAC **263**

264 **FROZEN FALL, ALASKA** 1919, OIL ON CANVAS ON PANEL, 34 x 28-1/4", SUNY COLLEGE AT PLATTSBURGH

TO THE UNIVERSE C. 1918–19, OIL ON CANVAS, 34-1/4 x 28", COURTESY OF THE AMERICAN HUMANIST ASSOCIATION **265**

266 VOYAGERS, ALASKA

1919–23, OIL ON CANVAS, 28 x 44″, COLLECTION OF ELTON ENGSTROM

NORTH WIND

1919, OIL, 41-1/2 x 31″, THE PHILLIPS COLLECTION, WASHINGTON, D.C. **267**

1923, OIL ON CANVAS, 33-1/4 x 44", COLLECTION OF KATHLEEN KENT FINNEY

ROCKWELL III, VERMONT

1921–23, OIL ON CANVAS, 38 x 44″, THE WHITNEY MUSEUM OF AMERICAN ART

MOUNT EQUINOX, WINTER   1921, OIL ON CANVAS, 33-1/4 x 43-1/2", COURTESY OF THE ART INSTITUTE OF CHICAGO

1921, OIL ON CANVAS, 34 x 44", THE WHITNEY MUSEUM OF AMERICAN ART

VERMONT HILLS   C. 1921, OIL ON CANVAS ON MASONITE BOARD, 22 x 38″, PRIVATE COLLECTION **273**

274 VIRGIN PEAKS, TIERRA DEL FUEGO

C. 1925, OIL, 34 x 44", THE KIEV MUSEUM OF WESTERN AND EASTERN ART

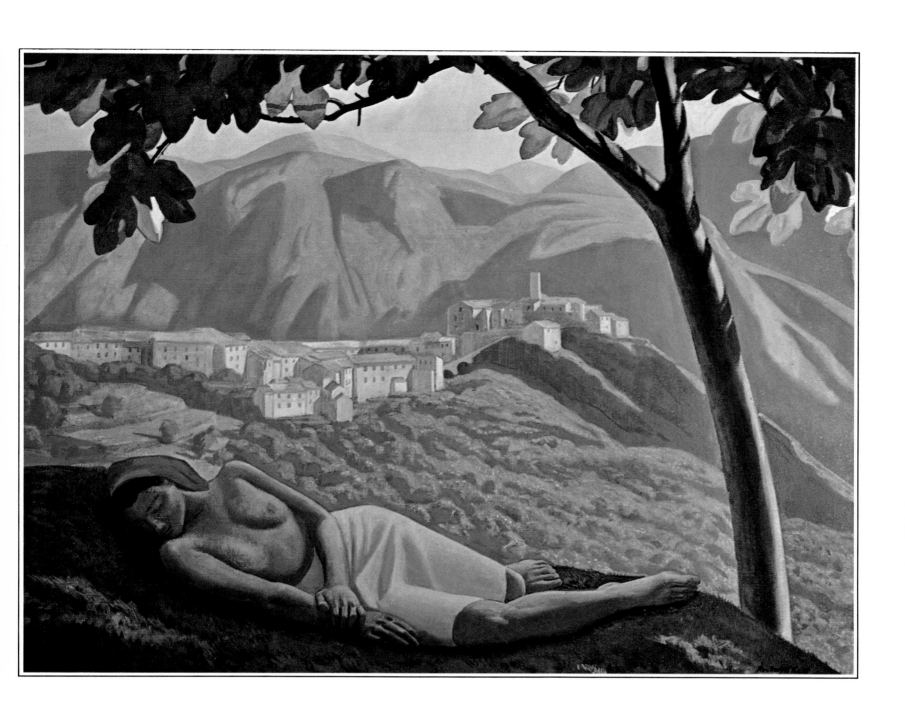

ALPES MARITIME   1925–56, OIL ON CANVAS, 34 x 44", COLLECTION OF SALLY KENT GORTON **277**

C. 1958, OIL ON CANVAS, COLLECTION OF JEAN AND LEONARD BOUDIN

SHRINE, THE MATTERHORN

C. 1925, OIL ON CANVAS, 27-1/2 x 44", COLLECTION OF KATHLEEN KENT FINNEY

DAN WARD'S STACK

282 BOY ON A CLIFF

1927, WATERCOLOR, 13-3/4 x 9-3/4", WORCESTER ART MUSEUM

MAN SEATED

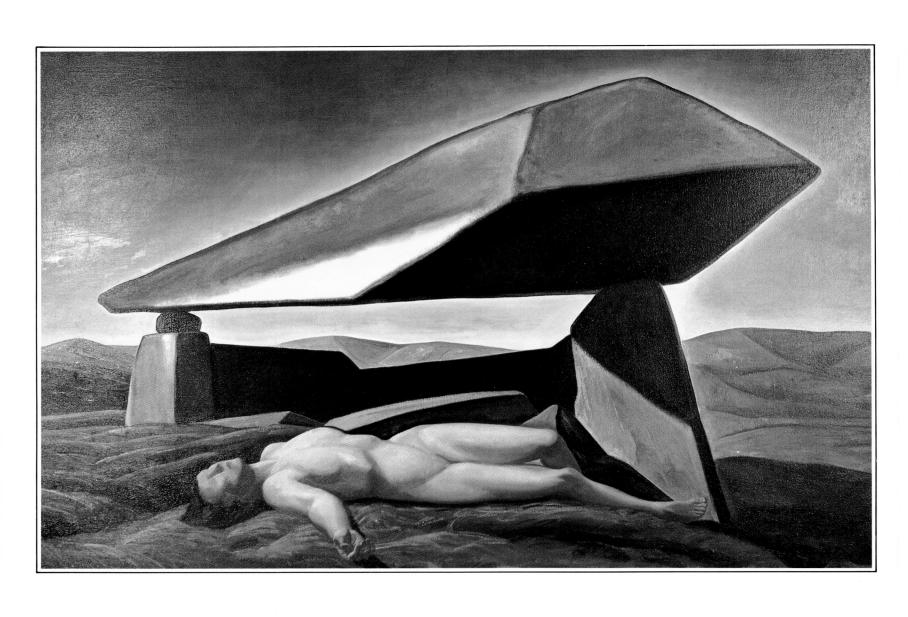

284 **CROMLEAGH (DRUID SACRIFICE)**   1926–27, OIL ON CANVAS, 33-3/4 x 51-7/8", PRIVATE COLLECTION

McGINLEY'S COTTAGE (IRELAND) 1926, OIL ON WOOD, 24-1/4 x 29-3/4", COLLECTION OF PAT EARGLE HAYES **285**

1926, OIL ON CANVAS, 38 x 54-1/4", COLLECTION OF ROBERT PETER MILLER

IRISH COAST 1926, OIL ON CANVAS, 33-1/2 x 43-11/16", THE PUSHKIN MUSEUM OF FINE ARTS **289**

1926, OIL ON CANVAS, 33-1/4 x 43-1/2″, COLLECTION OF SETH AND GERTRUDE W. DENNIS

292 HIGHWAYS, NORTH GREENLAND   1933–37, OIL ON CANVAS, 34 x 44-1/4", SUNY COLLEGE AT PLATTSBURGH

NORTH (GREENLAND)   C. 1931, OIL ON CANVAS, 33-15/16 x 44-1/16", COLLECTION OF PETER BRADY **293**

1935, OIL ON CANVAS, 34 x 44", COLLECTION OF MR. AND MRS. DAN BURNE JONES

CITADEL, GREENLAND

296 GODHAVN, GREENLAND

1934, OIL ON CANVAS ON PANEL, 27 x 48", SUNY COLLEGE AT PLATTSBURGH

GREENLAND PEOPLE, DOGS, AND MOUNTAINS C.1935, OIL ON CANVAS, 28 x 48-1/4", BOWDOIN COLLEGE MUSEUM OF ART **297**

1932, OIL ON CANVAS ON BOARD, 40 x 64", COLLECTION OF JOSEPH M. ERDELAC **299**

300 **THE ARTIST IN GREENLAND** 1929, OIL ON CANVAS ON PANEL, 33-1/2 x 43-5/16″, THE PUSHKIN MUSEUM OF FINE ARTS

DEAD CALM: NORTH GREENLAND

1932, OIL ON CANVAS ON WOOD, 34 x 44″, THE HERMITAGE **301**

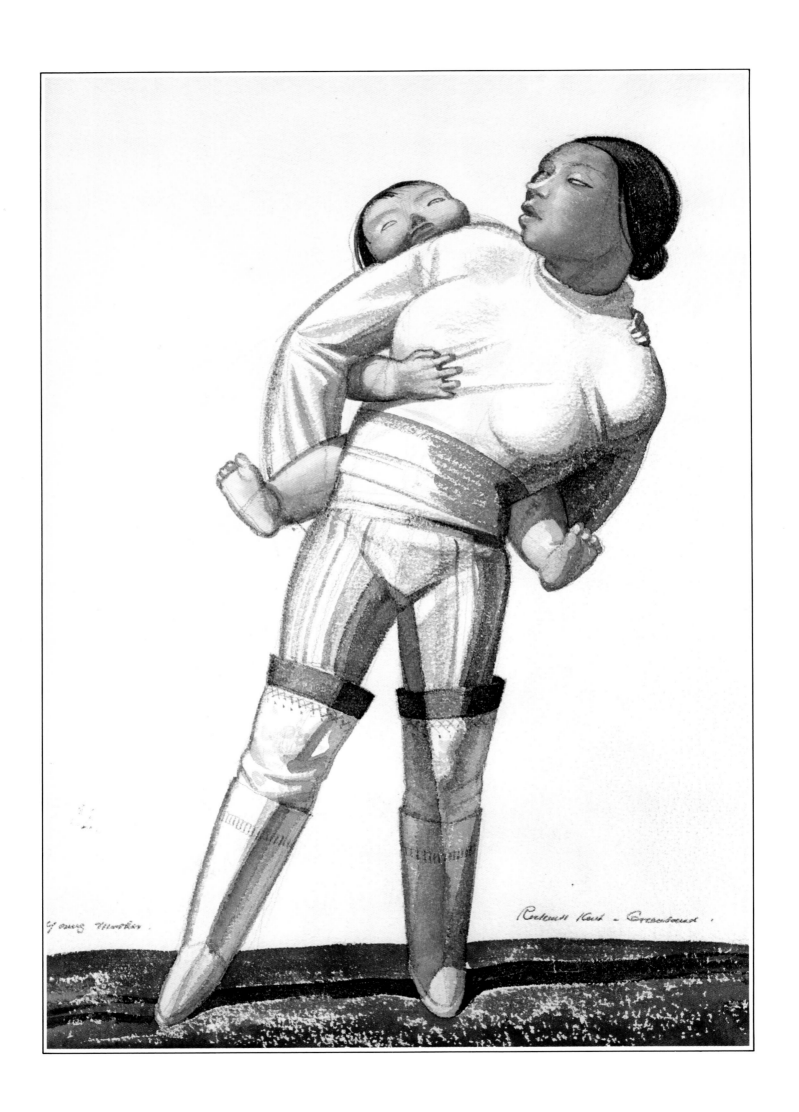

302 YOUNG MOTHER

C. 1935, WATERCOLOR, 14 x 10″, COLLECTION OF SALLY KENT GORTON

THIS IS THE STUDY SKETCH FOR HELENA, FROM THE
COLLECTION OF MR. AND MRS. DAN BURNE JONES,
THAT SHOULD HAVE APPEARED WITH THE
CAPTION FOUND ON PAGE 303.

HELENA C. 1934, TOP: WATERCOLOR, 10 x 14″; BOTTOM: STUDY SKETCH, COLLECTION OF MR. AND MRS. DAN BURNE JONES **303**

304 **GREENLAND SUMMER** C. 1930, OIL ON CANVAS ON PLYWOOD, 34 x 44", COLLECTION OF MR. AND MRS. DAN BURNE JONES

SUNDAY, GREENLAND 1933, OIL ON CANVAS ON PLYWOOD, 28 x 34", COLLECTION OF MR. AND MRS. DAN BURNE JONES **305**

306 MOUNT WEDGEWOOD, BRITISH COLUMBIA   C. 1952–53, OIL ON CANVAS, 28 x 34", COLLECTION OF PETER BRADY

1956–59, OIL ON CANVAS, 28 x 34-1/8″, COLLECTION OF SALLY KENT GORTON

AU SABLE RIVER RAPIDS 1950, OIL ON CANVAS, 34 x 44″, SUNY COLLEGE AT PLATTSBURGH **309**

310 CORN AND OATS, GRAY DAY 1945, OIL ON CANVAS, 28 x 44", COLLECTION OF SALLY KENT GORTON

C. 1960, OIL ON CLOTH

AU SABLE RIVER, WINTER

1960, OIL ON CANVAS, 28-3/32 x 39″, THE HERMITAGE **313**

SNOW-LADEN PINES

1967, OIL ON CANVAS, 38 x 44″, COLLECTION OF SALLY KENT GORTON

OIL ON CANVAS, 43 x 70″, SUNY COLLEGE AT PLATTSBURGH

PICNIC IN THE PINES

1956, OIL ON CANVAS, 28 x 43-13/16″, COLLECTION OF SALLY KENT GORTON **319**

1966, OIL ON CANVAS, 34 x 44", PRIVATE COLLECTION

BOMBS AWAY!

C. 1942, OIL ON CANVAS, 34 x 44″, PRIVATE COLLECTION **323**

324 **HEAVY, HEAVY HANGS OVER THY HEAD** 1949, OIL ON CANVAS, 28 x 34″, COLLECTION OF JOSEPH M. ERDELAC

ON EARTH, PEACE (STUDY FOR MURAL), 1944, GOUACHE, 10 x 13", COLLECTION OF JOSEPH M. ERDELAC

RUSSIAN MASS, AU SABLE FORKS, NEW YORK 1928, OIL ON CANVAS, 34-1/4 x 44-1/2″, COURTESY OF STEINWAY & SONS
ENTRANCE OF THE GODS TO VALHALLA 1927–28, OIL ON CANVAS, 33-1/4 x 43″, COURTESY OF STEINWAY & SONS

326 FIRE BIRD 1928, OIL ON CANVAS, 34-1/4 x 44-1/2″, COURTESY OF STEINWAY & SONS

ANGEL

MAID AND BIRD

C. 1918, OIL ON GLASS, 7-1/2 x 9-5/8″, COLUMBUS MUSEUM OF ART

C. 1918, OIL ON GLASS, 9-3/8 x 7-3/8″, COLUMBUS MUSEUM OF ART **327**

(PUERTO RICAN PANEL OF MURAL), 1937, OIL ON CANVAS, 7 x 13-1/2′, WASHINGTON, D.C. **329**

1940, WATERCOLOR ON PAPER, 6-1/8 x 9-1/4", COLLECTION OF JOSEPH M. ERDELAC

CHRISTMAS MORNING (STUDY FOR CALENDAR), 1946, GOUACHE, 10-1/2 x 14-1/2", COLLECTION OF JOSEPH M. ERDELAC **331**

332 BACCHUS   C. 1950, TEMPERA ON ILLUSTRATION BOARD, 24-1/4 x 13″, COLLECTION OF SALLY KENT GORTON

MOUNTAIN PINES (FABRIC DESIGN), 1950, TEMPERA, 26 x 28″, COLLECTION OF SALLY KENT GORTON **333**

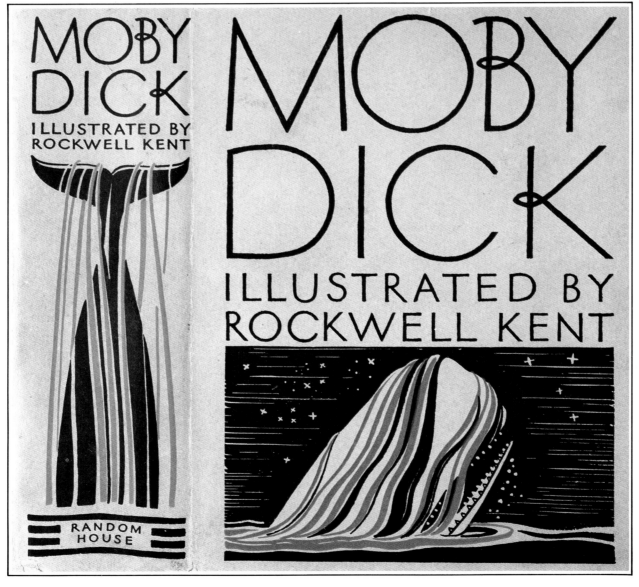

ROCKWELL KENT'S GREENLAND JOURNAL
ARCHITECTONICS
334 MOBY DICK

JACKET, IVAN OBOLENSKY, INC., 1962
BINDING, THE WILLIAM T. COMSTOCK COMPANY, 1914
JACKET, RANDOM HOUSE, 1930

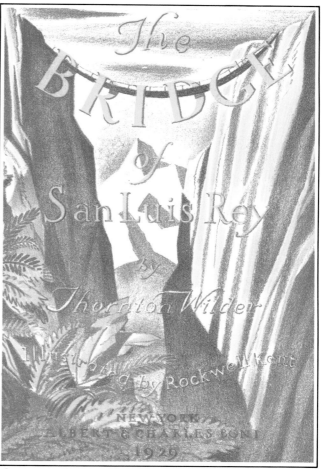

A NORTHERN CHRISTMAS
THE BRIDGE OF SAN LUIS REY
A BIRTHDAY BOOK

May ~ 1923

Condé Nast *Publisher*

35 cts · 3.00 a year

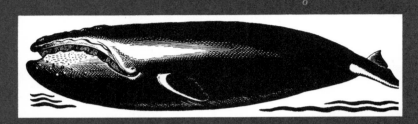

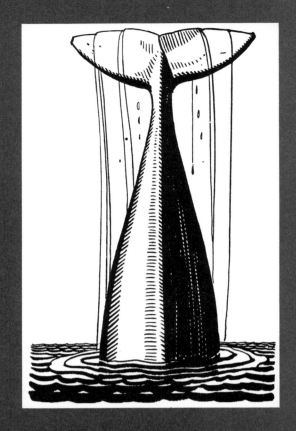

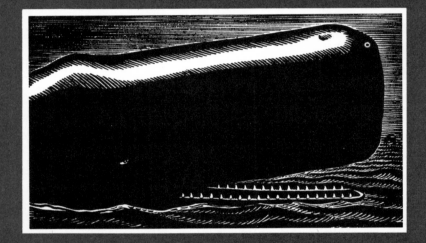

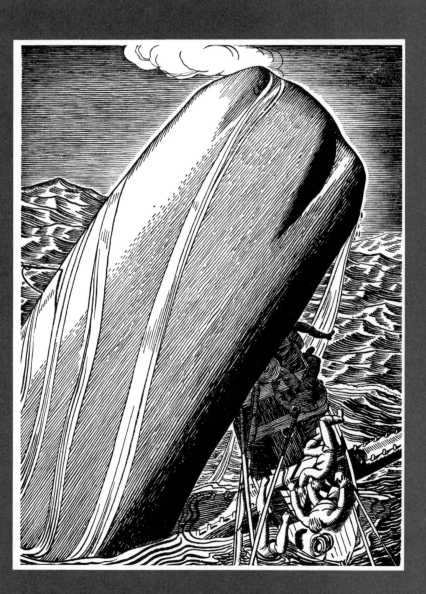

PRECEDING PAGE: AHAB, ILLUSTRATION FROM <u>MOBY DICK</u>, 1930

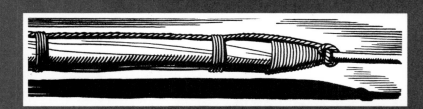

OPPOSITE AND ABOVE: ILLUSTRATIONS FROM <u>MOBY DICK</u>, 1930

Candide also blushed. She bade him good-morning in a hesitating voice; Candide replied without knowing what he was saying. Next day, when they left the table after dinner, Cunegonde and Candide found themselves behind a screen; Cunegonde dropped her handkerchief, Candide picked it up; she innocently held his hand; the young man innocently kissed the young lady's hand with remarkable vivacity, tenderness and grace; their lips met, their eyes sparkled, their knees trembled, their hands wandered. Baron Thunder-ten-tronckh passed near the screen, and, observing this cause and effect, expelled Candide from the castle by kicking him in the backside frequently and hard. Cunegonde swooned; when she recovered her senses, the Baroness slapped her in the face; and all was in consternation in the noblest and most agreeable of all possible castles.

WHAT HAPPENED TO CANDIDE AMONG THE BULGARIANS

CHAPTER II

CANDIDE, expelled from the earthly paradise, wandered for a long time without knowing where he was going, turning up his eyes to Heaven, gazing back frequently at the noblest of castles which held the most beautiful of young Baronesses; he lay down to sleep supperless between two furrows in the open fields; it snowed heavily in large flakes. The next morning the shivering Candide, penniless, dying of cold and exhaustion, dragged himself towards the neighbouring town, which was called Waldberghofftrarbk-dikdorff. He halted sadly at the door of an inn. Two men dressed in blue noticed him. "Comrade," said one, "there's a well-built young man of the right height." They went up to Candide and very civilly invited him to dinner. "Gentlemen," said Candide with charming modesty, "you do me a great honour, but I have no money to pay my share." "Ah, sir," said one of the men in blue, "persons of your

There was born, not so long ago,
a little girl to whose christening came
not one but two fairy godmothers.

a Good one,   and

a bad one. Now evil flies
fast and the bad fairy
got there first. She took
one look at the baby
and said:

"But for all of that," croaked the bad one, "you shall fall into the very pit of despondency."

Nothing could escape the good fairy. "Very well," she said, "and so that you may have somewhere to fall from, you shall climb the highest peaks of happiness."

The bad fairy was by now simply livid with rage. Gnashing her tooth, she screamed:

"Die young!"

"Alas!" murmured the good fairy. "So it must be!

And that you may fulfil that destiny, BE young all the years of your life — even though you live to be a hundred!"

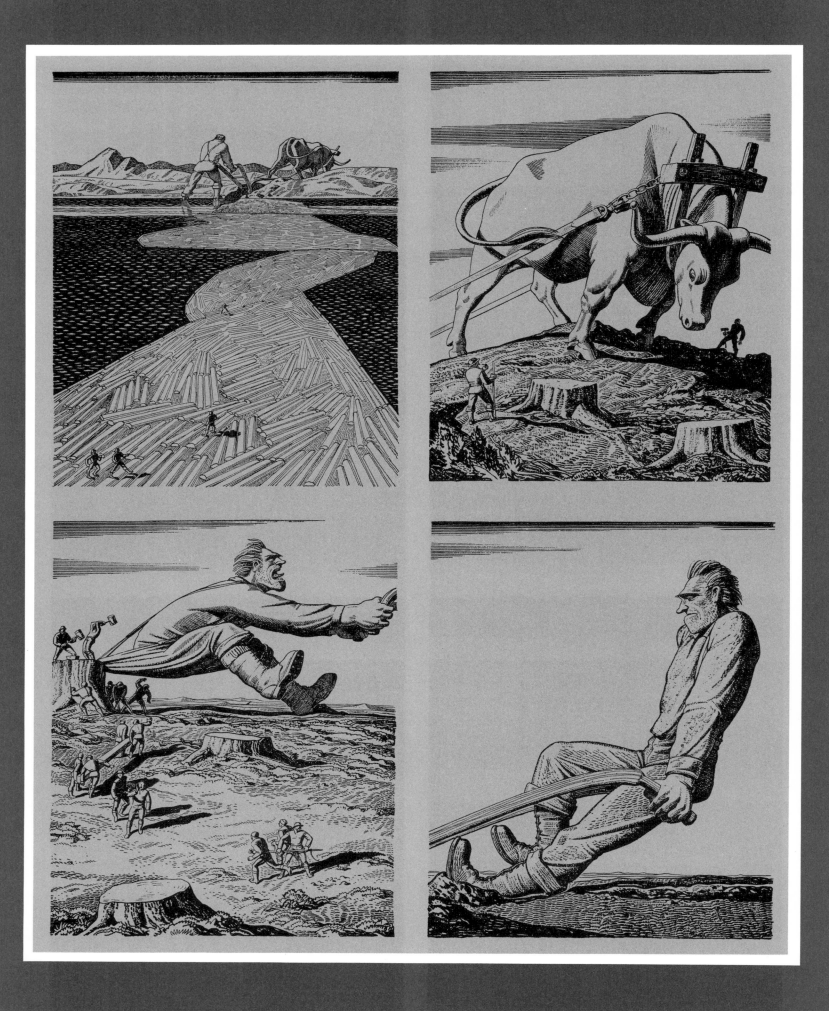

ILLUSTRATIONS FROM PAUL BUNYAN, HARCOURT, BRACE & CO., 1941

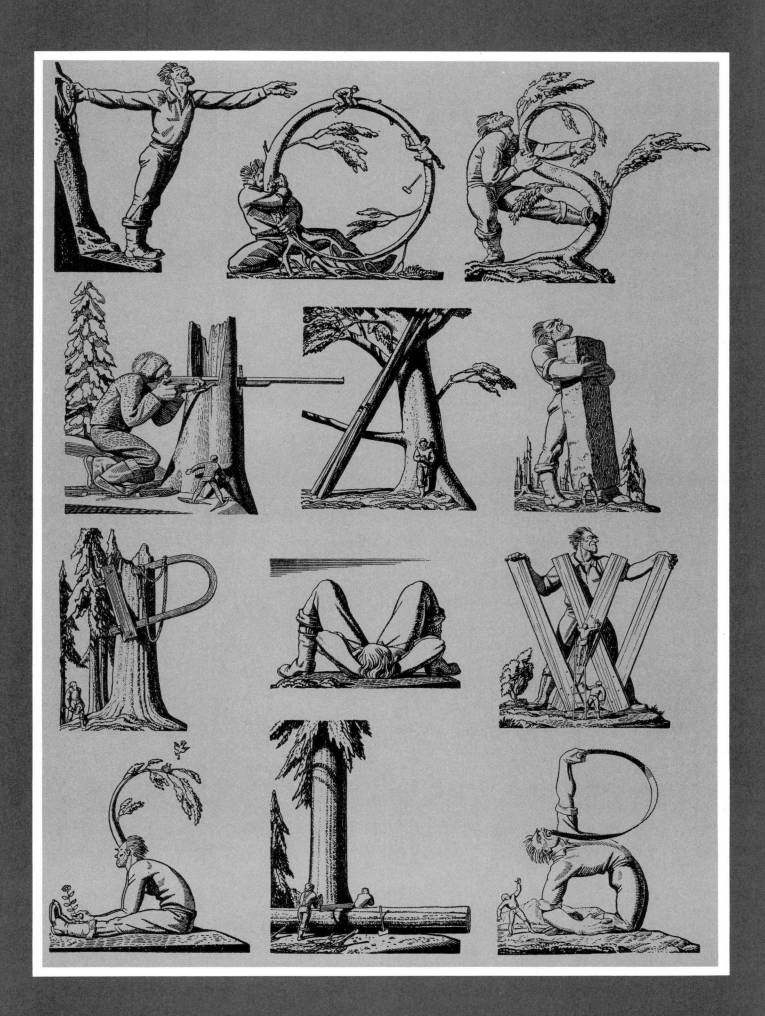

ILLUSTRATED INITIAL LETTERS FROM <u>PAUL BUNYAN</u>, 1941

ILLUSTRATIONS FROM <u>THE COMPLETE WORKS OF WILLIAM SHAKESPEARE</u>, DOUBLEDAY, DORAN & CO., 1936

FROM TOP, LEFT TO RIGHT: <u>HAMLET</u>, <u>THE SONNETS</u>, <u>HENRY IV, PART II</u>, <u>HENRY IV</u>, PART I

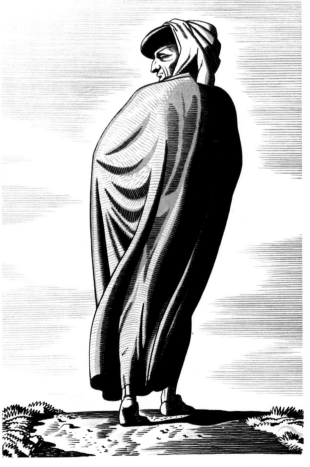

ILLUSTRATIONS FROM THE CANTERBURY TALES OF GEOFFREY CHAUCER, COVICI-FRIEDE, 1930

FROM TOP, LEFT TO RIGHT: THE PARDONER, THE PLOWMAN, THE MANCIPLE, THE LAWYER

OPPOSITE AND ABOVE: ILLUSTRATIONS FROM THE DECAMERON OF GIOVANNI BOCCACCIO,
GARDEN CITY PUBLISHING COMPANY, 1949

BEOWULF AND GRENDEL'S MOTHER, LITHOGRAPH MADE FOR <u>BEOWULF</u>, RANDOM HOUSE, 1932

BEOWULF AND THE DRAGON, LITHOGRAPH MADE FOR <u>BEOWULF</u>, 1932

ILLUSTRATIONS FROM GOETHE'S FAUST, NEW DIRECTIONS, 1941

ROCKWELL KENT: SELECTED CHRONOLOGICAL BIBLIOGRAPHY

The books listed here represent but a small part of Kent's enormous productivity as a writer and artist. Similarly, the list of books devoted specifically to him and his work can only suggest that he has been the subject of countless articles, citations, and reviews in magazines, newspapers, and books.

1914 *Architectonics: The Tales of Tom Thumtack, Architect* (Frederick Squires). The William T. Comstock Company, New York, 1914. 8vo. Bound in decorative cloth. 174 pages; 85 illustrations, besides initial letters, by Rockwell Kent. The artist's name does not appear in the book.

1920 *Wilderness: A Journal of Quiet Adventure in Alaska,* by Rockwell Kent, with drawings by the author and an introduction by Dorothy Canfield. G. P. Putnam's Sons, New York and London, Knickerbocker Press, 1920. 4to. Bound in gray linen with gold stamping. 240 pages; 64 illustrations and decorative endpapers. Second printing, 1924; third painting, 1927. Reset for 8vo. edition of the Modern Library in 1930. Subsequent reprints, including German and Russian editions. See 1970 for revised edition.

1922 *Rollo in Society: A Guide for Youth,* by Walter E. Traprock. G. P. Putnam's Sons, New York and London, 1922. Bound in light blue cloth with decorative paper labels. 194 pages; 19 full-page illustrations by Hogarth, Jr. (pseudonym for Rockwell Kent).

1924 *A Basket of Poses,* verses by George S. Chappell; pictures by Hogarth, Jr. (Rockwell Kent). Albert & Charles Boni, New York, 1924. 4to. Bound in decorated boards with paper label. 112 pages; 48 illustrations by Hogarth, Jr.

1924 *Voyaging: Southward from the Strait of Magellan,* by Rockwell Kent, with illustrations by the author. G. P. Putnam's Sons, New York and London, Knickerbocker Press, 1924. 4to. Bound in tan buckram with decorative stamping. 204 pages; 100 illustrations and decorated endpapers. Also deluxe edition, bound in blue paper, limited to 110 copies, signed and numbered, with additional original signed woodcut in two colors. Second printing, 1924; third printing, 1926. Reprint, 1936. Russian edition, 1966. Grosset & Dunlap edition, 1968.

1925 *The Memoirs of Jacques Casanova de Seingalt,* privately printed for Aventuros, New York, 1925. Large 8vo. 12 volumes, 1,026 numbered sets: 150 in half maroon morocco; 26 sets in full crushed maroon Levant and accompanied by a portfolio of 12 illustrations matted and signed by Kent; the remaining 850 sets bound in black cloth and decorated with gold stamping. 3,524 pages. 2-volume edition, Albert & Charles Boni, New York, 1932. 8vo. Expurgated and in reduced format,

2,264 pages, with only 8 of the 12 illustrations made for the first edition. 3-volume paper edition, Dover Publications, New York, 1961.

1927 *Dreams and Derisions,* privately printed by Pynson Printers for John Burke (Ralph Pulitzer), 1927. 4to. Bound in brown half morocco with marbled paper sides. 100 pages; 64 illustrations and decorations printed in brown ink. 200 numbered copies signed by the artist. The first 100 copies contain 3 more poems, 3 more illustrations, and an additional spot of a cupid.

1928 *The Ballad of Yukon Jake,* by Edward J. Paramore, Jr. Coward-McCann, New York, 1928. 12mo. Bound in cream paper over boards, with decoration stamped in black. 52 unnumbered pages; 2 illustrations by Hogarth, Jr., with one repeated on binding and dust jacket. Privately printed edition by Lincoln & Smith Press for E. R. Grabow, no place, no date, decorative orange paper over boards, pasted label in red and black.

1928 *Candide,* by Jean François Marie Arouet de Voltaire, illustrated by Rockwell Kent. Random House, New York, 1928. 4to. Bound in gold-embossed maize buckram. 122 pages; 81 illustrations, and decorative initials, endpapers, and paragraph marks. Printed by Pynson Printers. 1,470 numbered and signed copies, as well as 95 special copies (bound in decorated linen and morocco) with the illustrations colored in the studio of the artist. Reset in Garamond type for the second edition, 1929 (bound in red cloth), and for the special edition issued by the Literary Guild, 1929 (bound in blue cloth). Halcyon House, Garden City, N.Y., 1959. Barron's Educational Series, Great Neck, Long Island, N.Y., 1963. Facsimile edition published by Random House in celebration of its 50th Anniversary, 1975. Bound in red cloth.

1929 *The Bookplates & Marks of Rockwell Kent,* with a preface by the artist. Made by Pynson Printers for Random House, New York, 1929. Small 8vo. Bound in blue cloth with gold stamping. 80 pages, French-fold Japanese paper; 85 illustrations printed in black and gray. 1,250 signed and numbered copies.

1929 *The Bridge of San Luis Rey,* by Thornton Wilder. Albert & Charles Boni, New York, 1929. 4to. Bound in decorative linen designed by Kent. 126 pages; 7 original lithographs and 3 decorations. 1,100 copies numbered and signed by the author and the artist.

1929 *Gabriel: A Poem in One Song,* by Alexander Pushkin. Covici-Friede, New York, 1929. 8vo. Bound in parchment stamped in gold. 48 pages; 5 illustrations and decorations. Limited to 750 numbered and signed copies.

1 9 3 0 *Moby Dick, or the Whale,* by Herman Melville, illustrated by Rockwell Kent. The Lakeside Press, Chicago, 1930. 3 volumes, 4to. Bound in black cloth stamped in silver. 1,000 sets in aluminum slipcase. Printed at The Lakeside Press. 316 pages in Volume I; 300 pages in Volume II; 304 pages in Volume III; 280 illustrations. The second, or trade, edition was reset in smaller format (thick 8vo.), black cloth with decorative silver stamping, complete in one volume, but containing only 272 illustrations. Printed at The Lakeside Press, issued by Random House, 1930. Also a deluxe edition, Garden City, and Modern Library edition. There are many foreign editions, including Swedish, Norwegian, German, Czech, Spanish, and Russian.

1 9 3 0 *The Canterbury Tales of Geoffrey Chaucer,* together with a version in modern English by William Van Wyck, illustrated by Rockwell Kent. Covici-Friede, New York, 1930. 2 volumes. Folio. Bound in brown linen. 262 and 194 pages; 24 full-page illustrations in 2 colors, and 55 head- and tail-pieces (many repeated). 1,000 signed and numbered copies, of which 75 were deluxe editions, bound in pigskin and accompanied by special portfolio of Kent plates. Trade edition by same publisher, 1934. Garden City reprint, with Modern English by J. U. Nicholson, 1934. English edition, 1934.

1 9 3 0 *N by E,* by Rockwell Kent. Random House, New York, 1930. 4to. Bound in blue linen with silver decorative stamping. 252 pages; 108 illustrations in blue-gray ink. Printed by Pynson Printers in an edition of 900 signed and numbered copies. Trade edition, reset in smaller format, 8vo., printed by The Lakeside Press, natural finish cloth with blue stamping, and issued by Brewer & Warren, 1930. Also special edition for the Literary Guild, same year, in gray cloth with green stamping. There was also a special author's edition of 100 copies, slightly larger, and containing one extra design and a presentation poem. Reprinted many times, including editions for Literary Guild, Blue Ribbon Books. Russian edition, 1962; Estonian edition, 1964. Facsimile reprint of first trade edition, Wesleyan University Press, Middletown, Conn., 1978.

1 9 3 1 *A Birthday Book,* by Rockwell Kent. Random House, New York, 1931. 4to. Bound in silk lithographed in blue and stamped in red. 56 pages; 20 illustrations in greenish black and white, set in frames of text and decorative designs in gray and olive green. 1,850 signed and numbered copies. Printed by Pynson Printers. Some of the black-and-white illustrations first appeared in *The Golden Chain: A Fairy Story,* which was privately printed in a limited edition of only 8 copies.

1 9 3 1 *Venus and Adonis,* by William Shakespeare, illustrated by Rockwell Kent. Printing House of Leo Hart, Rochester, N.Y., 1931. 4to. Bound in tan silk with leather back. Printed by Leo Hart and Will Ransom.

90 pages; 21 illustrations in black and red. 1,250 signed and numbered copies. Trade edition by same publisher in reduced format, 1934. Also a pirated edition printed in Paris.

1 9 3 1 *City Child,* by Selma Robinson. Colophon, Ltd., New York, 1931. Narrow 8vo. Bound in decorated paper over boards, blue cloth back, pasted label. Printed by Pynson Printers. 74 pages; 42 decorations and original lithograph frontispiece by Kent. 300 copies signed by the author and by the artist (his thumbmark in red ink through a heart-shaped stencil). Trade edition, Farrar & Rinehart, New York, 1931. Bound in henna cloth with gold stamping, 41 illustrations.

1 9 3 2 *Beowulf,* verse translation by William Ellery Leonard. Random House, New York, 1932. Large 4to. Bound in rough gray linen with white decorative stamping. 156 pages; 8 original lithographs by Kent, printed in offset, and numerous initial letters in blue and red. Text handset in American Uncial. Printed by Pynson Printers in an edition of 950 copies signed with Kent's thumbprint.

1 9 3 3 *Rockwellkentiana: Few Words and Many Pictures by R.K. and, by Carl Zigrosser, a Bibliography and List of Prints.* Harcourt, Brace & Co., New York, 1933. Printed by The Lakeside Press, Chicago. 4to. Bound in white cloth lithographed in blue. 162 pages. Frontispiece in full color; copiously illustrated with reproductions of Kent's prints, drawings, and paintings. Numerous articles by Kent reprinted from catalogues, periodicals, books, or printed for the first time from manuscripts; checklist of wood engravings and lithographs and a bibliography by Carl Zigrosser. Reprint, same format, same publisher, 1939.

1 9 3 4 *Erewhon,* by Samuel Butler, with a special introduction by Aldous Huxley. Limited Editions Club, New York, 1934. Large 4to. Bound in light tan silk lithographed in blue. 252 pages; 10 full-page illustrations in two colors, and 29 chapter heads, title-page, and colophon designs printed in light brown ink. Printed by Pynson Printers in an edition of 1,500 signed and numbered copies.

1 9 3 5 *Salamina,* by Rockwell Kent, illustrated by the author. Harcourt, Brace & Co., New York, 1935. 8vo. Bound in natural linen stamped in blue. 370 pages, plus 20 tipped-in sheets bearing full-page illustrations printed in reddish brown; 62 chapter headings with initials. Printed at The Lakeside Press, Chicago. Author's edition limited to 100 copies. First trade edition, same format as above, but with slight variations and bound in dark blue cloth with silver stamping. English edition, Faber & Faber, London, 1936; text and illustrations all printed in black. Subsequent editions vary considerably in content and bindings, and include translations into Danish, Icelandic, and Russian. An Estonian edition was published in 1966.

1936 *The Complete Works of William Shakespeare,* Doubleday, Doran & Co., Garden City, N.Y., 1936. 2 volumes, 4to. Bound in blue buckram with parchment label printed in gold. 1,574 pages; 40 full-page illustrations, including 2 frontispieces, in 2 colors, plus title-page decoration. Limited edition of 750 copies signed by Kent. First trade edition, Garden City Publishing Company, Garden City, N.Y., 1936. 4to. Bound in green buckram stamped in gold. 1,548 pages. One-volume edition, Garden City Publishing Company, 1948. Doubleday, Doran also issued a limited edition of the illustrations alone, matted and boxed, with one illustration signed.

1936 *The Saga of Gisli, Son of Sour,* translated from the Old Icelandic by Ralph B. Allen, illustrated by Rockwell Kent. Harcourt, Brace & Co., New York, 1936. 8vo. Bound in natural buckram stamped in black. 160 pages; 14 illustrations, including 2 double-page spreads.

1936 *Leaves of Grass,* by Walt Whitman, illustrated by Rockwell Kent. Heritage Press, New York, 1936. 4to. Bound in green morocco stamped in gold. 570 pages; 126 illustrations and a frontispiece in two colors. 1,000 copies, signed by Kent. Trade edition the same but bound in green cloth and dated 1937.

1937 *Later Bookplates & Marks of Rockwell Kent,* with a preface by the artist. Made and published by Pynson Printers, New York, 1937. Small 8vo. Bound in rust-brown cloth stamped in gold. 84 pages; 96 illustrations, of which more than half are printed in two colors. 1,250 signed and numbered copies.

1940 *This Is My Own,* by Rockwell Kent, with drawings by the author. Duell, Sloan & Pearce, New York, 1940. 8vo. Bound in natural finish buckram with dark blue stamping. 410 pages; 101 illustrations. Second impression, 1941, with corrections and minor changes. There was also a special edition given as a subscription gift for the newspaper *Friday,* which contains an introduction by Kent not found in the other editions.

1941 *Paul Bunyan,* by Esther Shephard, illustrated by Rockwell Kent. Harcourt, Brace & Co., New York, 1941. 8vo. Bound in tan cloth with blue stamping. 234 pages; 22 full-page illustrations, plus title-page drawing and 38 illustrated initials and other smaller illustrations. Reprints by same publisher.

1941 *Goethe's Faust: A New American Translation,* by Carlyle F. MacIntyre, with illustrations by Rockwell Kent, together with German text. New Directions, Norfolk, Connecticut, 1941. 4to. Bound in natural buckram stamped in red and gold. 436 pages; 9 double-page illustrations by Kent. Designed by Ward Ritchie and printed at the Stratford Press in an edition of 100 signed and numbered copies. Trade edition by same publisher issued simultaneously; also reprint in small format, 1950.

1946 *To Thee, America!* a toast in celebration of a century of opportunity and accomplishment in America 1847 – 1947, written and illustrated by Rockwell Kent for Rahr Malting Company, Manitowoc, Wisconsin. Privately printed, 1946. 4to. Bound in coral-pink laid paper over boards with blue cloth back, gold stamped decorations. 60 pages; 48 illustrations and decorations by Kent. Printed by A. Colish, New York.

1948 *A Treasury of Sea Stories,* compiled by Gordon C. Aymar, illustrated by Rockwell Kent. A.C. Barnes & Co., New York, 1948. 8vo. Bound in sea-green buckram stamped in white. 480 pages; 10 illustrations by Kent.

1949 *The Decameron of Giovanni Boccaccio,* translated by Richard Aldington, illustrated by Rockwell Kent. Garden City Publishing Company, Garden City, N.Y., 1949. Large 8vo. Bound in maroon buckram with gold stamping. 2 volumes, boxed. Total of 596 pages, with 32 full-page illustrations in black with washes of two colors, plus title-page drawing and section heads. Limited edition of 1,500 signed and numbered sets. Trade edition in maroon and tan cloth. Later editions in green cloth and tan back.

1955 *It's Me O Lord: The Autobiography of Rockwell Kent.* Dodd, Mead & Co., New York, 1955. Large 8vo. 617 pages. Bound in dark blue cloth stamped in gold. 354 illustrations, including 94 chapter heads, reproductions of prints and drawings, as well as 56 black-and-white halftones and 8 color plates of paintings by Kent. A facsimile reprint, complete in every respect except for the 8 color plates, which are here printed in black-and-white halftone, was published by Da Capo Press, New York, in 1977.

1959 *Of Men and Mountains,* by Rockwell Kent, being an account of the European travels of the author and his wife, Sally, following their release from continental imprisonment. Asgaard Press of Ausable Forks, N.Y., 1959. 8vo. Bound in light green wrappers. 48 pages; 17 illustrations. 2,500 copies printed by A. Colish, Mount Vernon, N.Y. Published simultaneously was a limited edition of 250 signed and numbered copies, printed on cream-colored handmade paper and bound in marbled paper over boards with terra-cotta spine stamped in gold.

1962 *Rockwell Kent's Greenland Journal.* Ivan Obolensky, Inc., New York, 1962. 8vo. 320 pages. Bound in blue-green cloth stamped in silver. 79 illustrations, including map endpapers. The limited edition of 1,000 numbered copies, printed simultaneously, is bound in natural finish cloth stamped in gold, and has a two-compartment slipcase also containing a folder with six original lithographs by Kent, one of which is signed by the artist. Because of delays in production the two editions were actually published in February of 1963.

1968 *After Long Years,* by Rockwell Kent, being a story of which the author, for a change, is not the hero. Asgaard Press of Ausable Forks, N.Y., 1968. 8vo. Light brown wrappers stamped in gold foil. 24 pages; 9 illustrations. 2,500 copies printed by A. Colish, Mount Vernon, N.Y. Published simultaneously was a limited edition of 250 signed and numbered copies, printed on cream-colored handmade paper and bound in marbled paper over boards with brown cloth spine stamped in gold.

1970 *Wilderness: A Journal of Quiet Adventure in Alaska,* by Rockwell Kent, including extensive hitherto unpublished passages from the original journal. Published by the Wilderness Press and distributed by the Ward Ritchie Press, Los Angeles, Calif., 1970. Revised edition in a completely new format and typography, with the previously unpublished portion of the text set in oblique type. Large 8vo. 228 pages. Bound in blue linen with pasted label printed in black on gray paper, backstrip stamped in gold. Same illustrations and map endpapers as in 1920 edition. Printed by the Ward Ritchie Press in an edition of 1,550 signed and numbered copies.

SOME BOOKS ABOUT ROCKWELL KENT

Rockwell Kent, by Merle Armitage. Alfred A. Knopf, New York, 1932. 8vo. 84 pages. Short biographical sketch and bibliography, and 13 reproductions of the artist's works in various media. 550 numbered copies.

Rockwell Kent, by Andrei Chegodaev. Academy of Arts, Moscow, 1963. 4to. Russian text. 130 pages; 22 reproductions in full color and 102 in black and white, of paintings, lithographs, wood engravings, and drawings. Photo-portrait frontispiece.

Rockwell Kent, 1882 – 1971. National Council of American-Soviet Friendship, Inc., New York, 1971. Fol. A 32-page memorial to Kent, with biographical sketches and tributes by various friends and artists, excerpts from Kent's writings, plus 27 loose sheets of reproductions, in a stiff gray paper portfolio. Printed by A. Colish.

The Prints of Rockwell Kent: A Catalogue Raisonné, By Dan Burne Jones. The University of Chicago Press, Chicago and London, 1975. Large 4to. 240 pages. Thorough documentation of all Kent's prints, including lithographic designs for bindings and fabrics, 28 drawings by Kent cut in wood by J. J. Lankes. Over 300 plates, including reproductions of preliminary sketches, working drawings, and other ancillary matter. Chronology of prints, exhaustive bibliographies of works by and about Kent.

The Illustrations of Rockwell Kent. 231 Examples From Books, Magazines and Advertising Art, Selected by Fridolf Johnson with the Collaboration of John F. H. Gorton. Dover Publications, New York, 1976. 4to. 144 pages. Introduction by Fridolf Johnson.

Masters of World Painting: Rockwell Kent. Aurora Art Publishers, Leningrad, and Harry Abrams, New York, 1976. Fol. Text in Russian and English. 48 pages, 22 illustrations, including 15 hand-tipped plates in full color, most of them double-page.

An American Saga: The Life and Times of Rockwell Kent, by David Traxel. Harper & Row, New York, 1980. 8vo. Bound in dark blue cloth. 248 pages; 8 reproductions in color and 32 in black and white, of paintings, lithographs, wood engravings, and drawings. Selected bibliography.

ABOVE: TITLE PAGE VIGNETTE FROM <u>MOBY DICK</u>, THE LAKESIDE PRESS, VOL. II, 1930

A NOTE ABOUT THE EDITOR

Fridolf Johnson was born in Chicago and studied at the Art Institute of Chicago. He has been a designer, art director, and calligrapher, and since 1958, has operated his own small press, The Mermaid Press. He is the author of *Ornamentation and Illustrations for the Kelmscott Chaucer* (1973), *200 Years of American Graphic Art* (with Clarence P. Hornung, 1976), *The Illustrations of Rockwell Kent* (1976), and *A Treasury of Bookplates from the Renaissance to the Present* (1977). From 1962 to 1970, he was executive editor of *American Artist* magazine. Mr. Johnson lives with his wife, the painter Heidi Lenssen, in Woodstock, New York.

GRAPHIC NOTE

The text of this book was set in V.I.P. Kennerley, a modern adaptation of Frederic W. Goudy's design for Mitchell Kennerley, publisher, in 1911. Thought by many to be among Goudy's finest efforts, it is an elegant bookface based on classic Venetian design.

This book was photo-composed by The Clarinda Company, Clarinda, Iowa. The text was printed by Rae Publishing Company, Cedar Grove, New Jersey. The color separations were printed by American Printers and Lithographers, Chicago, Illinois. Four-color separations by Dai Nippon (DNA) America, in Tokyo, Japan. Two-color separations and duotones by Color Associates, St. Louis, Missouri. The book was bound by American Book – Stratford Press, Saddle Brook, New Jersey. Ellen McNeilly directed the production and manufacturing. R. D. Scudellari designed and directed the graphics. Naomi Osnos designed and coordinated the graphics.